From *Camelot* to *Spamalot*

From *Camelot* to *Spamalot*

Musical Retellings of Arthurian Legend on Stage and Screen

MEGAN WOLLER

OXFORD

UNIVERSITY PRESS

OXFORD
UNIVERSITY PRESS

Oxford University Press is a department of the University of Oxford. It furthers
the University's objective of excellence in research, scholarship, and education
by publishing worldwide. Oxford is a registered trade mark of Oxford University
Press in the UK and certain other countries.

Published in the United States of America by Oxford University Press
198 Madison Avenue, New York, NY 10016, United States of America.

Library of Congress Cataloging-in-Publication Data
Names: Woller, Megan, author.
Title: From Camelot to Spamalot : musical retellings of Arthurian
legend on stage and screen / Megan Woller.
Description: New York : Oxford University Press, 2021. |
Includes bibliographical references and index.
Identifiers: LCCN 2020042108 (print) | LCCN 2020042109 (ebook) |
ISBN 9780197511022 (hardback) | ISBN 9780197511039 (paperback) |
ISBN 9780197511060 | ISBN 9780197511046 | ISBN 9780197511053 (epub)
Subjects: LCSH: Arthur, King—Legends—Drama—History and criticism. |
Musicals—History and criticism. | Musical films—History and criticism. |
Arthur, King—Legends—Songs and music—History and criticism.
Classification: LCC ML2054 .W67 2021 (print) | LCC ML2054 (ebook) |
DDC 782.1/4—dc23
LC record available at https://lccn.loc.gov/2020042108
LC ebook record available at https://lccn.loc.gov/2020042109

DOI: 10.1093/oso/9780197511022.001.0001

1 3 5 7 9 8 6 4 2

Paperback printed by Marquis, Canada
Hardback printed by Bridgeport National Bindery, Inc., United States of America

Contents

Acknowledgments

As a project that began as an extension of my dissertation but turned into something completely new, this book has been completed with a ton of support throughout many years.

Since 2016, Gannon University has provided not only the working conditions but also the institutional support for me to conduct research and write my manuscript. A faculty research grant awarded in the spring of 2018 allowed a trip to Washington, DC, in order to consult archival materials on *Camelot* and *A Connecticut Yankee* at the Library of Congress. Additionally, the combination of scholarly release time and a Research Assistant during the 2019–20 academic year resulted in the completion of my manuscript. This backing has been invaluable, but it is the individual professional support that I have received, especially from my friends and colleagues in the School of Communication and the Arts, that have made Gannon my educational and scholarly home over the past several years. My Research Assistant, Abigail Ritchie, was an absolute blessing as I was writing this book. Self-directed, detail-oriented, comprehensive, and unendingly positive, Abbey did everything from hunt down sources, format, read and edit and read again, learn Sibelius in order to transcribe my examples, and countless other tasks. I could not have written as quickly or as smoothly without Abbey's help, and it was always a pleasure to see her smiling face.

I would also like to thank the many people who have read pieces of my manuscript or offered advice along the way. Gayle Magee and Jeff Magee have been a strong team of support and help since graduate school and continue to offer their perspectives and advice whenever I need it. The 2018 AMS Popular Music Study Group Junior Faculty Symposium offered a wonderful writing workshop, and the feedback received from my peers and especially mentors, Daniel Goldmark and Lori Burns, helped to refine the structure of my *Camelot* chapter and ultimately, the entire book. Special thanks for Daniel Goldmark for putting me in touch with Miles Kreuger, who graciously spoke with me over the phone about *Camelot*. The archival materials used in this book were studied with the help of the staff from the Library of Congress's Music Division and the Manuscript Division as well as the UCLA

Library Special Collections. Thank you very much to Emily Altman from the Frederick Loewe Foundation and Loren Plotkin from the Alan Jay Lerner Foundation for their enthusiasm and especially their help in refining my analysis. The anonymous reviewers provided useful and supportive feedback that shaped the final version of this book. Norm Hirschy has also offered a wonderful foundation of support throughout this process and has been quick to answer any and all questions, as has Lauralee Yeary.

Last but never least, my family are always my best and loudest cheerleaders. My parents, Jim and Kathleen Bolander, have fostered my love for music and always encouraged my pursuits. My in-laws Valerie and Basil Woller have also been incredible and interested advocates throughout this process. And none of this would have been possible without my husband and partner, Alex. As my most stalwart champion, friend, and colleague, Alex has encouraged, talked through every little thing, and heard more Arthurian musical songs than he has ever wanted to in his life; his input and encouragement sustain me every day.

Introduction: Arthur Adapted

Chivalrous knights roaming the land on adventures, illicit love affairs, and above all, a utopian kingdom with its leader's unrelenting search for inherent goodness: for hundreds of years, Arthurian legend has captured imaginations throughout Europe and the Americas. From the tragedy of Tristan and Iseult to the Quest for the Holy Grail, varying nations and generations have told its stories. Although the breadth of myth consists of a number of offshoots with their own protagonists, the core of so-called Arthurian legend is, of course, King Arthur. The legendary king of Britain, who—though hotly debated over the centuries—likely never existed, is at turns a conqueror, a lover, a scholar, and a political idealist. Arthur's deeds and personality traits have developed over the course of the years. Like so many before me, I, too, have become fascinated with the intricacies of Arthurian legend during the course of my research, especially as it appears in media throughout the twentieth and into the twenty-first century. Using adaptation theory as a framework, *From Camelot to Spamalot: Musical Retellings of Arthurian Legend on Stage and Screen* considers how musical versions in popular culture interpret the legend, presenting King Arthur in a particular way for modern audiences.

The seed of this project stems from my dissertation and subsequent work on Alan Jay Lerner and Frederick Loewe's *Camelot* (1960 Broadway; 1967 film).[1] The dissertation as a whole explores Hollywood adaptations of Broadway musicals throughout the 1960s and into the early '70s. Delving into how the film versions changed their stage counterparts, I investigate not only the alterations but also the potential reasons behind them. As such, my initial work on *Camelot* focused on the shift from the stage production to the much-maligned film. From this research, my interest in adaptation studies has grown. From my original research on *Camelot*, a renewed interest in T. H. White and then additional perspectives on the legend began. The ever-shifting, age-old tale of King Arthur and his world is one which thrives on adaptation for its survival. The continued presence—one might almost say continuous—of Arthuriana in popular culture both surprises and delights. Throughout the decades (even centuries), new generations tell the story in their own ways, updating or enhancing the relevance for a new audience.

From Camelot to Spamalot. Megan Woller, Oxford University Press (2021). © Oxford University Press.
DOI: 10.1093/oso/9780197511022.001.0001

This book explores musicalizations of Arthurian legend as filtered through specific versions of the tale as told by Mark Twain, T. H. White, and Monty Python. My research includes musical adaptations by creators such as Rodgers and Hart, Lerner and Loewe, and, of course, the members of Monty Python. These figures are not only important for musical theater but also provide representative versions of Arthurian legend for the twentieth and twenty-first centuries. From covers to remakes, audiences have a thirst for that "perfect" combination of familiarity and novelty, making the study of adaptations a culturally relevant enterprise. As such, my work concentrates on the process and result of adaptation. Musicals often adapt a previous source, including novels and plays.

Indeed, literary adaptations present a distinct case as the work changes medium. As noted by Linda Hutcheon, this type of adaptation involves shifting the material into new modes of presentation and practices typical of the new medium.[2] In other words, what works on the page may not have the same impact on stage or screen. Hutcheon uses the metaphor of the palimpsest to describe the intricate layering of meaning as various versions accumulate, accruing dense intertextual meaning.[3] Certainly, intertextuality is at the heart of all Arthuriana, and the musicals discussed throughout this study draw on a rich history of layered legend.

While Dudley Andrew and other scholars have shown that fidelity as an evaluative tool is detrimental to the study of adaptation, looking at how adaptations change their source material offers a lot of valuable information regarding approach and context.[4] More recently, some scholars have called for a re-evaluation of fidelity in light of continued tenacity in referring to an adaptation's relationship to source material. David L. Kranz proposes a way to discuss comparatively without resorting to the type of evaluation which certain approaches to fidelity might imply.[5] Bradley Stephens argues that "recognising an adaptation's relationship to its source remains a necessary step if we hope to understand a work's reception."[6] For Stephens, audience interpretation represents an important part of the process of adaptation. As such, I contend that fidelity provides a good point of departure as a comparative tool for rich analysis. While my analysis involves alterations to story and characterization in various versions of Arthurian legend, I do not seek to privilege any single version of the tale.

In dealing with a legend as sprawling and old as Arthuriana, Lisette Lopez Szwydky's use of the concept of culture-texts in her discussion of canonization and adaptation is useful. Szwydky argues that adaptations do not merely present "popular forms of canon extension or canon preservation," but have a more active role as "an equal player in the process of canonization."[7] She discusses literary classics as culture-texts, which she notes, "exist beyond the scope of their respective 'original.' In some cases, the original source itself is contested, forgotten, or otherwise ignored."[8] For contemporary audiences, Arthurian legend is so vast that any concept of an original seems a moot point for popular culture adaptations. Instead, adaptations add their own voice—their own versions—to the myth. This fact does not mean, however, that comparison does not provide its own insights. When choosing to take on this legend, creators have their pick of storylines and retellings. An exploration of what they chose and why, as well as any changes they made to those stories, can tell us much about contemporary interpretations of Arthur and why the tale continues to be popular.

Due to the propensity for creators to interpret or reimagine existing works from various mediums, the concept of adaptation has long been a part of film and musical theater discourse. Indeed this book develops from my own previous work on film musical adaptations of Broadway shows.[9] The importance of this process is reflected in Geoffrey Block's inclusion of "stage to screen" chapters in his 2009 revised edition of the seminal work *Enchanted Evenings*.[10] He observes the varying approaches to adapting a stage work to film, particularly that before the Rodgers and Hammerstein era, Hollywood musical adaptations were often "footloose and fancy free and at times unrecognizable vis-à-vis their stage counterparts," while film adaptations since the famed duo "tend to be relatively faithful."[11] More recent collected editions on adapting Frank L. Baum's *The Wizard of Oz* and Victor Hugo's *Les Misérables*, as well as *The Oxford Handbook of Musical Theatre Screen Adaptations*, confirm the place of adaptation in the related fields of musical theater and film.[12] As the essays on *The Wizard of Oz* and *Les Misérables* particularly illustrate, certain works permeate popular culture for long periods of time. My research on Arthurian legend complements these collections, considering the enduring popularity of Arthurian legend in popular culture with a musical focus.

Given that Richard Rodgers, Lorenz Hart, Alan Jay Lerner, and Frederick Loewe are all Broadway giants, a wealth of scholarship exists that deals expressly with the shows discussed in this book. Scholars such as Raymond Knapp, Geoffrey Block, Dominic McHugh, and Dominic Symonds all provide foundational discussions on these figures as well as specific musicals.[13] While the Disney Company has garnered a great deal of scholarship, less work has been done on *The Sword in the Stone*. James Bohn's monograph on music in Disney films through *The Jungle Book* touches on *Sword*, incorporating a relatively small passage in the context of the work.[14] The continued popularity and influence of Monty Python has similarly spawned both popular and academic research on the British comedy troupe. Indeed, *Holy Grail* crops up in Arthurian scholarship, especially research on film retellings.[15] Due to their humorously irreverent (yet sincere) interpretation, Andrew Lynch describes Monty Python as "White's natural inheritors."[16] Additionally, the popularity of the *Holy Grail* means that many British and American audiences in the twentieth century experienced the myth as filtered through Monty Python. However, this wealth of scholarship regarding all of these musicals rarely discusses how music shapes the interpretation of legend, instead focusing on *either* their status as musicals *or* Arthuriana. This book combines these approaches, looking at various stage and film musicals as *musical Arthuriana*.

As alluded to earlier, the concept of an "original" source is particularly complicated when dealing with Arthurian legend. The sprawling epic encompasses multiple storylines and varying central characters in hundreds of versions in multiple languages. What constitutes an "authentic" version of Arthurian legend? This question can never adequately be answered, and I further argue that one need not try. At the core of the appeal of Arthuriana is the legend's versatility and changeability. Given this context, any attempt to focus on fidelity as a source of value seems especially disingenuous. Even concentrating on my selected, highly idiosyncratic renderings of the myth from the late nineteenth and twentieth centuries presents ample issues. While a portion of my analysis does consider how the case studies change aspects of their particular sources, interpretation remains the primary concern. In each of these works, music plays a remarkable role in guiding the audience to understand this well-known tale in new and unexpected ways. Therefore, the goal of this monograph is to foreground the role of music in these Arthurian adaptations.

The first section of the book looks at two musicalizations of Mark Twain's *A Connecticut Yankee in King Arthur's Court*. In contrast to the later examples, these works involve an additional layer of reimagining as mediated by Mark Twain. Due to this fact, a prelude which examines Twain's novel and its relationship to "classical" Arthurian legend will open my analysis. Twain blends time periods in a more sustained way than either T. H. White's or even Monty Python's Arthurian world, both of which already are rife with anachronisms and modern intrusions. In "transporting" a contemporary character into ancient Camelot, Twain uses the tale to comment on society and technology in very obvious ways. This overt melding of time periods has made the novel a popular work to adapt.

Chapter 1 explores Richard Rodgers and Lorenz Hart's *A Connecticut Yankee* (1927; 1943 revival). While the 1927 original Broadway production represents my starting point, the 1943 revival with significant revisions and the 1955 television adaptation form the basis for how Rodgers and Hart, along with book writer Herbert Fields, depict Arthurian characters. Significantly, the later versions of the show include an increased musical presence for the villainous Morgan Le Fay, making the revival a prime focal point for my topic. As a Tin-Pan-Alley-era musical, *A Connecticut Yankee* conforms to common musical writing practices, including a lighter plot and conventional songwriting style. The use of a twentieth-century protagonist, who "travels" back in time to King Arthur's court, allows for the suspension of disbelief needed to swallow the contemporary lyrics and musical language.

Chapter 2 discusses the 1949 film *A Connecticut Yankee in King Arthur's Court*, starring Bing Crosby. This later film does not adapt the Rodgers and Hart musical; instead, it acts as a star vehicle for Crosby and features new songs by Jimmy Van Heusen and Johnny Burke. Less influential and enduring than the other works featured within this book, this 1949 film nonetheless provides an interesting counterpoint to the Rodgers and Hart revival of a few years earlier. The film was a commercial success, and this chapter considers it in that light. Furthermore, I examine the role of Bing Crosby and consider the purpose of this musical film as a star vehicle. With Crosby singing in four of the five surviving songs within the film, the music utilizes the crooner's voice and star persona in order to tell the story and sell the film.

The second section of the book considers two well-known adaptations of T. H. White's *The Once and Future King*: Alan Jay Lerner and Frederick Loewe's *Camelot* (Broadway 1960; Film 1967) and Disney's *The Sword in the Stone* (1963). Building on my previous work, Chapter 3 looks at how Lerner and Loewe adapt White for the Broadway stage. While Lerner revised *Camelot* well into the 1980s for revivals of the show, this chapter focuses specifically on two versions from the 1960s in considering the original Broadway stage production and the Hollywood film adaptation. Drawing on archival research completed at the Library of Congress, this chapter examines the process of adapting this long, unwieldy myth into a musical. Although Loewe did not work on the 1967 film, Lerner wrote the screenplay. Since the film version remains fixed and widely available, it is worth investigating how the changes made further adapt the tale. This chapter looks at how the musical *Camelot* interprets White's version of Arthurian legend, tracking the changes Lerner and Loewe made and especially how song affects characterization. Since Lerner and Loewe chose to focus on the love triangle between Arthur, Guenevere, and Lancelot, this chapter pays particular attention to how Lerner and Loewe alter their characters.

Chapter 4 examines *The Sword in the Stone* (1963). While Lerner and Loewe explore the rise and fall of the adult King Arthur, Disney tackled White's account of the future king's childhood. Although the animated film was released after *Camelot* premiered on Broadway, Walt Disney had obtained the rights to White's first Arthurian book in 1939. Since White published several versions of *The Sword in the Stone* before Disney produced the film, the portions of the fantasy that the film presents mark an important starting point. The final film features six songs written by Robert B. Sherman and Richard M. Sherman, designed to add to the tone of Disney's adaptation as a fantasy for children. This chapter considers how the Disney version alters the characters depicted in White's book. Unsurprisingly, the animated film abridges White's story for its seventy-nine-minute runtime. Despite the numerous changes, *The Sword in the Stone* contributes to the musical retellings of T. H. White's interpretation that enter into popular culture in the 1960s.

The final section of the book looks at Arthurian legend as told by the comedy troupe Monty Python. The British comedy troupe and Eric Idle's later musical adaptation focus on the comedic possibilities of King Arthur running around Britain, along with firmly anachronistic insertions. These properties are, first and foremost, funny and wonderfully successful in that regard. Much of the brilliance of this humor, however, is that it is incredibly layered. Monty Python manages to be silly yet intellectual at the same time. As such, the use of Arthurian legend as a loose backdrop matters for understanding the deeper layers of humor, often strengthening the cerebral aspects of the comedic approach. Furthermore, the Arthurian backdrop plays a role in the status of *Monty Python and the Holy Grail* and *Monty Python's Spamalot* in American popular culture. While fidelity to traditional Arthurian legend may not be a major goal of these works, I argue that it does not need to be in order to work as a piece of modern Arthuriana.

Chapter 5 deals with the 1975 film *Monty Python and the Holy Grail*. As Monty Python's first full-length film, *Holy Grail* combines the sketch comedy style of the troupe with a loose interpretation of Arthurian legend. The film follows King Arthur and his Knights of the Round Table as they quest for the Holy Grail, following familiar figures, such as Lancelot and Galahad, mixed in with Python creations, such as Sir Robin. Although chock-full of anachronisms and outright mockery, Monty Python's version of Arthurian legend nonetheless represents a valuable addition to the retellings of the story in the twentieth century. While the literature on *Holy Grail* offers a foundation for considering the film as an adaptation of Arthurian legend, little work has been done on the film's music and how it enhances the story. This chapter will emphasize the role of the music, especially the film's songs, arguing that they not only provide atmosphere but augment the narrative (such as it is). In this way, this chapter will also lay the groundwork for examining *Holy Grail* as the basis for Eric Idle's later musical, *Spamalot*.

The final chapter of the book shifts to *Monty Python's Spamalot*. In 2005, *Spamalot* premiered on Broadway; as an adaptation of the earlier comedy film *Holy Grail*, *Spamalot* enriches the version of Arthuriana as told by Monty Python. *Spamalot*, as a full-blown musical theater piece, adds numerous songs written by Idle and John Du Prez. These songs attach extra meaning as they send up not only Arthurian legend but also common musical theater tropes, augmenting the "meta" tone of the show for fans of musical theater history as well as Monty Python. While the earlier musical *Camelot* employs conventions of musical theater for dramatic purpose, *Spamalot* exploits the connection for humorous reasons. Furthermore, the musical incarnation increases many of the roles from the original film and includes new characters, extending the connections to the world of Arthurian legend. The musical's expanded pantheon of references and musical theater send-ups highlight the interpretive layering in a meaningful way. My analysis triangulates the legend with *Holy Grail* and *Spamalot*, arguing that while Monty Python may play fast and loose with ideas of fidelity, their versions of Arthurian legend remain true to the malleable spirit of the tale.

Hundreds of musical works have dealt with Arthurian legend throughout Western musical history. In some ways, the longevity of this tale and its continued widespread popularity across history are remarkable. To some extent, all of the creators and/or performers considered in this book, including Lerner and Loewe, the Disney teams, Monty Python, Rodgers and Hart, and Bing Crosby, are widely understood as pillars in their respective areas of musical theater or film. I further argue that these productions have shaped understandings of Arthurian legend and therefore consider them specifically as adaptations of Arthuriana. As its own area of research, Arthurian Studies is a robust field. Journals, book series, and countless monographs have been dedicated to the subject, exploring the impact of Arthurian legend on literature and media. My book contributes to this field of study but from a musicological standpoint. While a wealth of scholarship discusses many musical works about King Arthur or related stories, including several of the musicals in my book, my work focuses on how select shows and films adapt the legend in a particularly musical way.

Rather than present a comprehensive study of musical Arthuriana throughout time, this project studies select musicals for their approach and impact on popular culture in the twentieth and twenty-first centuries. While some selections, including *Camelot* and *Monty Python and the Holy Grail*, have had more success than others, I contend that all of the musicals chosen greatly contribute to the continuation of Arthurian legend. I have limited my study to Broadway shows or films that can be considered musicals; each of my selections contains newly written songs that adapt the tale. Another imposed limit is to only include shows or films in which King Arthur figures prominently (if not always as the main protagonist) and Camelot as place looms large (if not always constituting the primary setting). In a massive, sprawling legend which includes tangential stories and characters, from Percival to Tristan and Isolde, this delineation becomes a necessary one. Furthermore, all of the productions considered in *From Camelot to Spamalot* include an overtly modern perspective on the legend, intruding and even commenting on the tale of King Arthur. The style of the music and lyrics within the songs enhance this modern interpretation, representing the main thrust of the project.

Note on spellings: With centuries of stories based on Arthurian legend, the spellings of various characters' names have changed. Throughout this book, I use the spelling of each individual edition or production. For instance, Mark Twain uses the spelling *Morgan le Fay* while Fields and Hart use *Morgan Le Fay*; similarly, T. H. White spells the queen's name as *Guenever* while Alan Jay Lerner prefers *Guenevere*. The result is an inconsistency in spelling across characters but one which encompasses the many issues of adaptation.

PART 1

ADAPTING MARK TWAIN'S
A CONNECTICUT YANKEE
IN KING ARTHUR'S COURT

PART I

Prelude

Twain as Adapter

Mark Twain's 1889 novel *A Connecticut Yankee in King Arthur's Court* offers a fascinating beginning to the study of musical adaptations of Arthurian legend. Similar and yet vastly different to the other sources considered in this book, Mark Twain harnesses the story of King Arthur and his Knights of the Round Table for a nineteenth-century American reader. Unlike T. H. White's *The Once and Future King* and subsequent adaptations or even Monty Python, Twain not only inserts anachronistic elements into the legend but also deposits an entire main character into the fictional past of Camelot. Of course, the incorporation of contemporary elements into the legend has occurred throughout the history of Arthuriana and represents part of what has made the story stay alive for numerous generations. At the same time, Twain's high concept of "time travel" in order to juxtapose nineteenth-century American with apparent sixth-century English ideals is a fresh take on the tale.

In *A Connecticut Yankee in King Arthur's Court*, Twain frames the story in the nineteenth century as though protagonist Hank Morgan has shared an account of a remarkable time travel experience. As the supposed "time travel" involves trauma, both in going back and returning to the future, coupled with the fact that Morgan's experience takes him to a legendary court, the tale reads more as a fantastical parable than science fiction. Throughout the tale, Hank Morgan variously feuds with the legendary Merlin, becomes the right-hand man of the good but simple King Arthur, and befriends many of the most noble knights in the land. More than this, Hank Morgan single-handedly attempts to take charge of what he views as a backward system via modern technology and educational ideals.

Literary scholars have long wrestled with meaning in Twain's *Connecticut Yankee*. Widely acknowledged as his most complex, even oblique, work, interpretations have varied throughout the decades. The ambiguity inherent in the narrative structure, treatment of fantasy and science fiction, and

From Camelot *to* Spamalot. Megan Woller, Oxford University Press (2021). © Oxford University Press.
DOI: 10.1093/oso/9780197511022.003.0001

general contradictions of character regarding "Yankee" Hank Morgan have all made the work a prime site for interpretive conflict. Many of these elements led a number of mid-twentieth-century literary scholars to denounce *Connecticut Yankee* as a failure. Indeed, Gary P. Hutchinson observes that often the perceived failure of the novel is linked with ageism, resulting in the problematic trend of criticism to claim that late works of authors suffer from creative decline.[1] More recent scholarship has acknowledged the intricacy of Twain's engagement with Arthurian legend in numerous ways. The use of language and storytelling as a device represents a key aspect of the narrative complexity. Lee Clark Mitchell and Lydia R. Cooper both point toward the circular nature of *Connecticut Yankee* as fundamental to the understanding of meaning in the work.[2] In Cooper's estimation, "the novel fuses time, place, and, ultimately, language in order to demonstrate the consistency of human nature."[3] In the end, the similarities between the fictional past of Arthurian England and the United States of the nineteenth century reveal more than their differences.

In this regard, the question of whether Twain employs his contemporary protagonist to criticize a medieval British past or current society becomes key. Frankly, it is difficult to read *A Connecticut Yankee in King Arthur's Court* as solely falling into one camp or another. The ambiguity, in part, lies with the characteristic mixture of serious subject matter and humor in order to convey the satire. Nevertheless, Everett Carter claims that the novel should be read as a "defense of democracy, technology, and progress," criticizing England and the abhorrent practices of the past.[4] Of course, the novel absolutely does do this. However, Twain's criticism extends to nineteenth-century British and even American society.[5] One explicit link involves Twain's concerted focus on the evils of slavery. With the effects of slavery and the American Civil War lingering at the end of the nineteenth century, the emphasis reads as decidedly American in its censure. More than that, Twain overtly bridges the slavery in Arthur's kingdom with the American south. In one memorable passage, Twain writes, "it reminded me of a time thirteen centuries away, when the 'poor whites' of our South who were always despised and frequently insulted by the slave-lords around them, and who owed their base condition simply to the presence of slavery . . ." nevertheless defended the oppressive institution.[6] Furthermore, the ending—though notoriously ambiguous—relates the mutual destruction of Camelot and the order of chivalry with Hank Morgan's industrial revolution, and indeed Morgan himself. Neither mode of living wins, and the reader is left to wonder about the so-called superiority of advanced technology, which includes weaponry.

Perhaps the most difficult aspect of Twain's novel is the Connecticut Yankee himself, Hank Morgan. Upon waking to find himself in a mythological past, the protagonist immediately dismisses the people of Camelot, constantly referring to their stupidity and "childlike" natures. At best, Morgan adopts a paternalistic attitude toward the citizens with whom he interacts. He delights in asserting his self-perceived superiority and role as "Sir Boss," explicitly stating his desire to impose his own will upon England. Although part of the humor, Hank Morgan's constant flippancy can come across as grating. More troublingly, he frequently exhibits callousness toward fellow humans and even a tendency to kill indiscriminately. For example, he condemns to death a group of musicians simply for not playing to his liking, and he displays no remorse.[7] Carter posits that Twain identifies with his main character, stating that he "treated his alter-ego sympathetically, weighing plot and characterization heavily in his favor."[8] Moreover, Carter claims that Morgan's callous behavior should be read as part of the "comic-epic tone."[9] Cooper, however, cautions against conflating author and character. Instead, she presents the view that Hank Morgan might be interpreted as a microcosm for the complexity of human nature. She argues that "perhaps Hank is both hero and villain, an embodiment of the human capacity for both malice and mercy, a man who both conquers and is conquered."[10] Hank Morgan is neither entirely morally good nor wholly bad. Often unlikable, the character has moments of empathy and understanding.

Through Hank Morgan, Twain overtly asserts an American perspective into Arthurian legend. While Arthuriana has shown the ability to morph, reflecting not only the time but also the place of its telling, the American viewpoint might seem incompatible with a story of ancient monarchal idealism and chivalry. Indeed, Twain plays with this very idea in his juxtaposition of King Arthur's England with a nineteenth-century New Englander. Hank Morgan not only attempts to usher in a sixth-century industrial revolution but also espouses ideals of democracy. In Morgan's voice, Twain writes,

I was from Connecticut, whose Constitution declares "that all political power is inherent in the people, and all free governments are founded on their authority and instituted for their benefit; and that they have *at all times* an undeniable and indefeasible right to *alter their form of government* in such a manner as they think expedient" [emphasis original].[11]

Although Hank Morgan's means of attaining democracy are somewhat dubious, the democratic ideals he expresses are never in question. Twain does more than simply employ contemporary American slang, though plenty of that can be found throughout the novel. He embeds a particularly American ethos into the novel, allowing the two worlds to collide yet also to learn from one another. As discussed earlier, *Connecticut Yankee* does not present a cut-and-dried juxtaposition of the "good" and the "bad," the "past" and the "present," but a complicated tale of human nature and progress.

Despite the seemingly incongruous use of modern language, ideas, and characters, Twain does make extended use of Arthurian legend via Thomas Malory's *La Morte d'Arthur*. Rebecca Umland and Samuel Umland make the claim that Twain's novel is a "great and influential literary work, but it is not a great Arthurian work."[12] Umland and Umland's reasoning underscores the fact that Twain's novel goes (and therefore, subsequent adaptations go) beyond the anachronisms and commentary inherent in retellings of the tale throughout the centuries. However, I disagree with their assertion. Mark Twain directly engages with the most well-known English language version of King Arthur's life, even quoting from Malory's text in several places throughout his novel in order to convey the world in which Hank Morgan finds himself.[13] More importantly, the malleability of the legend, with its updating and revising throughout the centuries, is what I argue makes it such an enduring tale. Thus, Twain enters into a long tradition of re-envisioning Arthurian legend, introducing contemporary concerns into it. Additionally, Twain's contribution to Arthuriana has been remarkably influential to twentieth-century iterations—both as discussed in this book and beyond.

A number of adaptations of *A Connecticut Yankee in King Arthur's Court* were made in the twentieth century on stage and screen. Indeed, Twain's book has proved remarkably well suited to adaptation as the titular Yankee and technological advances can be continually updated. Actors as diverse as Will Rogers and Whoopi Goldberg have taken on the role of the time-traveling character, and in 1995, Walt Disney Studios released *A Kid in King Arthur's Court*. For the most part, these adaptations have employed the loose concept of the novel without adhering to the complex depiction of humanity or moral ambiguity of the original. On a basic level, *Connecticut Yankee* provides the fun and fantastical intersection of two disparate time periods while referencing Arthurian legend. Unsurprisingly, the musical adaptations discussed in the opening two chapters tend to soften Morgan's character or simplify the political and social satire.

Twain's novel greatly influenced the myriad works of Arthuriana created in the twentieth century, not just those that specifically adapt it. Alan Lupack and Barbara Tepa Lupack posit that as the foundational text of American Arthuriana, Mark Twain's "approach not only allowed for parody but also suggested possibilities for less romantic treatments of the Arthurian stories."[14] Both T. H. White and Monty Python can be considered inheritors, extending the possibilities of Arthurian legend for twentieth-century consumers. Additionally, White and the Pythons each incorporate contemporary perspectives in their own ways. White, of course, uses the conceit that Merlin "lives backwards" through time in order to juxtapose the time periods as well as simply inserting his own authorial voice in order to relay his pacifist message. Similar to Twain's device, Monty Python introduce modern characters into *Monty Python and the Holy Grail* in the form of minor, yet pivotal characters: the Historian and the British police. In all cases, the Arthuriana discussed throughout this book represent clear comparisons between the mythical world of Camelot and contemporary society, often associating the different time and settings for commentary or humor. As Twain's work does this in the most sustained way, the musical adaptations of his novel present an interesting starting point.

1

Musical Storytelling and Revision in Rodgers and Hart's
A Connecticut Yankee

In one of the hit tunes of the musical, the titular Yankee and his lady love sing "thou swell, thou witty," introducing the most famous of the language juxtapositions that thread throughout Richard Rodgers and Lorenz Hart's *A Connecticut Yankee*. In 1927, the songwriting team opened their biggest success on Broadway to date with their musical adaptation of Mark Twain's novel. With a successful score by Rodgers and Hart and a book by Herbert Fields, the show ran for 421 performances in its initial run. Sixteen years later, the duo would revisit their hit show, even writing six new songs for the revival. The overt merging of time periods within Twain's novel presents a number of possibilities for wordplay, various musical styles, and characterization in the musical adaptation.

This chapter focuses on Rodgers and Hart's depiction of the Arthurian myth in a musical comedy setting. With this in mind, I do not aim to re-hash previous scholarship but to consider Rodgers and Hart's musical from a different angle.[1] Given my emphasis, this chapter highlights the changes made in the 1943 revival since Rodgers and Hart enhance the musical presence of common Arthurian characters. As such, I study materials from multiple versions of the musical *A Connecticut Yankee* in order to tease out the complicated relationship between a contemporary American musical and Arthuriana. As Dominic Symonds's research has illustrated, *Connecticut Yankee* epitomizes Bruce Kirle's premise that musicals are always "works-in-process": incomplete as text, open to variation, and realized in performance.[2] Although materials for the 1920s version of the show are incomplete, which Symonds contends "represent both a frustrating lacuna and a tantalizing invitation to speculate," the aforementioned author does an admirable job of pooling knowledge from multiple sources in order to present the most comprehensive discussion of the show to date.[3] Of course, the 1927 Broadway

From Camelot *to* Spamalot. Megan Woller, Oxford University Press (2021). © Oxford University Press.
DOI: 10.1093/oso/9780197511022.003.0002

production represents my starting point. However, as previously mentioned, the revisions made for the revival engage with existing Arthurian characters in a more sustained way. Therefore, the 1943 revival and 1955 televised production will represent a significant portion of my analysis. I intend not only to complement the previous scholarship on this show but also to illustrate the ways in which Rodgers and Hart influenced later retellings of Arthurian legend. As such, my analysis begins by discussing how the musical adapts Twain's novel with a focus on the Arthurian characters.

Adapting Mark Twain and Arthuriana Engagement

Taking their cue from Twain's novel, Fields, Rodgers, and Hart's musical adaptation features the Yankee as the protagonist. The character, however, undergoes a number of changes as a result of the adaptation process. First of all, Twain's Hank Morgan becomes Fields and Hart's Martin. Although a seemingly small detail, the name change indicates a larger alteration of character traits. As discussed in the Prelude, Hank Morgan emerges as an incredibly complex picture of humanity throughout the course of the novel. He displays compassion and lofty ideals while also indulging in a troubling amount of violence in his quest for power. The surname Morgan even implies a special affinity with the Arthurian world in the form of Morgan le Fay. Stephen Knight asserts that the name is doubly "ominous. First it suggests, in non-abbreviated, non-Yankee terms, Henry Morgan the notorious pirate. Secondly it makes him kin with Morgan le Fay, the cruel aristocrat."[4] Of course, neither Rodgers and Hart nor librettist Herbert Fields came up with the name change. By the 1921 silent film, Hank Morgan had shifted into Martin Cavendish. Since this early film version inspired the Rodgers and Hart musical, the adoption of Martin as the Yankee's name comes as no surprise.[5]

Narratively, the kinship between Morgan le Fay and Hank Morgan presents itself when Hank sends an entire group of musicians to their deaths during his short residence in the Queen's castle. While this episode remains in the musical, Martin is generally less morally ambiguous than his literary counterpart. Arguably, Martin comes across as slightly more likable, but the alteration largely occurs as a result of the simplification inherent in adapting a literary figure into a musical theater one. In fact, the twentieth-century incarnation of Martin agrees to marry one woman despite being in love with another—hardly admirable behavior. And even from the perspective of the first decades of the twentieth century, Martin's obvious penchant for youth, beauty, and stupidity in women is not overly noble either. At the same time, the musical includes fewer indications of Martin's power-hungry nature. Neither, however, does it show his moments of compassion and disdain for slavery. On the whole, the character feels typical of 1920s American musical theater, playing his casual misogyny and generally cavalier attitude for laughs.

Furthermore, the plot only loosely adapts Twain (and, of course, the title is shortened). Herbert Fields expands the frame story in order to accommodate a thoroughly musical-theater-type love triangle. As a matter of fact, Symonds cites the romantic conventions of musical comedy as a possible reason for the amplification of the romantic storyline.[6] On the eve of his wedding to Fay Morgan, Martin feels conflicted due to his love for Alice. Upon finding another woman in her fiancé's lap, Fay knocks him over the head with a champagne bottle. Fields invented all of this backstory, giving the framing device less mystery than Twain. The musical's version also sets up the Camelot dream as a means for Martin to resolve his romantic difficulties. All the figures he meets in Camelot have an analog to his real-life friends, including Alice as Alisande/Sandy and Fay Morgan as Morgan Le Fay. Given that so much of the first act is spent in the contemporary era, it can hardly be surprising that the majority of the episodes described in Twain's novel are cut or simplified for the musical.

In each of the major versions discussed in this chapter, the frame story, and consequently Martin, exemplifies its current contemporary setting. As such, both Martin's characterization and his topical allusions refer to the late 1920s, early 1940s, or mid-1950s, depending on the time of production. One of the most notable changes from the 1927 original Broadway production to the 1943 revival involves the wartime setting. The 1943 revival introduces Lieutenant Martin Barrett, U.S.N., and his various military colleagues, including both Fay and Alice. As a result of this frame, some of Martin's modern advancements to medieval English life include costumes, behaviors, and artillery drawn from twentieth-century US military life. The 1955 televised production further reflects its own time. While it more or less takes the 1943 revival as its source, this production once again removes the wartime framing.

Moreover, the televised production excises some of the troubling or outdated aspects from the earlier stage versions. For instance, this updated frame story makes it clear that Martin is marrying Fay partly due to the fact that Sandy left him six months before. He does not simply decide to marry for mercenary reasons while in love with a woman in town. While Martin is clearly settling for Fay, the 1955 production sets up his situation as more sympathetic. In general, 1955 Martin is a more likeable character. He is a lot less condescending and casually sexist throughout the entire production and makes self-referential jokes about television tropes and film. These three versions of the Rodgers and Hart adaptation illustrate one of the aspects that make Twain's concept almost infinitely adaptable: the modern character can continually be updated to fit contemporary sensibilities.

The relationships and scenes chosen from Twain's novel indicate a particular emphasis within the musical production. In the novel *A Connecticut Yankee in King Arthur's Court*, Merlin represents the main antagonist for Hank Morgan's idea of progress (other than the larger institution of the Church). Merlin persistently attempts to surpass Hank/Martin in magic, but Martin's remarkable foreknowledge and technological prowess consistently thwart those attempts. In the musical, Merlin remains an antagonistic presence but takes a backseat to the villainous Morgan Le Fay. Both the novel and musical depict Morgan Le Fay as particularly bloodthirsty, while the musical changes her into a stereotypical black widow. In making the Arthurian character an equivalent for Martin's modern fiancée, she becomes the driving "evil" force, kidnapping Sandy in order to remove her from Martin's life. While select situations come from the source novel, such as ordering the death of the musicians as discussed previously, much of Morgan Le Fay's villainy was created specifically for the show. Although a few additional narrative aspects from the novel make their way into the show, *A Connecticut Yankee* should be considered a loose adaptation, less concerned with fidelity to the source material than a contemporary romp through Arthurian England.

Similar to most stage and film adaptations of *A Connecticut Yankee in King Arthur's Court*, Herbert Fields removes the majority of the political and social satire inherent in the novel. Writing from his specific historical perspective, Twain infused his fantasy with scathing commentary on an idealized British past as well as aspects critical of the present in both the United Kingdom and the United States.[7] In the musical, superficial elements remain without engaging in the serious commentary present in the novel. As in the book, Martin often remarks on the stupidity or childishness of Camelot's residents. However, his educational reforms, including the "man-factories," are downplayed in favor of the anachronistic technological marvels of telephones and radio in a medieval past. Similarly, the monarchs own slaves—and King Arthur and Martin are even briefly enslaved as in the source novel; however, Martin displays no particular disgust or need to abolish slavery. The presence of slaves merely adds to the setting and acts as a catalyst for the final confrontation with Morgan Le Fay rather than an overarching condemnation of slavery as a historical practice.

Perhaps most significant of all the changes made for the Rodgers and Hart musical, Martin does not hasten Camelot's fall. In the novel, Mordred reveals Lancelot and Guinevere's affair during a dispute over stocks with Sir Lancelot. In the ensuing war, all of the main figures of Camelot die. Hank Morgan returns from a voyage to Camelot in order to wage war on Merlin, the Church, and the remaining knights, proceeding to lay waste to his opponents only to become mortally wounded at the end. None of this final conflict occurs in the musical. Instead, Martin engages in a confrontation with Morgan Le Fay, declares his love for Sandy, and wakes to find he unconsciously (literally) married her real-life counterpart, Alice. This ending scene resolves the love triangle while also leaving the dreamworld of Camelot intact. Martin leads no revolution in an attempt to bring democracy to the people. He simply spends time with well-known Arthurian characters as a psychological means of working out his relationship problems.

As an adaptation of a revisionist Arthurian work, the musical version of *A Connecticut Yankee* has a somewhat convoluted relationship with the larger body of Arthuriana. Mark Twain engages with several stages of Arthurian literature. The deglamorized Arthurian world represents a direct opposition to the romanticism of Alfred, Lord Tennyson's *Idylls of the King*. Tennyson's epic Arthurian poetry would have been the most well-known version of the myth to contemporaneous readers, and Twain offers an American response. At the same time, Twain also engages with the older *Le Morte d'Arthur* by Thomas Malory, even using passages from that text. In this way, *A Connecticut Yankee in King Arthur's Court* enters into a dense intertextual web and places itself in the English-language Arthurian tradition. The musical removes any explicit connection to Malory but mentions Tennyson in the dialogue.

As such, *A Connecticut Yankee* the musical keeps the nineteenth-century reference but lacks the intertextual density of Twain's novel. Given that Tennyson would likely have been the best-known version of Arthuriana to audiences, the reference makes sense.[8] Additionally, the Tennyson reference brings to mind one of Rodgers and Hart's earlier forays into musicalizing

Arthurian legend, "Idles of the King" from *The Garrick Gaieties* (1926).[9] The musical also alludes to the story of Tristan and Isolde, suggesting a link to Richard Wagner's musical treatment of the Arthurian stories. The love potion that Merlin brings to Morgan Le Fay in order to seduce Martin is the same recipe used in the Tristan legend. This narrative link acknowledges the primary musicalization of Arthuriana at the time without resorting to musical quotations. These fairly minor mentions place Fields, Rodgers, and Hart's *A Connecticut Yankee* firmly in the Arthurian tradition, alluding to a rich intertextual history of the legend.

Unlike the films and stage musicals discussed in the final two sections of this book, King Arthur is only a minor character in the Rodgers and Hart musical. Twain depicts the famous monarch as backwards, ignorant, and vain, yet surprisingly kindhearted. In the most affecting segment of the novel, Sir Boss and King Arthur roam the English countryside disguised as peasants. During this sojourn, King Arthur cares for a woman dying of smallpox with no regard for his own health or concern about the squalor. The pair also are captured and sold as slaves, and while the king is initially more disturbed by his low asking price, he comes to understand the ills of slavery. Twain's portrayal of Arthur is a far cry from the mythical king, but nevertheless, takes an affectionate view of the misguided monarch as a good man. The musical keeps the conceit of disguising the king as a commoner, and even briefly selling him into slavery, but eliminates the most humanizing aspects of the episode. This version of Arthur remains backwards in his thinking and is presented more as a pal to Martin. Overall, he is nearly inconsequential, simply providing legendary flair. As I will discuss further in the next section, his musical presence is also lacking, which further marginalizes him as a character.

In both Twain's novel and Fields, Rodgers, and Hart's musical adaptation, a number of additional Arthurian characters pepper the plot without figuring heavily into it. Several Knights of the Round Table are mentioned to various extents, including Sir Kay, Sir Galahad, and the exemplary Sir Lancelot. In the source novel and musical versions, Sir Kay finds and captures the Yankee, bringing him to Camelot. Kay typifies the ridiculous knight-errant, making up a fantastical story about fighting dragons and defeating Hank/Martin in a glorious fashion. Subsequently, the stage musical shows very little of the knight. The 1955 television adaptation, however, increases this character's role through song as discussed in the next section. Both the 1927 and 1943 stage adaptations adopt the pure Sir Galahad as the male half of the secondary romantic couple. As such, he is given more characterization than any of the other knights.

Interestingly, Fields's libretto openly acknowledges Galahad as Lancelot's son by Elaine. Fields represents Galahad as naïve and unsure in love, while portraying Lancelot as a lothario. In a brief father-son discussion, Lancelot exclaims "thou hast my glamorous reputation to live up to, thou are my son— I hope."[10] Lancelot shows obvious dismay that his acknowledged son has yet to sleep with his love interest, Evelyn. Galahad's traditional purity, which leads him to find the Holy Grail in several stories throughout the literature, is treated with humor and disdain in the musical; his chaste relationship with Evelyn acts as an obstacle in their love. While his son enjoys a prominent place in the show, Lancelot himself figures very little beyond his interactions with Galahad. In Twain's novel, Lancelot is presented as the best knight in true Arthurian fashion as well as a close friend of Hank Morgan after his years in Camelot. The musical sidelines Lancelot even more. Guinevere is married to Arthur and is, therefore, Queen of England, but she barely appears in either the novel or musical. She merely provides Arthurian flavor and presents another example of silly femininity in Hank/Martin's eyes.

Furthermore, the famous love triangle between Arthur, Lancelot, and Guinevere is merely a fringe plot point in both the novel and musical adaptation. Twain's novel acknowledges the affair between Lancelot and Guinevere as an open secret, and it does play a role in the ultimate downfall of Arthur's reign. In *A Connecticut Yankee* the musical, the love triangle merely become a side gag. In order for the jokes to land, however, Fields presumes some knowledge of the affair between Lancelot and Guinevere on the part of the audience. In Fields's libretto, Arthur actually orders Martin to burn at the stake because he reveals foreknowledge of the affair between Queen Guinevere and Sir Lancelot. Arthur decries the statement as slander and sentences Martin to death (until he claims to cause the eclipse, which saves him at the end of Act I). In Act II, Arthur asks the telephone operator Evelyn to connect him with Guinevere, and she calls Lancelot's suite. Arthur maintains his ignorance, but members of the court—and, of course, the audience—understand that the couple is engaging in an affair. Unlike in the literary tradition, the show ends before the illicit affair becomes anything more than an inside joke.

Most of the discussion thus far has centered on plot and character points as found in the 1927 and 1943 Broadway versions of *A Connecticut Yankee*. The 1955 television broadcast makes a number of further changes and is representative of an extant, available performance of the Rodgers and Hart show. Generally speaking, the televised production sanitizes the Twain novel even further and removes additional problematic aspects from the earlier Broadway productions. As mentioned earlier in this section, this version updates Martin and makes him a more likeable lead. At a running time of only one hour and seventeen minutes, the televised *A Connecticut Yankee* also makes a number of cuts and changes. The largest narrative edit is the elimination of the secondary romantic couple, Sir Galahad and Evelyn. Galahad is mentioned once on the telephone but never makes an onscreen appearance. As I will tease out further, his songs are either cut or reassigned to the now larger role of Sir Kay.

This production also does not make Sandy a temporary proto-feminist—a character arch that causes romantic strife between her and Martin. Instead, she criticizes his tendency to overwork. This marks a parallel between the medieval Sandy and the modern version, since Sandy initially left Martin due to his prioritization of business over their relationship. Significantly, the 1955 version also changes the ending. Fay simply breaks off the engagement, leaving Martin free to declare his love for Sandy. Sandy does not, however, marry Martin while he remains unconscious. In many ways, the alterations reflect the changing audience values from 1943 to 1955 in such a way that the television adaptation represents a different relationship to Twain's novel and Arthurian legend as a whole.

Like the source novel, *A Connecticut Yankee* represents an American take on the thoroughly British myth. Unlike Twain's work, the musical does not use a distant, imaginary British past to comment on changing social orders or contemporary mores. Alternatively, Herbert Fields, Richard Rodgers, and Lorenz Hart employ the mythical past as a psychological tool for the main character to resolve his romantic troubles. Each of the real-world characters appearing in the dreamworld as Arthurian figures affirms that fact. In strongly depicting Martin's sojourn in Camelot as a result of his being knocked unconscious, the collaborators justify the overtly anachronistic elements. William A. Everett asserts that the

> integration of dissimilar elements is central to both Hart's approach to lyric writing and many nineteenth- and twentieth- century interpretations of the Arthurian legend, including Twain's. Hart's genius at achieving dichotomatic juxtaposition made him an ideal creator of specific lyrics that would amplify the ideology of Twain's novel.[11]

Many commentators have noted the use of juxtaposed language styles as a running—if perhaps tiresome—gag throughout the show.[12] Additionally, Martin's sensibilities, influence on his surroundings, and topical references all similarly reflect the time and place of production. As such, the musical represents a lighthearted insertion into the Arthurian canon, targeting contemporary US audiences in such a way that assumes a basic knowledge of the legend in order to provide an entertaining backdrop for the romantic entanglement.

More importantly, *A Connecticut Yankee* fits into the mold of twentieth-century American musical theater. As Symonds asserts, "perhaps more than any other cultural idiom, the Broadway musical strained the fault lines between European and American culture."[13] As such, the form might be viewed as the perfect means to tell an age-old European tale in an American voice. Ethan Mordden emphasizes that by the end of the second half of the 1920s, "Rodgers and Hart seemed so immutable, prolific, and unique that it was probably their work . . . that announced the arrival of a native art."[14] Rodgers and Hart's American style made them the perfect songwriting team to turn Twain's version of Arthurian legend into a Broadway musical. *A Connecticut Yankee* conforms to the conventions of Tin-Pan-Alley-era musicals. As was common in the 1920s, Rodgers employed the songwriting style of the time by focusing "almost entirely on simple tunes and accompaniments in fixed musical forms."[15] In its topicality, *A Connecticut Yankee* also includes a distinctly Broadway intertextuality. For example, Dominic Symonds discusses the numerous intertextual allusions to recent Broadway musicals in the song "Evelyn, What Do You Say?" from the 1927 Broadway production.[16] Thus, the musical contains the recognizable stamp of the Tin Pan Alley era, presenting an example of a thoroughly contemporary American form of musical theater.

Arthurian Characters and Song

It would be easy to dismiss the depiction of Arthurian legend and the associated characters as "inauthentic," particularly in terms of musical style. The fact of the matter, however, is that none of the films or stage musicals considered throughout this book offer any semblance of medieval musical authenticity, nor even attempt to construct such a thing.[17] My analysis, then, does not seek to set up a strong dichotomy between the modern styles used for the contemporary frame setting/Martin and the Arthurian world. As Dominic Symonds and others have observed, the stylistic differences between imagined past and the present exist but in a resoundingly American popular idiom.[18] Instead, I consider in this chapter how the songs performed by traditional Arthurian figures portray these characters, focusing on their characterization in order to illustrate how Rodgers and Hart adapt the larger myth.

In a mode typical of the time period, *A Connecticut Yankee* ultimately produced three hit songs across its two main versions. As a Tin-Pan-Alley-era musical, *A Connecticut Yankee* fits into the mold of contemporary shows, including other Rodgers and Hart musicals, in that the popular song industry helped to drive the writing style and ultimate success of individual songs. Larry Stempel states, "show songs, by contrast, might prove more durable [than the shows themselves]: A much bigger market existed for them outside the theater than in it."[19] This has proved true for three of *Yankee's* songs: "My Heart Stood Still," "Thou Swell," and "To Keep My Love Alive." The first two especially have become standards of the Great American Songbook.

In the case of "My Heart Stood Still," the impact of the popular song industry and the practice of reusing material can be seen since Rodgers and Hart initially wrote the song for the earlier show *One Dam Thing after Another*. Rodgers also recalls that they decided to use the pre-existing song in their new show in order to keep it away from actress Beatrice Lillie; Rodgers claims that "once we used the excuse, we had to make sure the song was really in the show."[20] Used in *A Connecticut Yankee* to signify the lingering love between Martin and Alice, "My Heart Stood Still" illustrates Richard Rodgers well-known ability to create inventive, memorable melodies using simple musical elements. Allen Forte's detailed analysis of the melodic and harmonic character of the song has further application in its romantic characterization, particularly in the song's well-known chorus.[21] The A section in the AABA chorus has a cascading melody in which Rodgers's applies descending, stepwise patterns of a minor third, effectively indicating longing.

At the same time, Rodgers's music for "My Heart Stood Still" contains an inherent sense of optimism. Each subsequent pattern begins on a higher pitch, inserting hope into the melodic construction. The use of the violin in the orchestration to double the melody emphasizes the melodic effect. The harmonic richness with an abundance of seventh chords, often leading into satisfying resolutions to the tonic at the beginning of each eight-bar phrase of the chorus, further highlights the optimism of the romance. The B and final A sections have a parallel melodic peak (D5); occurring on the word "thrill" toward the end of the song, this peak illustrates Rodgers's focus on the thrill of love rather than the pain of longing. Although the song is a lovely romantic ballad, "My Heart Stood Still" appears in the modern portion of the show. It does have a reprise in the Arthurian section of the show but links Sandy with Martin's modern love interest. Therefore, the song bears no markers of the imagined Arthurian past.

"Thou Swell," on the other hand, is the most conscious combination of "old" and "new" language in the show, wrapped in a catchy, jazz-inspired musical package. Both "My Heart Stood Still" and "Thou Swell" are sung by Martin and Alice/Sandy, and the typical love song format makes them successful songs in their own right. Although "Thou Swell" includes both Shakespearean-style language and typically twenties slang, the lyrics remain broad enough to apply to romantic feelings outside of the show. In his light-hearted seduction of the Lady Alisande, Martin charmingly combines words she understands with his own colloquialisms. The resulting song showcases Hart's lyrical inventiveness. Rhyme and language juxtapositions are apparent from the outset with the line, "babe, we are well met as in a spell met." A great deal of the song's fun stems directly from Hart's delightful contrasts throughout "Thou Swell."

Rodgers's music enhances the lighthearted enjoyment this song brings with a buoyant, catchy melody and a chorus that features syncopation in either the melody itself or accompaniment. While Hart's lyrics purposefully contrast "old sounding" language with contemporary jargon, Rodger's music is some of the most willfully modern in the entire show—even as the entire score should be understood within the framework of American popular song. The rhythmic complexity and pentatonic emphasis highlight Martin's very Americanness.[22] By using elements of jazz as assimilated by American popular music, Rodgers inserts his distinctive, highly American style into the Arthurian world.

Unsurprisingly, "My Heart Stood Still" and "Thou Swell" have not only been recorded numerous times but have garnered the most scholarly attention. Both tunes have been recorded by jazz musicians and popular song interpreters throughout the decades. Artists as disparate as Frank Sinatra, Rod Stewart, and The Supremes all have a version of "My Heart Stood Still," and a similar, lengthy list could be made for "Thou Swell." Typical Tin Pan

Alley songs, specifically those of Rodgers and Hart, allow for countless interpretations, though jazz tends to be the favored style for recordings. Historically, scholarship on Rodgers and Hart has favored their songs over entire shows; given this, these two songs have received consideration, which Geoffrey Block has collected in his thorough *Richard Rodgers Reader*.[23] A great deal of insightful analysis has been done on both of these songs, and they each are excellent examples of Richard Rodgers's compositional style and Lorenz Hart's witty, complex lyric writing. Yet neither "Thou Swell" nor "My Heart Stood Still" depict any of the Arthurian characters. Important as they are in the Rodgers and Hart catalogue, neither song really interprets Arthurian legend in any meaningful way.

"To Keep My Love Alive," on the other hand, was written for the Arthurian star Morgan Le Fay. As such, I discuss the song in the context of the show later in this section. It is also worth briefly considering its life outside of the show. As the only "hit" to come out of the 1943 revival, "To Keep My Love Alive" has been recorded by several popular song interpreters, including Ella Fitzgerald, Anita O'Day, and Pearl Bailey. Dorothy Rodgers wrote of the song: "in a flashback to his old brilliance Larry wrote one of his wittiest lyrics, 'To Keep My Love Alive'; it was to be his last."[24] That witty list of a black widow's tricks likely helped the song survive, though it has not had the same amount of success as the two original standards.

Although Martin Barrett and his Twain-created true love Alisande represent the main characters in *A Connecticut Yankee*, pre-existing Arthurian characters also populate the musical to different degrees. Furthermore, Rodgers and Hart give musical numbers to some of these characters, emphasizing them to varying degrees depending on the version. Given that the most important characters in a musical invariably sing and dance, the decision to give songs to well-known figures of the myth or not tells us much about the treatment of the legend in the musical *A Connecticut Yankee*. And importantly, Rodgers and Hart adapt the characters through song in an intertextual contribution to the pantheon. All of the productions discussed in this chapter include ensemble numbers that feature the knights and ladies of Camelot; the solo numbers and duets, however, vary greatly, interpreting the characters in multiple ways (see Table 1.1). In the following discussion, I consider several songs listed in Table 1.1 with a focus on solo numbers and duets in order to look at how Rodgers and Hart represent the familiar individuals from the Arthurian tradition.

Table 1.1 Songs Featuring Arthurian Characters in Three Versions of
A Connecticut Yankee

Original Broadway Production, November 3, 1927	Broadway Revival, November 17, 1943	Live Telecast, March 12, 1955
Act I	Act I	Act I
At the Round Table (Ensemble; Members of Camelot's Court)	At the Round Table (Ensemble)	At the Round Table (Ensemble)
On a Desert Island with Thee (Galahad with Evelyn)	On a Desert Island with Thee (Evelyn, Galahad)	To Keep My Love Alive (Morgan Le Fay)
Finale; "Rise and Shine"***	To Keep My Love Alive (Morgan Le Fay)	Rise and Shine/Hymn to the Sun (Ensemble)
Act II	Act II	Act II
Opening (Ensemble)	Ye Lunchtime Follies (Galahad and Ensemble)	Ye Lunchtime Follies (Sandy and Ensemble)
I Feel at Home with You (Galahad with Evelyn)	Can't You Do a Friend a Favor? (Morgan Le Fay with Martin)	Can't You Do a Friend a Favor? (Morgan Le Fay with Martin)
The Sandwich Men (Knights)	I Feel at Home with You (Galahad, Evelyn, Sir Gawain and Ensemble)	I Feel at Home with You (Sir Kay, Switchboard Operator, and Ensemble)
Evelyn, What Do You Say? (Evelyn with Knights)	You Always Love the Same Girl (Martin and King Arthur)	You Always Love the Same Girl (Martin and King Arthur)
	The Camelot Samba (Merlin and Ensemble)	The Camelot Samba (Merlin and Ensemble)

Ensemble Numbers

All of the productions considered in this chapter include ensemble numbers that feature the Knights of the Round Table as well as the ladies of the
court. Within each version of the show, the lords and ladies of Camelot provide a background for Martin's psychological journey. Indeed, all the major
productions of *A Connecticut Yankee* include the ensemble number "At the
Round Table." This song acts as the introduction to the court of Camelot,
coming after Martin and Sandy's jazzy love duet "Thou Swell." Labeled in
the current piano-conductor score rental as "Knight's Opening," the listed
Arthurian characters comprise Tristan, Sagramore, and Merlin among
the more general ensemble. In a nod to medieval musical tropes, the instrumental introduction opens with a short trumpet motive in a brisk $\frac{2}{4}$,

as shown in Example 1.1, which Rodgers identifies as "Allegro Marziale."[25] Despite the superficial use of a trumpet call, Symonds observes that "this is clearly not Arthurian music, nor does it pretend to be."[26]

Alternating between a simple common time and the rousing, martial $\frac{2}{4}$, this song introduces life in Camelot. In a toast, the knights sing a straightforward march with a repetitive melody about food and fighting before praising the nobility and purity of King Arthur. The knights and ladies' praise shifts into a regal, homophonic choral style when addressing Merlin or the king directly. In one of his few musical moments, Merlin further expounds on the virtues of the king. When the knights and ladies announce that the king will speak, the rhythmic motive of a triplet commemorates the moment. Humorously, Arthur has nothing to say; he flounders for a moment before thanking the court and sitting down. The ensemble, however, praises it for a "mighty speech" in song, further highlighting the absurdity of the monarchy and court life. As a whole, the song sets up Camelot as a self-important, indulgent, but ultimately ridiculous place.

The Camelot ensemble participates in several other numbers across each version, though none characterizes the knights and ladies in quite the same way as their first appearance. Two additional chorus song and dance numbers, however, deserve comment due to how their anachronistic musical styles are used to depict the Arthurian background. The first, "Rise and Shine / Hymn to the Sun," a gospel song that celebrates the sun returning after the eclipse at the end of Act I, is a joyous chorus act finale. "Rise and Shine" begins in a slow, sustained homophonic hymn style before building in tempo and rhythmic complexity for the exuberant finale. Symonds asserts that the song works on a number of levels within the show. It both alludes to the "primitive" nature of the Arthurian characters and aligns with the trend of including gospel-style numbers in musicals in the 1920s. In associating this type of worship with gospel, the song "suggests a commentary on the primitivism of black culture" in such a way that Symonds contends that though

Example 1.1. "Knight's Opening" Trumpet Motive. Herbert Fields, Lorenz Hart, and Richard Rodgers. *A Connecticut Yankee.* New York: R&H Theatricals, 1977.

Example 1.2. Basic Samba Rhythm Used in the "Camelot Samba."
Herbert Fields, Lorenz Hart, and Richard Rodgers. *A Connecticut Yankee.*
New York: R&H Theatricals, 1977.

Fields, Rodgers, and Hart may have been "oblivious to the problematic racial overtones of their work, their theater, like much of the period, was deeply entrenched and complicit in perpetuating the ideologies of the time."[27] Indeed, they continued to engage in this type of problematic musical stereotyping in an added number for the revival.

For the 1943 revival, Rodgers and Hart wrote the "Camelot Samba" as a set piece for Queen Morgan Le Fay's court. Using the musical stereotypes of samba, coupled with exaggerated costumes and dancing, this song dovetails with the popularity of samba and other "Latin" dance styles in the 1930s and 1940s. By likening "old Camelot" to Brazil and referencing "ye Latin lovers," the lyrics set up the broad usage of samba for this number. Once the opening verse ends, the song and subsequent dance employ a basic samba rhythm, shown in Example 1.2, with minor variations. The samba in *Connecticut Yankee* strongly resembles the highly stylized Brazilian persona as exemplified by Carmen Miranda during this time period. Miranda began starring in films in the early 1940s, including Busby Berkeley's *The Gang's All Here* (1943). These films helped to disseminate particular stereotypes of Latin American music and samba, in particular. Once again, Rodgers and Hart are utilizing a trendy musical style, importing it into their show (as Broadway musicals are prone toward doing). And yet again, the result is problematic, exoticizing the Arthurian characters and appropriating this Brazilian style in order to do so. Interestingly, Merlin leads the "Camelot Samba," highlighting his role as a royal lackey. Through both of these songs, Rodgers and Hart present the people of Camelot as "Other," differentiating them from the modern, white background of Martin Barrett.

Sir Galahad

While various minor knights have small solos in ensemble numbers, Sir Galahad is the only knight to have a significant singing role in *A Connecticut*

Yankee.[28] Galahad represents an interesting choice in a number of ways. Fields, Rodgers, and Hart choose to depict King Arthur, Queen Guinevere, and Sir Lancelot as the older generation. In fact, Arthur's contemporary counterpart is Fay Morgan's father. As such, the romantic entanglement between the legendary trio has been a fact of Camelot for many years before Martin's "arrival." Rather than presenting the famous love triangle as the secondary romance, the collaborators focus on Lancelot's adult son by the absent Elaine. Although Galahad is an extremely marginal character in Twain's novel, the knight has a long and prominent history in English Arthuriana. In many stories, Galahad finds the Holy Grail and ascends into Heaven upon the discovery. His purity, embodied through virginity, allows the illegitimate son of Lancelot to attain the perfection that his father never could. Fields, Rodgers, and Hart turn the typical virginal characterization of Galahad into a comedic situation. Galahad's inexperience with women and fear of sex irk both his womanizer father and, significantly, his lover Evelyn. Indeed, one of the primary anxieties for the secondary romantic couple is Galahad's reticence. Two songs, "On a Desert Island with Thee" and "I Feel at Home with You," illustrate Galahad's musical characterization. These two love duets appear in both the 1927 and 1943 Broadway productions.

The Act I duet, "On a Desert Island with Thee," occurs after the show's official introduction to King Arthur and his knights. Although Arthur and Lancelot propose a match between Queen Morgan Le Fay and Sir Galahad, the young knight already has a love interest in Lady Evelyn. Symonds observes that "much of the comedy suggests that Galahad is gay . . . Thus, the gender expectations are reversed, sexualizing Evelyn and emasculating the bold knight."[29] While the literary tradition marries a chivalric masculinity with chastity and religious purity, Fields, Rodgers, and Hart imply that a virginal young man signifies closeted homosexuality. This shift represents both the differing time periods and genre expectations for understanding Sir Galahad. Galahad's unwillingness to have sex with Evelyn is not purity but fear—one that must be overcome in a heteronormative musical comedy but provides comedic opportunities. Indeed, the fantasy woven in "On a Desert Island with Thee" is one of sexual bliss.

The verse of "On a Desert Island with Thee" begins with Galahad attempting to reassure Evelyn of his love, as well as her reluctance to be seen by others. Both vocal lines are descending and stepwise, reflecting the concerns and fears of their real world. Soon, however, Galahad spins a beautiful fantasy of the two of them alone on an island. As Galahad claims to "care not a jot" for other people's judgments, his vocal line confidently leaps up a minor seventh then down a minor sixth. The melody shifts to a much more disjunct character with a clear arched phrasing. The end of the verse leads into the song's refrain, which is a typical AABA, 32-bar form. The melodic character of the A section emphasizes the cheery use of C major in the piano-vocal score by outlining the tonic triad then descending with a dotted rhythmic motive (Example 1.3). The refrain's B section strongly emphasizes the dominant, moving back and forth between ii^7 and V^7 in each of the eight measures. When the lovebirds sing of their invented island, the song takes on a dancelike character with only hints of the jazz influence inherent in Martin and Sandy's "Thou Swell." A trio section separates two statements of the chorus, not adding much melodically in its use of the tonic triad and repeated notes but with some harmonic interest. For example, Rodgers emphasizes E minor for several measures when Evelyn sings about the "prudish" people who may disapprove of their love. Shifting to the relative minor of V underlines the acknowledgment of disapproval, briefly interrupting the fantasy (which is characterized by the otherwise relentless optimism of C major).

"On a Desert Island" fits into the prototype of a secondary love duet in that it is fun and upbeat but lacks the inventiveness of Martin and Sandy's parallel tune. "Desert Island" is much more repetitive, especially in terms of its melodic and harmonic profile. Although lacking the overt slang used by Martin and later adopted by his cohorts, the song nevertheless contains a number of obviously modern references. Evelyn asks what "ten books" they should pack—a palpably non-medieval query and one that presupposes literacy. While clearly a Tin-Pan-Alley-style tune, "Desert Island" focuses less on the recognized sense of modernism that applies to Martin's songs. Instead, the song functions to characterize Galahad and Evelyn, using common musical theater stylistic hallmarks.

In the Decca 1943 Cast Revival recording, elements of performance illustrate potential interpretations of Galahad and Evelyn. Chester Stratton's

Example 1.3. Motive from "On a Desert Island with Me." Herbert Fields, Lorenz Hart, and Richard Rodgers. *A Connecticut Yankee.* New York: R&H Theatricals, 1977.

Galahad has a light tenor voice, and he has to reach for the high notes. Given the melodic leaps and disjunct character of the chorus's melody, the limitations of Stratton's voice enhance the comedic aspects of the song without undermining the confidence implied in Rodgers's compositional style. Contrasted with Vera-Ellen's harsher, unpolished timbre and often flat singing in both her higher and lower registers, Stratton's singing style is competent if inconsistent, though certainly stronger than his romantic partner's. The bouncy tune feels lighthearted but lacks the inventiveness present in "Thou Swell."

Although the lyrics focus on their physical relationship, the performance highlights the comedic aspects of their romance rather than any hint of sex appeal. Vocally, Vera-Ellen's Evelyn is not aesthetically appealing. At the same time, Vera-Ellen exhibits a cutesy quality slightly reminiscent of Betty Boop but without the extreme attempt at "sexiness." Of course, the musical follows this song with a dance number, accentuating the area in which Vera-Ellen did excel. While the song itself heightens the comic aspect of the secondary couple, the dance portion further allows for the romance to bloom onstage. With its bouncy rhythmic character, "On a Desert Island with Thee," presents a solid foundation for this cheery, romantic song and dance. Regardless, Galahad's virginity and Evelyn's sexuality are lampooned in the surviving recording.

This song highlights the decision to turn Galahad's sexual inexperience into a humorous situation. Unlike the literary tradition, Galahad's chastity does not illustrate his perfection. In *A Connecticut Yankee*, the collaborators present the same character trait as perhaps a marker of homosexuality but overtly as an obstacle to be overcome in order to enter into the expected heteronormative romance of an early-to-mid-twentieth-century Broadway musical. "On a Desert Island with Thee" is Galahad's first foray into the socially "appropriate" realm of heterosexuality, albeit presented in a comedic light (thus, potentially negating the supposed normativity).

"I Feel at Home with You" is Galahad and Evelyn's second act duet. The song grows out of a discussion about marriage. After some mild resistance, Galahad declares his love for Evelyn and praises her for changing him from a "milquetoast" to a lover. Marked to play with "bright bounce," this fun and catchy love duet with an AABA chorus is extremely characteristic of secondary couple love songs. The dotted rhythms, moderately quick tempo, and memorable tune offer a cheerful declaration of affection, listing all the traits each member of the couple loves about the other. Once again, humor dominates the lyrical approach. "I Feel at Home with You" plays on the "cozy cottage trope" as identified by Jeffrey Magee.[30] Instead of pinpointing a specific place as home, the couple acknowledges each other as home no matter where they go. As Galahad lists the reasons why he loves Evelyn, a dated sexism comes through as he notes how she "fit[s] on the knees" and flatters him. Some elements of passion are involved, though seemingly taking a back seat to companionship. For her part, Evelyn calls Galahad an idiot in five different ways. She notes that "our minds are featherweight," expressing delight in their mutual lack of intellectual capacity.

In the Revival Cast recording, the performance style once again enhances the purpose and characterization of the song. Chester Stratton sings the verse and chorus in an old-fashioned style with a good deal of rapid vibrato, straining less than in "On a Desert Island with Thee." Since Rodgers's melodic writing includes fewer large leaps, Stratton's ease with the simpler tune stresses the couple's shift from romantic fantasy to domesticity. His bright timbre is again juxtaposed with Vera-Ellen's less polished singing. Significantly, the pair never sings together. Galahad and Evelyn always alternate their statements, singing about each other but never vocalizing as one. As Galahad states outright, their romance seems based more on companionship than physicality (although that aspect is not absent). With their cheery romantic duets, Chester Stratton and Vera-Ellen depict a fun secondary couple through their performance. Using this performance as a model, *A Connecticut Yankee* characterizes Galahad not as the religious and chivalric symbol of Arthurian legend but a typical comedic male character of American musical comedy.

In addition to his romantic duets, the 1943 revival adds another musical number for Galahad in the second act opening, "Ye Lunchtime Follies." Galahad and the Camelot ensemble illustrate the changes that Martin has wrought during his time as Sir Boss. The shift from the spiritual gospel-style "Rise and Shine" to a modern song-and-dance number exemplifies Martin's influence. Galahad and the others have adopted customs, habits, and language from Martin's twentieth-century idiom. Galahad sings the song over the radio as a means of announcing a work break and introducing the entertainment, which will segue into a dance number by the factory workers. The lunch break entertainment taking the form of a "follies" makes explicit reference to the revues of the early twentieth century, particularly the Ziegfeld Follies. Rodgers references a number of musical and dance styles throughout the sequence, including swing, boogie woogie, and crooning. On the whole,

"Ye Lunchtime Follies" is a typical musical comedy syncopated song-and-dance number. The song modernizes Galahad, showing his connection to Martin and removing him from his primary role as hapless lover.

In the 1955 television production, the secondary romance—and, therefore, the characters of Galahad and Evelyn—is removed in order to shorten the running time. An instrumental version of "On a Desert Island with Thee" accompanies a short court jester dance at Queen Morgan Le Fay's court. In the jester performance, "Desert Island" is bookended by the more familiar "Thou Swell." Used as a brief dance instrumental, "On a Desert Island with Thee" lacks the association with Galahad as discussed previously in this chapter. Instead, it acts as a sort of bridge for "Thou Swell" (which incidentally lacks a bridge) in a court entertainment. The televised production does retain "Ye Lunchtime Follies," performed by Sandy, and "I Feel at Home with You," now sung by Sir Kay. In the 1955 production, "Ye Lunchtime Follies" retains the same purpose. It shows the modernization of Camelot. The song does little to add to Galahad's characterization in the 1943 revival, simply giving him additional stage time. Given the jazzy musical persona of Sandy, it makes sense to give her the second act opening. The song turns into a female solo with chorus girls, which additionally works as a "follies" number. Janet Blair, who plays Sandy, is a belter, and the song showcases her vocal style.

Sir Kay

The televised production elides Sir Galahad with Sir Kay. In the literary tradition, Kay is the son of Sir Ector and Arthur's foster-brother. Although Malory and others often depict Sir Kay as particularly unpleasant, he is also one of Arthur's most loyal knights. Like in the Twain novel and stage adaptations, Kay captures Martin and brings him to Camelot. In making up a daring tale of dragons and fighting, the Kay of *A Connecticut Yankee* is emblematic of the simplistic minds of Camelot's residents. In the 1955 televised production, he also sings the song "I Feel at Home with You," directed largely to the Switchboard Operator (whom Kay briefly refers to as "Miss Windemere"). Accompanied by a small ensemble and featuring syncopated brass, Kay seduces with his song. He interrupts the Switchboard Operator at her work and weaves a domestic fantasy for their future (Figure 1.1). As such, the televised production reassigns the function of the song. Additionally, the

Figure 1.1. Sir Kay Seduces the Switchboard Operator. Herbert Fields, Lorenz Hart, and Richard Rodgers. *A Connecticut Yankee*. Directed by Max Liebman. Pleasantville, NY: Video Artists International, 1955. DVD.

characterization of Kay as a charming flirt is wholly new—more musical comedy than Arthurian legend.

This version omits the opening verse, beginning on the more familiar chorus with the line "I feel at home with you." Although Galahad's lyrics remain the same when translated for Kay, Evelyn's portion is removed. Instead, the Operator sings Galahad's original line about respecting his partner. Unlike the Broadway production, Kay and his romantic interest sing together in harmony. However, Figure 1.2 shows him as a womanizer as Kay sings the song to other women working in the factory. The tune becomes a call and response between Kay and his conquests before the Operator returns to finish the song, usurping her competition. In this version, "I Feel at Home with You" is kept more for its own sake than any real characterization. In true Tin Pan Alley style, the upbeat love song is generic enough that any number of characters could sing it in the context of the show. Although it functions as a resolution in the mildly rocky relationship of Galahad and Evelyn, "I Feel at Home with You" works just as well as Kay's means of seduction.

Figure 1.2. Sir Kay as Womanizer. Herbert Fields, Lorenz Hart, and Richard Rodgers. *A Connecticut Yankee*. Directed by Max Liebman. Pleasantville, NY: Video Artists International, 1955. DVD.

Morgan Le Fay

In regard to engagement with Arthurian legend especially, the most significant change made for the 1943 Broadway revival is the addition of songs for Morgan Le Fay's character. Of the six new songs written for the revival, three belong to Fay Morgan/Morgan Le Fay. "This is My Night to Howl" occurs during the contemporary setting of the prologue. Both "To Keep My Love Alive" and "Can't You Do a Friend a Favor?" are sung by Queen Morgan Le Fay. Vivienne Segal played the villainous queen in the Broadway revival— a performance that has been preserved on the Revival Cast recording. In 1940, Segal had originated the complicated Vera Simpson in the Rodgers and Hart classic *Pal Joey*. When the team decided to return to *A Connecticut Yankee*, they had Segal in mind for Morgan Le Fay. As such, Rodgers and Hart wrote the character's songs, in particular "To Keep My Love Alive," for Segal. Rodgers composes for her mature mezzo-soprano, and Hart utilizes the sexually aware image developed in songs like "Bewitched, Bothered, and

Bewildered" and "Den of Iniquity" from *Pal Joey*. In this way, Rodgers and Hart harness Segal's capabilities in order to enhance the character of Morgan Le Fay.

In both the 1927 and 1943 productions, Morgan Le Fay is the primary antagonist of *A Connecticut Yankee*. This represents a marked change from Twain's novel, which introduces Merlin as Hank Morgan's principal rival. Twain includes an episode spent in Morgan Le Fay's castle in which her cruelty and love of torture are exhibited; she is clearly depicted as a villain. However, she does not compete with Hank or represent magic in the Yankee's ongoing battle between magic and science in the way Merlin does. Indeed, the incident involving the execution of the musicians does more to align Hank Morgan with Morgan Le Fay than to place the two at odds. The musical *A Connecticut Yankee* presents Merlin as a bit of a joke with his magician's tricks, and while somewhat villainous, he is only a henchman for the nefarious Morgan Le Fay. Exchanging the role of antagonist reinforces Martin's contemporary romantic dilemma, since Morgan Le Fay is the medieval counterpart to his real-life fiancée Fay Morgan. In making Morgan Le Fay the "villain" in Martin's fantasy, she represents the undesirable romantic partner in both worlds, leading to the dissolution of the engagement. At the same time, the development of her role in *A Connecticut Yankee* becomes another point of reference with pre-existing versions of the character.

Morgan le Fay has a long and complicated history in Arthurian literature. In many English-language accounts of Arthuriana, the foundation for the basic character traits and background of Morgan le Fay is rooted in Malory's *La Morte d'Arthur*. Morgan le Fay is Arthur's half-sister; the siblings share their mother, Igraine. Malory depicts Morgan le Fay as a remarkably complicated character. She is a sorceress, seductress, and nemesis of Arthur until she bears him to Avalon at the moment of his death. In the past several hundred years, Morgan le Fay rarely has been depicted as simplistically evil. Although some stories paint her as more sympathetic than others do, the character is often complex in her motivations and actions. Mark Twain's interpretation of the character, like all his Arthurian characters, shows an unschooled and ignorant woman. Morgan le Fay is almost innocent in her wickedness, and her portrayal includes a humorous juxtaposition of allure and malice. Upon the brink of meeting the infamous queen, Hank Morgan describes her thus:

> I knew Mrs. Le Fay by reputation, and was not expecting anything pleasant.
> She was held in awe by the whole realm, for she had made everybody believe

she was a great sorceress. All her ways were wicked, her instincts devilish. She was loaded to the eyelids with cold malice. All her history was black with crime; and among her crimes murder was common.[31]

Once he meets and spends time with Morgan le Fay, Hank expresses surprise at her beauty and charm. With an even temper and a lot of grace, she casually orders tortures as entertainment, sends commoners to the dungeons, and even murders. Twain's Queen Morgan le Fay actively hates her brother, even attempting to order Hank to the dungeon after he gives the king a casual compliment in conversation. In the novel, the queen is also married to the older Uriens, as in typical Arthurian stories, and the two have a son, Sir Uwaine. The collaborators of *A Connecticut Yankee* take Twain as their starting point while coloring the character with traits outside the Arthurian tradition.

In the 1943 version of *A Connecticut Yankee*, Morgan Le Fay retains her love of cruelty but undergoes a number of character changes. Morgan Le Fay's first appearance occurs when she visits her brother, coming to Camelot in order to find a new husband. Her animosity toward her brother becomes apparent when she pretends not to recognize him in disguise in her castle at the end of the second act. Her behavior is clearly power-driven in both her desire to marry the Boss and wrest control from King Arthur—aided by the wicked, yet incompetent, Merlin. By the end of the show, Morgan Le Fay becomes a stock villain in her actions. She kidnaps Sandy and tries to administer a love potion to Martin. In regard to the original Broadway production, Symonds writes that "pitting his Connecticut hero against the evil Queen in a finale aping Hollywood at its silent best, Fields makes of Le Fay's castle a macabre film studio."[32]

The biggest alteration made to Morgan Le Fay from Twain's version is her representation as a black widow. Fields's version of the queen is not married to the old King Uriens, like in Twain's novel, but has been widowed three times. She names Mordred, Mark, and Athelstane as her deceased husbands. All three come from Arthurian legend; the most interesting in terms of relationship to Arthur himself is Mordred. Traditionally, Mordred is Arthur's illegitimate son by his other sister Morgause, who grows up hating his father and orchestrates the downfall of his reign. In *A Connecticut Yankee*, Arthur explicitly calls Mordred too old for his sister, easily removing any hint of their customary relationship. Tellingly, Morgan Le Fay straightforwardly admits to killing each of her husbands.

The 1927 Broadway production illustrates a fascinating look at musical characterization for Fay Morgan/Morgan Le Fay. The modern character, Fay Morgan, does sing "Ladies' Home Companion" in the prologue. The song "establishes the engaged couple as rather jaded and presents a cynical version of their future."[33] Fay Morgan, while not a love match for Martin, is not a villain. Therefore, she receives some musical characterization. Her medieval counterpart, however, ultimately does not sing. The queen's musical presence underwent some revision throughout the development process of the Broadway production. Initially, a song titled "Morgan, Morgan Le Fay" held a place in the second act when the action shifts to the queen's castle. Narratively, the placement of a song for Morgan Le Fay makes sense, but the song was reassigned to Evelyn (now called "Evelyn, What Do You Say?").[34] In the end, the 1927 production left Morgan Le Fay as an entirely unmusical character. Given that unlikable or "evil" characters often do not sing in musicals, the result highlights the queen's malevolent nature and points out her unsuitability for Martin. Unlike the sweet-voiced Sandy, Morgan Le Fay—and, therefore, Fay Morgan—is not a viable romantic partner for the hero. In casting Vivienne Segal as the malicious queen, however, the musical presence and characterization of Morgan Le Fay develops further in the 1943 revival.

Morgan Le Fay's introductory song, "To Keep My Love Alive," presents the bloodthirsty queen as a black widow. This was apparently the last song Lorenz Hart ever wrote, and the lyrics reflect his wry wit and humor as Morgan Le Fay calmly lists all of the ways in which she has killed her many lovers. She boasts of her fidelity, simply killing her husbands in order to maintain her vows (i.e., "till death do us part"). The song uses a relatively slow tempo, focusing on the amusing, yet murderous, lyrics. Hart's clever rhymes and delightful inventiveness are on full display in this song as Morgan Le Fay lists her annoyances and murderous ways of dealing with them. Indeed, Morgan turns her grievances back on her many husbands in a homicidal version of poetic justice. For example, Sir Thomas's insomnia caused his deadly wife to buy a "little arsenic, he's sleeping well alright." And no less than two husbands were killed for their music-making habits—one even hit over the head with his own harp. Rodgers's pleasant, repetitive melody supplies a diverting juxtaposition to the laundry list of murders. The chorus utilizes the familiar AABA form, a stepwise melody, and simple harmonic profile. The first four measures of the A section stay on the tonic before ending the phrase on the common ii–V^7–I cadence.

Although the B section is not quite so static, Rodgers clearly keeps the emphasis on Hart's amusing, crafty lyrics. Accompanied by a string heavy ensemble, the music is sweetly pleasurable, and it is easy to see why this tune became the one additional hit from the show with its focus on lyrical wit.

"To Keep My Love Alive" is closely tied to Morgan Le Fay's characterization, and the references to various knights as "Sir" George and so on certainly give it an older or British affect. At the same time, the subject matter is broad and funny enough to be pulled from the context of the show pretty easily. Giving Morgan Le Fay a musically sweet-sounding ballad as an introductory song renders her character appealing to some degree and softens her vicious nature. In this way, Rodgers and Hart's depiction of Morgan Le Fay aligns with Twain's. Queen Morgan Le Fay is both charming and cruel, and her song comically highlights these seemingly opposing traits. Without a musical number, her role as a villain takes precedence. The addition of "To Keep My Love Alive," on the other hand, sets the character up as a much more comical antagonist, as well as a more important character.

Vivienne Segal's performance of the song on the recording further highlights this characterization of Morgan Le Fay. As the longest track on the recording at nearly seven minutes, "To Keep My Love Alive" emphasizes Vivienne Segal's prominence, and, therefore, Morgan Le Fay's, in the context of the revival. Oddly enough, the recording cuts the opening verse but does include the encore. Written specifically for Vivienne Segal, it comes as no surprise that "To Keep My Love Alive" largely sits in her vocal wheelhouse. She employs a clear, mezzo-soprano tone with a fairly wide vibrato, highlighting the character's maturity. The entire track is ably sung, and Segal tends to stretch her best notes, particularly a C-♯ or D5 both of which showcase her voice. Indeed, Segal often takes a little extra time on quarter notes that lie in this part of her range. Similar to her performance of "Bewitched, Bothered, and Bewildered," Segal's recording emphasizes her particular vocal abilities, comedic timing, and, of course, the lyrics.

Humorously, the end of each verse thwarts expectations by dropping down the octave. In the recording, the end of these final phrases goes down to a low F, adding an additional element of comedy to the song and illustrating Segal's range. The dip into the lower range removes Morgan Le Fay from the lyrical soprano into an earthier chest voice. Using this lower end of Segal's range on the lyrics "to keep my love alive" makes the otherwise predictable melody sound ironic; Rodgers simply but cleverly emphasizes the lyrics and Morgan Le Fay's characterization. The final note of the song takes this trend to an extreme with a D3. Expectations would assume an ending that stresses the star's vocal ability. For a strong mezzo-soprano, such as Segal, ending on a higher pitch would certainly conform to these expectations. The existing piano-conductor score ends each verse with a descending line; however, these phrases consistently end on the tonic but never go lower than the D above middle C. In Rodgers's piano-vocal sketches for the song, he does notate the low F in the second ending of the song, illustrating his familiarity with Segal's vocal range as well as the comedic possibilities.[35] As such, the humorously low notes represent a combination of Rodgers's writing for her voice and a performance choice by Segal to return to and even extend the joke. The mixture of Segal's lyrical mezzo-soprano, low final notes, and matter-of-fact description of her murders emphasizes her character as not just a villain but a charming and amusing one.

In "Can't You Do a Friend a Favor?," Morgan Le Fay expresses her romantic interest in Martin. This duet shows the queen's attempt to seduce Martin, as well as his attempt to avoid her advances. While Sandy quickly adopts Martin's jazz-inflected style in "Thou Swell," Morgan Le Fay sings in a more "old-fashioned" style. In reality, "Can't You Do a Friend" is a typical Tin Pan Alley song. It features a declamatory opening verse and a 32-bar form chorus (ABAC). In a straightforward common time and again sitting directly in Segal's comfortable range, the song illustrates her desire for and attempted manipulation of Martin. In his turn, Martin assumes Morgan Le Fay's musical style in order to redirect her attention and stay "just friends" with the acknowledged black widow. Appearing early in Act II, "Can't You Do a Friend a Favor?" comes directly after Morgan Le Fay has made plans with Merlin to kidnap Sandy. As such, the audience is under no illusions about the queen's intentions, understanding her to be the main antagonist. Although performed straight by Segal, the song takes on an ironic edge since she plans to force her way into Martin's affections. The song also tempers the argument between the newly feminist Sandy and Martin in the next scene. Additionally, Morgan Le Fay reprises the song when Martin and Arthur enter her castle poorly disguised as slaves. Recognizing both her brother and Martin, she sings "Can't You Do a Friend a Favor?" in a final attempt to seduce the latter before giving him a love potion.

In the 1943 revival production, Vivienne Segal's Morgan Le Fay became the most musical female lead. In fact, "To Keep My Love Alive" is the only truly solo number in the entire score—excepting a very brief reprise of "My Heart Stood Still" sung by Martin. Although Martin sings in the most songs, they are invariably duets. Only Morgan Le Fay gets a song describing herself without the input of another character. Harnessing the star power of Vivienne Segal, the revival enhances Morgan Le Fay's character. Taken together, her two songs depict her as fascinating, even potentially appealing, yet cruel and manipulative. This interpretation dovetails with both common representations of the character in Arthuriana and Twain's specific version of her. At the same time, the musical alters the queen from an unfaithful wife to a deadly faithful one in order to underscore her inappropriateness for Martin in the real world—it would be an unmitigated mistake for Martin to marry Fay Morgan.

Taking its cue from the Broadway revival, the 1955 television production retains all of Fay Morgan/Morgan Le Fay's songs. Gale Sherwood plays Morgan Le Fay and was known for singing with Nelson Eddy. Although Sherwood also showcased the upper part of her range in operetta and musical theater recordings, her style and timbre have a number of similarities to Segal's strong mezzo-soprano with a wide vibrato. In casting Sherwood, the 1955 television production keeps a similar enough voice type to Segal as to draw comparisons. Sherwood's performance of "To Keep My Love Alive" adheres to the score more than Segal's does but infuses it with mischief through her interactions with Arthur's knights. She remains poised throughout, alternately singing directly to the camera and looking at the hapless potential suitors, even engaging in a short, courtly dance during an instrumental interlude as shown in Figure 1.3. Rather than sink down in pitch at the end of the chorus like Segal, Sherwood ascends on the final phrase only to drop down the octave on the final note. This choice highlights her higher range, while maintaining the humor. "Can't You Do a Friend a Favor?" starts with the chorus and takes a much slower tempo than the Segal recording does, stressing Morgan Le Fay's seduction attempt. Overall, the 1955 performance is capable but adds little to Le Fay's characterization. Interestingly, while the characterization of Morgan Le Fay remains stable, Sandy's vocal range is lowered and the production assigns her "Ye Lunchtime Follies." As such, she represents a starker contrast to the queen and receives additional screen time, overshadowing the importance of Morgan Le Fay's character in the televised production.

Figure 1.3. Gayle Sherwood's Performance of "To Keep My Love Alive."
Herbert Fields, Lorenz Hart, and Richard Rodgers. *A Connecticut Yankee.*
Directed by Max Liebman. Pleasantville, NY: Video Artists International,
1955. DVD.

King Arthur

King Arthur himself is an extremely minor character in *A Connecticut Yankee*. Of course, dozens of Arthurian stories from across time focus on other characters, such as Tristan and Isolde or Grail stories featuring Perceval or Galahad. Arthuriana does not need to simply tell the tale of King Arthur. As such, Mark Twain's use of Camelot, and its various figures, as a backdrop certainly qualifies as an Arthurian contribution. In Twain's novel, Arthur obviously takes a back seat to Hank Morgan. As discussed before, Twain does include an episode where Hank and Arthur travel the countryside in disguise and eventually end up as slaves. During this portion of the novel, the reader gains additional insight into the king's character. While still silly, as seen through Hank's perspective, Twain reveals a kindness in Arthur that fleshes him out as more than just an ineffectual and uneducated monarch.

Even more than Twain does in his novel, Fields, Rodgers, and Hart turn the king into a minor character. In the contemporary world, Arthur is Fay Morgan's father—representing a similar (but different) familial connection as the king and his sister queen. The musical's Arthur is a part of the older generation. As such, young knights, such as Galahad, take precedence in the musical comedy iteration. The show does retain aspects of Arthur and now Martin's sojourn in disguise. However, it becomes a plot device, which serves to get the pair into Morgan Le Fay's castle in order to rescue Sandy, rather than further exploration of Arthur's character. In the 1927 Broadway production, Arthur's musical presence is virtually nonexistent. At best, he participates as part of the ensemble in numbers featuring the knights. Since a lack of songs denotes a lack of importance in a musical, King Arthur's role is extremely marginalized in the original Broadway production. The presence of the king simply places the audience in the correct mindset for the mythological background.

The 1943 revival does include a duet between Martin and King Arthur during their time outside Camelot. "You Always Love the Same Girl" represents Martin's acknowledgment that Alice and Alisande/Sandy are quite literally the same girl. Both Geoffrey Block and William Everett discuss the significance of this particular song in regard to changing musical theater ideals. Everett observes that the function of "You Always Love the Same Girl" as a plot song was "atypical in the Rodgers and Hart of the 1920s," reflecting how expectations and norms had changed."[36] Given that the revival of *A Connecticut Yankee* opened in the same year as Rodgers first collaboration

with Oscar Hammerstein II, *Oklahoma!*, Block's description of musical similarities to Rodgers and Hammerstein's style also makes sense.[37] The subject
of the song directly references Martin's love story, yet Arthur's contribution
is a significant one.

Arthur responds to Martin's musings in a more figurative manner, positing
that all girls one loves are the same (or else you wouldn't love them). Arthur
claims that you are not "untrue" if you love many women because they are
somehow all the same. Arthur's participation in Martin's reflection on his
strange situation has two major effects on his portrayal. The main purpose
of the song is to enhance the comradery between King Arthur and Martin.
The pair passes the melody back and forth between each other, and they sing
in unison at the end of each chorus statement. They have a musical rapport
that heightens their similar ways of thinking as well as their friendship. In the
recording, Dick Foran as Martin and Robert Chisolm as King Arthur have
remarkably similar timbres, highlighting their compatibility. Secondarily,
Arthur's attitude about loving several women trivializes Guinevere's affair
with Lancelot. In this song, Arthur not only does not particularly display devotion to his wife but explicitly justifies loving more than one woman. If both
the king and queen have extramarital affairs, her perceived betrayal lessens.
Given that *A Connecticut Yankee* ends its sojourn in Camelot before the
downfall, the audience leaves with a much more optimistic feeling regarding
the mythical reign of King Arthur.

Influence and Legacy

While Mark Twain's *A Connecticut Yankee in King Arthur's Court* and the
later silent film adaptation form the basis for the Rodgers and Hart musical,
the musical treatment of the Arthurian characters contribute their own interpretation to the larger pantheon of Arthuriana. As mentioned earlier in
this chapter, the additional use of Arthurian legend most likely comes from
Tennyson as several references and character interpretations imply. Although
not as dense in its intertextuality as its source material, Fields, Rodgers, and
Hart do include some clear influence from Malory. The creators' versions of
the Arthurian characters, however, also draw on common musical comedy
tropes. The 1943 depiction of Morgan Le Fay, in particular, is a unique one
even as it alludes to earlier versions of her. Since the modern Martin Barrett
and his love interest are the main characters, they have the most songs. Yet

the musical characterization of the familiar figures of Arthurian legend creates an influential imprint that impacts the understanding of later musical retellings.

As a Tin-Pan-Alley-era musical, Rodgers and Hart's *A Connecticut Yankee* represents a typical "work-in-process." From tryouts through Broadway opening and a later revival, the show has undergone a number of alterations throughout its performance life. As such, the musical's engagement with Mark Twain's novel and Arthurian legend writ large has changed throughout its lifetime. As Block has explored, the original Broadway production garnered more success than the 1943 revival.[38] From a twenty-first-century perspective, however, the revival version is both more complete and the only version available for performance.[39] While "My Heart Stood Still" and "Thou Swell" have become standards of the Great American Songbook, *A Connecticut Yankee* has not entered American popular consciousness or even the common musical theater repertory in the same way *Pal Joey* has, for example, or indeed in the same way later Arthurian musicals considered in this book have. At the same time, *A Connecticut Yankee* exemplifies an important piece of Arthuriana for two primary reasons. First of all, this musical represents a twentieth-century engagement with Arthurian legend by one of the most foundational teams of songwriters in American musical theater. Their interest in the legend and the show's initial popularity helped to perpetuate the myth in American culture. Similarly, Rodgers and Hart's contribution has illustrated a number of possibilities for musical treatment of Arthuriana.

Rodgers and Hart's reimagining of Arthurian legend via Mark Twain set up a number of trends that come through in later musicals. While Lerner and Loewe take an earnest approach to the tale, Rodgers and Hart treat the world of King Arthur with lightheartedness and humor. In sidelining the love triangle between the king, Queen Guinevere, and Sir Lancelot even more than the novel does, Fields, Rodgers, and Hart reduce the sense of tragedy inherent in the legend. Instead, Guinevere and Lancelot's affair becomes a running joke, focusing on comedy over drama. Additionally, the treatment of Galahad includes potentially coded homosexuality, subverting the heteronormative subplot typical of musical comedy. Most importantly, the show contains an intertextual approach central to all Arthurian stories. Although less dense than Twain, the anachronistic intertextuality, in particular, represents a key part of musical retellings. All of these aspects come through in later films and stage musicals. *Spamalot*, for instance, takes much from the approach to

Arthuriana seen in 1927 (plus 1943 and 1955) to extremes. Given that Eric Idle explicitly cites musical comedy of the 1920s as inspiration for his musical treatment of *Holy Grail*, the similarities to Rodgers and Hart's musical is important.[40] The earlier duo lays the groundwork for comedic musical interpretations of Arthurian legend in the twentieth century and beyond.

2

Bing Crosby's Stardom and the Depiction of Legend in Paramount's *A Connecticut Yankee in King Arthur's Court*

A mere six years after the revival of Rodgers and Hart's Broadway adaptation, Paramount released the 1949 Bing Crosby vehicle *A Connecticut Yankee in King Arthur's Court*. Appearing at the height of Crosby's contract with Paramount Pictures, the film capitalizes on the singing actor's popularity and appeal in its adaptation of Mark Twain's novel. Arguably the least influential and enduring of the musicals considered in this book, this film version of *A Connecticut Yankee in King Arthur's Court* nevertheless offers a fascinating look at the continued interest in Arthuriana in addition to being an intertextual reference point for adaptations of Twain's novel. Similar to the Rodgers and Hart stage musical, Paramount's version of *A Connecticut Yankee* employs Arthuriana as a colorful background for a romantic musical comedy. Since the film acts as a vehicle for Crosby, *A Connecticut Yankee* highlights his individuality while displaying a sense of ease in integrating himself into the world of Arthur. In short, Crosby's performance depicts Hank Martin as remarkably likeable. Singing four of the five songs in the film, Crosby's Hank dominates the musical landscape and becomes the standard by which the Arthurian characters are measured.

Unsurprisingly, the film garnered a good amount of commercial success as well as praise for Crosby's performance from contemporary critics. According to *Variety*, Paramount's *A Connecticut Yankee* grossed $3 million in its initial release, making it the nineteenth highest grossing film of 1949.[1] Indeed, the Twain adaptation beat out Crosby's other 1949 release, *Top O' the Morning*. Although Crosby's status as a singing film star guaranteed a certain amount of popularity, the film could not compete with the Al Jolson biopic, *Jolson Sings Again*, which was the highest grossing film of the year, or significantly, with the Rodgers and Hart musical biopic, *Words and Music* (1948). Critics found Crosby's performance predictably able but generally

From Camelot *to* Spamalot. Megan Woller, Oxford University Press (2021). © Oxford University Press.
DOI: 10.1093/oso/9780197511022.003.0003

considered the film itself to be a bit lackluster. Both the *Variety* reviewer and Edwin Schallert of the *Los Angeles Times* described the film as having pleasant qualities.[2] *Variety*, however, noted that the "film also falls down in some of the technical work, which doesn't help to carry out the illusion of the romantic days of 528."[3] Bosley Crowther effusively praises Crosby, stating "we can thank Bing Crosby, primarily and above all, because it is Bing in the role of the Yankee who gives this film its particular charm," further observing that it is "Bing's delightful personality, his mild surprises and sweet serenities, and his casual way of handling dialogue that makes this burlesque a success."[4] Clearly, for many critics, Bing Crosby represented the primary draw of the film adaptation.

Casting and Persona

As Crosby's thirty-second feature film with Paramount Pictures, *A Connecticut Yankee in King Arthur's Court* takes advantage of an over fifteen-year film career. Since 1934, Crosby had starred in eighteen films that made the list of the highest grossing films of their year, including *Holiday Inn* (1942), *Going My Way* (1944), and several of the so-called Road films that teamed Crosby with Bob Hope.[5] For his performance of Father Chuck O'Malley in *Going My Way*, Bing Crosby earned his only Academy Award for Best Actor. The partnership with Hope became an immensely popular franchise, not only at the time, but as Gary Giddens observes, these films have been "endlessly recycled on television and at repertory theaters, still fresh, still funny."[6] Crosby's commercial and critical success in film coupled with his recording and radio career made him one of the biggest stars in the United States by the end of the 1940s. Gary Giddens remarks that Crosby "ranked in the top-ten for the better part of two decades and scored as the nation's most popular film star five years running, something no one else in his generation, or those that followed—until the 1970s—accomplished."[7] Although his film career traditionally gets less attention than his recording and radio career, Crosby was integral to American popular culture as an actor. In his analysis of Crosby's tenure at Paramount, Bernard F. Dick discusses the importance of Crosby's time at this studio together with the types of films he made. Dick notes,

> With the coming of sound, Paramount embarked upon a new kind of
> movie that was neither a musical nor a straight film, but one with musical

numbers that were rarely integrated with the plot and were, for the most part, diversions. In other words, these films were not musical comedies, but comedic musicals.[8]

And it is in this style of "comedic musical" that Bing Crosby became known for in the 1930s and 1940s.

The Paramount style of musical helped to shape Crosby's persona; along with the studio's marketing strategies, these musicals developed his image in a specific way. These so-called comedic musicals differentiated Paramount's films from the lavish productions of studios such as MGM. Instead, Paramount relied heavily on the personality and comedic timing of stars, especially Bing Crosby. The crooner couples his smooth, naturalistic vocal style with casual wit. Even when not paired with a louder personality, such as Bob Hope, Bing Crosby often exudes a laidback humor. Given the straightforward persona and the seeming ease with which Crosby approached not only his singing but also his acting, Paramount actually had to combat the charge of laziness in their marketing approach of their biggest star.[9]

One relevant aspect of Crosby's persona as it relates to *A Connecticut Yankee* is the depiction of children's affinity for the actor. Paramount films often included child characters or a nameless gaggle of kids who follow Crosby's character around, illustrating that he is good with kids. Due to the later controversy surrounding Bing Crosby's treatment of his own children, the development of the star as a wholesome, father-like figure is an interesting facet of his image.[10] Gary Giddens's comprehensive (and ongoing at the time of this writing) multi-volume biography examines the complexity of Crosby's life, presenting a more nuanced picture than either his contemporary persona or later detractors suggest.[11] Regardless of the realities of the detached star, Bing Crosby's persona conveys warmth and a fatherly nature. Crosby's version of Hank Martin utilizes the accumulated popular image of the actor/crooner, harnessing his persona in order to shape the film.

Crosby's singing style famously takes advantage of recording technology, shifting away from the brash stage style of singers like Al Jolson to one which utilizes the potential of the microphone. Will Friedwald calls the crooner "one of the great innovators of twentieth-century style," further stating, "Crosby forever changed the way we hear the human voice, and he was the first great musician to develop a performance style in response to technology."[12] Not only do Crosby's crooning vocals come across well in recording or on the radio, but his style feels natural in the context of his Paramount musicals. The audience, of course, expects the star to sing in his signature style. During the so-called Golden Age of the Hollywood musical, Crosby's easy, comedic approach provided an enjoyable contribution to the genre. And while Crosby's legacy tends to focus on his voice, his prominent film career certainly has much to do with the star's centrality to American popular culture in the mid-twentieth century.

While *A Connecticut Yankee in King Arthur's Court* is first and foremost a Bing Crosby vehicle, some additional casting has an important effect on the interpretation of Arthurian legend within the film. Sir Cedric Hardwicke plays King Arthur, lending the film his experience on stage and screen and infusing the character with a sense of authority. On stage, Hardwicke had a number of credits to his name, including several Shakespeare plays, but was most known as an interpreter of George Bernard Shaw's works. Furthermore, at age forty-one, Hardwicke became the youngest actor to receive a knighthood. In a *New York Times* article commemorating his career, the author states, "in the years that followed, he became known to American audiences for mature and dignified characterizations entirely suitable for a 'Sir.'"[13] By the time he played Arthur, Hardwicke had appeared in just over fifty films, including Alfred Hitchcock's *Rope* in 1948. As such, Sir Cedric Hardwicke was a familiar and well-respected addition to *A Connecticut Yankee*. While Hardwicke's experience and persona lend a sense of gravitas, the actor's portrayal of Arthur focuses on the possibilities of ridiculousness in the king. Additional Arthurian characters, Sir Sagramore and Merlin, were played by William Bendix and Murvyn Vye, respectively. Both actors specialized in character parts, and Bendix, in particular, had a number of supporting roles under his belt prior to *A Connecticut Yankee*. Taken as a whole, the actors playing each of the legendary characters support Crosby's leading man, bringing their respective talents to add humor to the film.

Relationship to Rodgers and Hart's Musical and Songwriters

Since Paramount's adaptation of Twain's novel comes close on the heels of Rodgers and Hart's Broadway revival, an understandable comparison arises between the two musicalized versions. In fact, one wonders why Paramount did not use any of the songs by the renowned duo. J. Roger Osterholm notes that Paramount actually could not use Rodgers and Hart's songs due to the fact that MGM owned the rights.[14] Indeed, the rival studio used the hit tune "Thou Swell" in their musical biopic of the songwriting team, *Words and Music* (1948). June Allyson performed the song as a "show number" in order to provide pseudo-medieval flair for the onscreen production. *Words and Music* grossed more than *A Connecticut Yankee* with its sanitized biographical subject matter, and more importantly, hit songs from Rodgers and Hart's catalog. Regardless, Paramount had to look elsewhere and hired their own contracted songwriting team.

James Van Heusen and Johnny Burke wrote the songs for the 1949 film version of *A Connecticut Yankee in King Arthur's Court*. The pair had worked on a number of Paramount musicals prior to this film, including several featuring Bing Crosby. In fact, Van Heusen and Burke wrote several songs for Crosby's award-winning film *Going My Way* and won the 1944 Academy Award for Best Song for "Swingin' on a Star" from that film. Given their experience with Paramount and Bing Crosby films, Van Heusen and Burke were a natural choice for *A Connecticut Yankee*. The songwriting team knew how to write for a Crosby vehicle and highlight Paramount's star. At the same time, the close proximity to Rodgers and Hart's revival—although it was not received with the same enthusiasm as the original 1927 production—invites comparison with the famous duo's songs. Crowther observes, "although [Van Heusen and Burke's songs] aren't up to the classics of Rodgers and Hart, [they] are obviously suited to be sung."[15] Yet David Carson Berry observes that Jimmy Van Heusen was an incredibly successful songwriter, not only in Hollywood but also more broadly. Berry surveys compositional trends in a number of his songs that reveal his "artistry and compositional ingenuity."[16] While the songs from this film are not among Van Heusen's most enduring, they adequately fulfill the needs of the film, and in some cases, help to interpret the characters of King Arthur and his knights in unique ways.

Adapting Twain

In the opening credits, the Paramount film calls itself *Mark Twain's A Connecticut Yankee in King Arthur's Court*, explicitly coupling this particular adaptation with Twain's novel. Of course, like all adaptations, this film's creators take their own liberties. At the same time, Paramount stays closer to the source material than earlier film adaptations do and closer even than Herbert Fields's treatment of the story does. The *Variety* reviewer, in particular, notes that the Paramount adaptation is "closer to the Twain story than the 1921 silent."[17] Nevertheless, the opening frame changes drastically. First of all, the diegetic present is not contemporary with the time of production but is set in 1912. In place of a modern Yankee and topical allusions, the film enters a nostalgic pre-war past. In its treatment of technology then, the film relies on a pre-WWI conception of progress and avoids the specter of technological advancement's destructive possibilities as represented by the world wars. Nevertheless, Umland and Umland observe, "in its final twenty minutes or so it does take a sobering turn towards social criticism similar to that found in Twain's novel."[18] The criticism, however, is not as pointed as in the novel, situated as it is in the past. The film opens with Hank touring a castle in England and disturbing the guides with his presumed (outlandish) knowledge of the past. The owner, Lord Pendragon, becomes interested and summons Hank who quickly embarks on his tale.

The framing device, which occurs before Hank's story begins, introduces Arthurian legend as "history." In the context of actual history, scholars agree that the existence of King Arthur is highly unlikely.[19] Additionally, Mark Twain invents certain characters, including Lady Alisande. The Paramount film treats the Knights of the Round Table as historical fact. Furthermore, the film defines Camelot as a surviving castle, which tourists can visit and explore. As such, the Paramount film does not treat Hank's adventure as a realization of legend but as a trip to the concrete past. Additionally, the film heavily implies that actual time travel takes place. In Twain's novel, the possibility of actual time travel is oblique at best; and in Rodgers and Hart's version, Martin's journey is an overt fantasy caused by being knocked unconscious. In the 1949 film, Hank walks through a real castle in 1912, revealing uncanny knowledge of the historical figures and actively correcting the tour guide's mistaken assumptions.

The film retains the affectation of having Arthurian characters double as contemporary ones as seen in the Rodgers and Hart stage musical. From the outset, Lord Pendragon and King Arthur are not only played by the same actor, but also both suffer from a chronic cold. Furthermore, the modern-day Lord Pendragon sets up a meeting between Hank and his niece Sandy after hearing the young man's story. Sandy, of course, turns out to be the spitting image of Lady Alisande, and even gives Hank a knowing wink at the end of the film. As such, the film simultaneously implies that the world of Camelot and King Arthur was real and that Hank Martin travels through time—making the film a true musical fantasy.

For the most part, the 1949 film musical can be understood as a vehicle for Bing Crosby. Since Twain's original novel heavily focuses on Hank Morgan's perspective, the source material provides a solid foundation for a strong emphasis on Crosby's portrayal of the character. Unsurprisingly, the Paramount film sanitizes a number of aspects of Twain's tale. Similar to Fields, Rodgers, and Hart's protagonist, the Yankee's name removes all unsavory associations. Unlike the stage musical, however, this film preserves the given name Hank. Bing Crosby's character becomes Hank Martin—a figure recognizable from the novel but without the troubling association with Morgan le Fay. Indeed, the film not only changes Hank's surname but omits the character's arbitrary ordering of musicians' deaths. Moreover, the 1949 Hank Martin makes very few active alterations to the running of Camelot. He does not set up factories of any kind or "invent" new technology on a mass scale. Susan Aronstein remarks that "unlike the literary Hank, he has no desire to 'boss' the country, he only wants to get the girl."[20] Hank's romantic goals—rather than his paternalistic desire to reform the medieval era—are what drive his actions in Camelot; he no longer remakes the country in his own image.

Instead, Hank Martin desires a simple life as a blacksmith, even requesting his own blacksmith's shop from the king. In the film's present, Hank Martin is a former blacksmith forced to become an auto mechanic due to the changing technologies of the early twentieth century. This version of Hank is not a technological wiz from a factory but a small business owner who is trying to keep up with the times. In order to do so, Hank bought an extraordinarily comprehensive almanac, which teaches him how to service an automobile and a number of other things throughout the film. Rather than a beacon of technological progress, Hank is often somewhat wary of technology as evidenced by his preference for his previous occupation of blacksmith to mechanic. Once in the medieval past, Hank does use his almanac to make a pistol but never resorts to weapons of mass destruction, or even larger guns, like his earlier counterparts. Hank's foray into weaponry is couched as a pet project, ultimately becoming a plot device that allows him to defeat Merlin in the final conflict. The film even contains a comedic scene in which Sir Sagramore fiddles with the pistol, not believing in its danger until it accidentally goes off and pierces a suit of armor.

Hank's desire for a simpler way of life represents a marked difference from his literary source. In addition to removing many of the disconcerting facets of his character, the Paramount film enhances his wholesome image. Hank Martin is a magnet for neighborhood kids, both in the present time and in the Arthurian past. The first song of the film shows Crosby singing to a crowd of children about inventions. At the end of the song, he states, "well, there's a moral somewhere, kids." This characterization is more about Bing Crosby's own star persona than it is about Hank. Stephen C. Shafer's analysis of cartoons featuring the American icon reveals a shift in his image that solidifies by the late 1940s when the crooner was depicted as "reliable, non-threatening, domestic, and mainstream."[21] Connecting with this persona, *A Connecticut Yankee* shows Crosby's bachelor character as a fatherly figure and moral educator to the youths. When he travels to Camelot, children still hang around his shop. In this way, the film displays Crosby as a wholesome, kid-friendly, masculine role model.

Of course, the Paramount film augments the romantic attachment between Hank Martin and Lady Alisande (aka Sandy). Previous adaptations similarly bow to mainstream conventions of popular entertainment in this way. Hank first encounters Alisande during her court performance in which she sings and dances for her uncle, King Arthur. The two are immediately attracted to one another, shown by a shot/countershot of their reactions toward seeing each other for the first time (Figure 2.1). At Hank's first ball, he seeks out Alisande and shows his affection for her by winking—an action the medieval lady does not understand at first but soon becomes their signature exchange (Figure 2.2). This scene also reveals that Lady Alisande is betrothed to the brave Sir Lancelot, who has gone questing. This love triangle becomes the main source of romantic strife throughout the film. Although Hank and Sandy fall in love, she feels obligated to keep her promise of marriage to Lancelot. Unlike either the Twain or the Rodgers and Hart musical, the 1949 version of Sandy is initially unavailable, leaving space for a romantic entanglement. Similar to the Rodgers and Hart version, on the other hand, Lady Alisande does have a modern-day counterpart: Lord Pendragon's niece, Sandy. At the end of the film, Sandy winks at Hank, leaving the audience to wonder at the sense of reality and her role in the doubled time periods.

While the filmmakers change Twain's novel in a number of significant ways, this film does retain several aspects not present in the earlier stage musical adaptation. Both adaptations include the episode in which King Arthur agrees to disguise himself as a commoner. In the Paramount film, the reasons Hank proposes this scheme are the same as in the novel; he wants Arthur to experience the poverty and strife of his subjects. The film also keeps the slave auction after Hank, Sagramore, and Arthur's capture. Similar to the description in Twain's novel, Arthur sells for less in the auction than Hank.

Figure 2.1. Shot/Countershot of Hank and Alisande's Meeting. Edmund
Beloin. *A Connecticut Yankee in King Arthur's Court*. Directed by Tay Garnett.
Universal City, CA: Paramount Pictures, 1949. DVD.

Figure 2.2. Hank's Signature Wink. Edmund Beloin. *A Connecticut Yankee in King Arthur's Court*. Directed by Tay Garnett. Universal City, CA: Paramount Pictures, 1949. DVD.

Unlike the stage musical, the Paramount film does allude to some version of Twain's creation of Clarence, Hank's trusty sidekick. The film, however, conflates Clarence with a minor Knight of the Round Table, Sir Sagramore. In this version, it is Sagramore, not Sir Kay, who captures Hank and spins a tale involving dragons to the court. The storytelling knight regrets causing the imminent execution of the newcomer, and ultimately, becomes Hank's squire once the crisis has passed. Although Hank affectionately refers to the knight turned squire as "Saggy," Sir Sagramore reveals that his given name is Clarence. Similar to his literary counterpart, this Clarence becomes Hank's right-hand man—a willing sidekick for all of Hank's schemes.

In keeping with Twain's novel, Merlin and Morgan le Fay are portrayed as villainous in the film. Both characters wear black in the manner of stock evil characters (Figure 2.3). Morgan le Fay represents the lesser villain with a more reduced characterization than she receives in either the Twain novel or Rodgers and Hart version. Like the earlier stage musical, however, Morgan le Fay is attracted to Hank when he arrives in Camelot. The film makes her

Figure 2.3. Merlin and Morgan Le Fay in Black Outfits in the Right of the Frame. Edmund Beloin. *A Connecticut Yankee in King Arthur's Court*. Directed by Tay Garnett. Universal City, CA: Paramount Pictures, 1949. DVD.

King Arthur's niece rather than his sister, so that she and Alisande are of a similar age. This version of Morgan le Fay is certainly bloodthirsty but mostly depicted as a scorned woman. She resents the fact that Hank prefers Alisande over her and was completely passed over at the ball when she asked Hank to dance.

However, Morgan le Fay's wickedness takes a backseat to Merlin's villainy during the course of the film. The Paramount film portrays Merlin as ambitious and jealous of Hank's "magic" tricks. Ultimately, Merlin stages a coup and enslaves both Arthur and Hank when the two are in disguise—knowing full well who they really are. When Sagramore kills a guard during his escape, Merlin orders the execution of Hank and the king. Once the two escape (through Hank's knowledge of a forthcoming eclipse via his remarkable almanac), Merlin takes Sandy hostage. The medieval portion of the film then ends with Hank's daring rescue and attack on Merlin's tower.

Like any piece of Arthuriana, additional characters from the world of King Arthur populate Paramount's *A Connecticut Yankee in King Arthur's*

Court. As mentioned earlier, Sir Sagramore doubles as Twain's original creation, Clarence. The film picks up on a minor Knight of the Round Table and conflates him with another figure in order to flesh out his characterization. The film also includes the renowned Sir Lancelot. When Hank arrives in Camelot, Lancelot is away from court questing. Interestingly, the film takes up the notion of Lancelot as a hapless member of a love triangle; however, since Hank and Sandy represent the main romantic couple, Lancelot becomes Lady Alisande's betrothed. Given this shift, Lancelot is a generation younger than King Arthur. The film interprets the famed knight as skilled yet pompous—a prime example of the backward Knights of the Round Table. The pre-existing engagement and Sandy's conviction regarding knightly honor form the main areas of conflict for the developing relationship between Hank and Sandy. Other than his knightly prowess, Lancelot receives very little characterization or development. Since Lancelot becomes the member of a more prominent love triangle in this particular story, the film simply removes Guinevere from the equation. As such, King Arthur appears to have no queen in this version—or, at least, she is never mentioned.

Arthur himself contains a number of resemblances to his literary and stage musical counterparts. As discussed earlier, King Arthur has a modern counterpart in the Paramount film in a similar vein to Fields, Rodgers, and Hart. In the 1949 film, the twentieth-century Lord Pendragon is a descendant of the illustrious King Arthur, still residing in the ancient king's castle. Of course, the legendary King Arthur was the son of Uther Pendragon. Therefore, the film draws on an existing mythical background. As mentioned earlier, both the modern Pendragon and the long-dead king suffer from chronic colds, linking the past and present for both Hank and the audience. Additionally, this character quirk enhances the portrayal of King Arthur. The constant sneezing and searching for cold remedies gives the king a ridiculous air. He also comes across as benevolent yet oblivious. Given his kind nature, Hank finds it difficult to believe the king would allow the injustices he encounters in Camelot. When confronted, Arthur reveals his ignorance, occasioned by selfishness and privilege. The king readily agrees to tour the country in disguise and vows to implement changes when he witnesses the behavior of his knights firsthand. The Arthur of this film is not the idealized ruler of the legends—although until confronted with the truth, the king believes that he is beloved and reigns over a perfect kingdom. In reality, Camelot is plagued with class inequality and poverty. As a genuinely kind man, however, Arthur accepts the true nature of his kingdom and promises real change. The film's version of Arthur is funny and preoccupied with his health yet a sound, if imperfect, ruler.

Song and Characterization

In the final cut of the film, Bing Crosby sings in all of the musical numbers but one. The only number that does not include Crosby is performed by the Lady Alisande (played by Rhonda Fleming). Her song and accompanying dance number, "When Is Sometime," is couched as a diegetic performance for the court's entertainment. Alisande's musicality introduces her as a viable romantic partner for Bing Crosby's Hank Martin, underlined by his obvious and immediate attraction to her. Understanding the film as a Crosby vehicle certainly explains the musical focus. Crosby's first song appears in the modern framing segment in order to set up Hank Martin's affinity for invention and appeal to children. As noted in the previous section, Hank exhibits a certain nostalgia for an earlier age through his partiality to his original profession of blacksmith. At the same time, the song, "If You Stub Your Toe on the Moon," represents his willingness to learn new technologies, which will serve him well in medieval England. The majority of the musical numbers, however, occur during Hank's sojourn in Camelot. As such, the crooner's signature style characterizes the sound of the film's Arthurian world.

Hank's influence on Camelot is explicitly musical, as evidenced in a scene where he teaches the court musicians how to "jazz" up their staid, $\frac{3}{4}$ time dance music with heavy use of strings. Unlike the book's Hank Morgan, this film's Hank Martin does not order the execution of the court musicians when he dislikes their music but instead goes to straighten them out. In altering the episode from Twain, the film takes advantage of Bing Crosby's musical persona in an extended set piece. Hank first whistles or sings a melody for individual instrumentalists in the ensemble. Amusingly, he attempts to whistle a motive for the penny whistle, which fails to sound good. Crosby punctuates the musical joke with the line, "let's file this away until 1776." Hank then identifies the zither as the "rhythm section" and asks him to switch the meter from three to four. When Hank comes to the lute, he actually picks up the instrument to demonstrate, adjusting the tuning and then briefly playing (Figure 2.4). And finally, he brings the trumpet player—who typically heralds arrivals or announcements—into the band. In this way, Hank turns the medieval ensemble into a big band suitable for his style of crooning

Figure 2.4. Hank Martin Demonstrates the Lute. Edmund Beloin. *A Connecticut Yankee in King Arthur's Court*. Directed by Tay Garnett. Universal City, CA: Paramount Pictures, 1949. DVD.

popular song interpretation. Hank's first influence on the Arthurian world is a musical one, not a technological one. Although Crosby sings at points throughout the film, this diegetic scene shows a blacksmith turned mechanic display an uncanny amount of musical skills. As such, the scene, by focusing on Hank's intimate knowledge of music and preference for a big band sound, telegraphs Bing Crosby's career as a singer.

Once Hank has exerted his influence on the court musicians, he introduces the court to couples dancing. While many of the knights and ladies appear scandalized at first, Arthur enjoys the new dance style and joins Hank and Sandy on the dance floor. Once the king breaks the ice, the rest of the court takes up the dance (quickly learning the steps). Throughout the dance scene, Hank's modernized band plays. Of course, the actual sound of the band does not match with the visual representation of a pseudo-medieval ensemble. For example, the music heard does not include a zither or natural trumpet. Soft use of a drum kit and typical modern brass instruments, on the other hand, are evident. The backbeat is apparent and indicates not only the change in meter as dictated by Hank but the typical characteristics of American popular music. Significantly, the full version of the transformed dance piece includes a syncopated, fast-paced version of the opening motive from the romantic song "Once and for Always" (Example 2.1). The use of this short melodic motive prefigures the full statement of the song, which occurs during the romantic encounter between Hank and Sandy in the following scene.

The romantic ballad, "Once and for Always," appears twice in the film. On the whole, the song is a typical Crosby crooner ballad. As the film's signature romantic song, "Once and for Always" invites comparison to Rodgers and Hart's similarly functioning song, "My Heart Stood Still." Although the context of the two songs differs in terms of narrative placement, both songs refer to the love between Hank/Martin and Sandy. In the Paramount film, Hank sings "Once and for Always" soon after meeting Lady Alisande. At this point in the film, neither Hank nor the audience have been introduced to Alisande's modern counterpart. Burke's lyrics, however, allude to the fact that this love is not confined to Hank's time in Camelot. Broadly, the sentiment of loving "once and for always" has a common metaphorical meaning. In *A Connecticut Yankee in King Arthur's Court*, however, it takes on a more literal significance. Claiming that "wishing days are over" and "don't you know that always isn't too much time," Hank signals a love that will literally span hundreds of years.

Similar to Rodgers's melodic writing in "My Heart Stood Still," Van Heusen's main melodic motive in "Once and for Always" utilizes a descending minor third. The motive begins, however, with a quick turn from B♭ to A♭ and back up to the B♭ before finishing the stepwise descent. In order to accommodate Crosby's range, the film's soundtrack version is in a lower key than the published piano-vocal score, and this motive begins on a D in the score's version rather than B♭ as in the film (see Example 2.1 for transcription of motive as it appears in the film). While the melodic motive on the lyrics "once and for always" bears some similarity to Rodgers's in "My Heart Stood Still," Van Heusen's melody typically utilizes a larger range with

Example 2.1. "Once and for Always" Opening Motive. Transcribed from Edmund Beloin. *A Connecticut Yankee in King Arthur's Court*. Directed by Tay Garnett. Universal City, CA: Paramount Pictures, 1949. DVD.

more leaps. Written for Crosby's vocal capabilities, Hank regularly jumps an octave in the transitions between one phrase and another—smoothly, of course, in true crooner fashion. Unlike the standard Tin Pan Alley, 32-bar form of Rodgers's ballad, Van Heusen's chorus is thirty-six measures with an AA′ formal structure. In the second A section, the melody changes from the original after ten measures and extends an extra four measures in order to reinforce the title sentiment and resolve the harmonic progression; the first A section ends on the dominant, leading into the repetition while the song itself ends on the tonic. In the final ending, however, Van Heusen employs his distinctive chromatic bass line as discussed by Berry.[22] Rather than the V–I harmonic progression that marks the transitions between the song's phrases, Van Heusen ends the song with a short chromatic descent from scale degree 2 through ♭ to end on the tonic. "Once and for Always" then fits with Van Heusen's emblematic popular music style as well as showcasing Crosby's signature croon.

Accompanied by sweet strings, Hank woos the Lady Alisande (Sandy) with the well-known smooth style of Bing Crosby's recording career. True to style, Crosby includes some light scat-singing. His gentle "doo-doos" successfully attract Sandy. When she sings the next phrase of the ballad, Sandy even imitates Hank's mild scatting. Her adoption of his style indicates that she has fallen in love with Hank. Significantly, only the two of them have sung in the film at this point. Hank and Sandy each have had a solo number, demonstrating their mutual musicality, and therefore, their suitability as a romantic pairing. Additionally, Hank's meddling with the court musicians and introduction of couples dancing served as his first major romantic moment with Sandy. In true musical fashion, Hank and Sandy's romance proceeds according to their mutual proclivity toward song and through musical numbers. Sandy's ability to quickly pick up on Hank's modern singing style demonstrates her viability as a partner for the famous crooner.

"Once and for Always" also occurs as the final song of the film, making it the only song with a reprise. The song begins with a short excerpt that weaves in and out of dialogue before Crosby sings a full statement. Narratively, Hank sings the song as a testament to his devotion after Merlin has imprisoned him and captured Sandy. Although neither Hank nor Sandy sing the song again, the underscoring utilizes the tune when Hank stages a daring rescue of Sandy. In fact, the underscoring includes fourteen total uses of strains from "Once and for Always." Including the opening prelude, the cue sheets show that the tune appears seven times before Bing Crosby initially sings the song in cue 21.[23] Given that "If You Stub Your Toe on the Moon" comes in second in terms of underscoring appearances with nine cues, the infusion of "Once and for Always" into the overall score highlights the centrality of the romance. Therefore, the romantic ballad unsurprisingly becomes the centerpiece of the film's musical approach. As a moderate, lyrical ballad, "Once and for Always" highlights Crosby's crooning style while simultaneously serving as a typical love song for the budding romance—Hank's primary concern in Camelot.

The only musical moment for the Arthurian characters occurs in the trio "Busy Doing Nothing," sung by Hank, Sagramore, and King Arthur. This song takes place when the king and his companions disguise themselves as peasants and travel across the English countryside. All three characters sing the light, catchy tune together throughout much of the number, either in unison or harmonizing during long-held notes. Since neither Sir Cedric Hardwicke nor William Bendix is a strong singer, Crosby's vocal skill forms the foundation for this pleasant trio. Rather than use his softer crooning style, Crosby sings full out (except in a contrasting soft portion of a verse), allowing his singing partners to match his vocal style if not timbre and ability.

The resulting ensemble sound is quite pleasant for this enjoyable, light-hearted number. The song begins with a section of "la-las," which act as a brief refrain. The use of "la-la" in a bouncy dancelike tune gives the song a particularly jovial, carefree feel while also superficially signifying an older style of song. The use of "la-la" in the tradition of English song has a long history, and while the songwriters may not be specifically referencing the English madrigal, for instance, the device nevertheless tracks with that tradition. Of course, the stylistic hallmarks of "Busy Doing Nothing" are that of a mid-century musical comedy film. As such, the musical number does not sound even pseudo-medieval—nor is it meant to.

"Busy Doing Nothing" also represents the only musical characterization given to Arthur and Sir Sagramore. As the title suggests, the song details the cheerful attitude of Hank and his Arthurian companions. Throughout the number, the group revels in their sense of freedom from responsibility and enjoyment in their travels, singing nonsensical lyrics about keeping nature in line. The simple musical elements and cute dancing work together to emphasize the male comradery depicted in "Busy Doing Nothing." Sagramore, especially, has been portrayed as Hank's close friend and helper, and the song solidifies their relationship. Arthur's participation also highlights his friendship with the other two men—ostensibly his social subordinates. Appearing during the king's social experiment, the song further levels the class distinction between the three men. In this number, the titles of king, squire, and "Boss" do not matter; they are simply three friends enjoying a vacation. While the film portrays both Sagramore and Arthur as likeable throughout its duration, this song enhances their appeal. Arthur, in particular, does not show symptoms of his chronic cold or self-pity in the musical number. He simply becomes "one of the guys" and has a pleasant, if inexpert, musical moment. Indeed, "Busy Doing Nothing" is the most fun song in the entire film. As such, the participation of classic Arthurian characters offers a joyful interpretation of them.

In all the musical numbers, Bing Crosby dominates while simultaneously setting a musical standard for the other characters to emulate. Whether Crosby sings alone or with others, his musical persona and ability reigns. Tellingly, the other characters either make specific adjustments to incorporate his style (e.g., Sandy's mild scatting) or simply take their cues from him. Of course, the scene with the court musicians turns this musical dominance into an extended diegetic witticism. Yet, even without this obvious reminder, the film exerts Bing Crosby's musical persona into the fabric of the film and interpretation of Arthurian characters. The medieval world of Camelot conforms to the prevailing influence of Hank Martin/Bing Crosby. This approach follows naturally from the status of *A Connecticut Yankee in King Arthur's Court* as a star vehicle. At the same time, it serves to transform Twain's modern technological influence into a primarily musical influence. The familiar figures of Camelot have a modern appeal, singing and dancing with one of the twentieth century's biggest singing film stars.

In the theatrical release, only Hank's love interest, Sandy, sings without Bing Crosby; originally, however, Merlin's characterization was enhanced through the song "Twixt Myself and Me." Through a 1947 Decca recording, the cut song survives—though it is extremely rare. Opening with high fluttering woodwinds and harp flourishes, the song immediately has a fairytale, mystical aura about it. Given that *A Connecticut Yankee in King Arthur's Court* represents magic as fake, the musical tropes for portraying a sense of the magical become ironic in the context of the song. The lyrics further emphasize the irony as Merlin admits—to himself alone—his fears and faults. Singing the line "mumbling words of magic while I knock on wood," Merlin privately reveals his insecurities regarding his status as a magician. Murvyn Vye's robust, yet untrained, baritone highlights Merlin's bluster. His singing style also has the capacity for a good deal of vocal character acting. When singing about his fear of discovery over the magical fakery, Vye manipulates his voice so that it almost sounds pouty—adjusting his timbre to emphasize the anxiety he feels. On the title lyrics, the lower range is highlighted as Merlin resolves to keep up appearances.

If it had been used, "Twixt Myself and Me" would have had several key effects on *A Connecticut Yankee in King Arthur's Court*. Importantly, the song turns Merlin from a flat, two-dimensional character into one with motivations beyond broadly drawn implications of greed and ambition. As discussed in a previous section, the film draws on Twain's depiction of Merlin while imparting a cartoonish quality to his stock evil nature. "Twixt Myself and Me" offers insight into the famous magician's belligerence. The song also would have given additional screen time to this central Arthurian character. By allowing Merlin a song, Arthuriana becomes less of a "window-dressing" for Hank's adventures and enriches the status of the film as an Arthurian interpretation. Of course, the increase in emphasis on Arthurian characters would have resulted in a decrease of Crosby's musical dominance. Ultimately, the filmmakers chose to highlight the star vehicle nature of the film.

Importantly, it also addresses the issue of magic from an Arthurian perspective. All modern retellings that include Merlin must contend with the element of fantasy indicated by the presence of a wizard. In Mark Twain's novel, Hank Morgan immediately dismisses magic as either phony or delusions of medieval England's ignorant residents. This assertion, however, remains entirely from Hank's viewpoint. The Paramount film takes strides to show these figures as more self-aware than Twain allows. In an earlier scene, Sagramore freely admits his tendencies to bend the truth after spinning a yarn about dragons when he captured Hank. Merlin himself is amazed at Hank's creation of fire through matches and surreptitiously steals a spent match in order to examine it. In "Twixt Myself and Me," Merlin reflects on his charlatanism to some extent, acknowledging to the audience that magic is not real in this world. Without the number, the film loses an additional Arthurian perspective on this matter, letting Hank's viewpoint guide the audience instead.

Conclusion

In some ways, the 1949 Paramount adaptation of *A Connecticut Yankee in King Arthur's Court*'s status as a fun but rather run-of-the-mill star vehicle mars its legacy. Unlike many of the later examples, including Lerner and

Loewe's *Camelot* and especially *Monty Python and the Holy Grail*, this film does not command a great deal of cultural resonance into the twenty-first century—either with scholars or general audiences. Neither were any of the songs hits like "Thou Swell" from Rodgers and Hart's musical. While the film did well at the box office, it was not a smash. Furthermore, *A Connecticut Yankee in King Arthur's Court* has not had the staying power of other Crosby films, such as *White Christmas* or *High Society*. Yet the film holds a certain niche popularity for Crosby film fans; Symonds states that this film is also "much loved" if not as popular as Rodgers and Hart's musical retelling.[24] The continued availability of this film as a product, especially in comparison to the incomplete 1927 stage musical if not the 1943 revival, means that the film has more accessibility. As such, the film has the potential to reach new audiences of Crosby fans or Arthurian enthusiasts.

Interestingly, the decision to set the "modern" portion of the film in the actual past results in a film that often feels less dated than the Rodgers and Hart stage musical. In both Broadway incarnations, Herbert Fields and the songwriting team sprinkle the show with topical allusions and jokes that can appear irrelevant at best or simply outright problematic to later audiences. Of course, the nature of theater means that subsequent productions might update the show in various ways. For the 1949 film, however, the entire original production takes on a patina of the past. Even in the framing story, a sense of nostalgia pervades, and, significantly, the audience is never situated in their own time period. Although the Paramount version has a style and approach typical of the studio in the 1940s, the "contemporary" setting in the past and then a further, mythologized past allows for a continued suspension of disbelief in later twentieth-century and twenty-first-century audiences. The film feels old—but it's *supposed* to feel old.

More importantly, the decision to make this film in the first place speaks to the popularity of the Arthurian world in American popular culture. At the time of production, Mark Twain's novel had enjoyed not only the Rodgers and Hart stage adaptation but also additional film adaptations, including the 1921 silent film and the 1931 remake starring Will Rogers. Aronstein's discussion of these films claims that they all "use the adventures of their Yankee in Camelot to celebrate American progressive values and confirm the nation as a land of democratic possibility . . . [the] 1949 release, reinforces these themes, emphasizing American optimism in a nation reeling from the traumas of World War II."[25] Thus, the film not only indulges in American fascination with the world of King Arthur but also co-opts the ideals for an

American sensibility and purpose. Furthermore, the Paramount adaptation uses the biggest star at its disposal, and one of the biggest film stars of the mid-twentieth century, to do so. In becoming a Bing Crosby vehicle, the 1949 musical film of *A Connecticut Yankee in King Arthur's Court* both draws on and cements the tale's importance in American popular culture.

In its depiction of familiar Arthurian figures as well, the approach is significant. Unlike the Twain novel, the filmmakers portray the famous king and accompanying characters as silly without resorting to the kind of condescension that the author engages in. While not the first adaptation to take this particular approach, the collective idea that we can poke fun at the legend without tearing it down is important. Inserting humor into the idealized monarch and chivalric lifestyle removes reverence without quite sneering, allowing audiences to experience the good while simultaneously implying that modern advances have improved quality of life as well as ways of thinking.

As a modern reinvention of Arthuriana, which inserts an explicitly American perspective on the familiar myth, Mark Twain's *A Connecticut Yankee in King Arthur's Court* represents an essential starting point for musical retellings in the twentieth century. Unsurprisingly, the musical adaptations discussed in these first two chapters are wholly American in nature—both musically and narratively. Only a few years after the 1927 Broadway production premiered, however, British author T. H. White published the first installment of what would become the most important entry of Arthurian literature of the twentieth century: *The Once and Future King*. Two prominent musical adaptations by resoundingly American creators become the next touchstones for musicalized engagement with Arthuriana, representing a much more complex relationship between the British legend and American popular culture than the Twain retellings represented.

PART 2
ADAPTING T. H. WHITE'S
THE ONCE AND FUTURE KING

3

Interpretation and Characterization
in Lerner and Loewe's *Camelot*

"Camelot, Camelot!" intones Arthur in a triumphant rising triadic motive, reminiscent of a bugle call. Throughout the title song of Lerner and Loewe's musical, the legendary king weaves a spell that entrances the audience, pulling us into a land of magic, idealism, and sensuousness. Alternating between imaginative description accompanied by gentle, lyrical musical lines and the rousing cry of joy led by the "Camelot" motive, the song "Camelot" encapsulates the long-held fascination with Arthurian legend. With multiple vocal reprises as well as instrumental allusions, the recurring theme from "Camelot" does much to tell the story throughout the musical. Most importantly, this song illuminates several fundamental aspects of King Arthur's character. Both the music and lyrics reveal an optimistic, idealistic man with a great love for his land and a charisma that draws others to his cause. "Camelot" thus does important narrative work in two distinct ways: it not only gives the audience insight into King Arthur's mindset but it also provides the seed that leads to both Guenevere and Lancelot's love for the great king, eventually bringing them all together for one of the most famed love triangles in literary history.

As the function of the song "Camelot" demonstrates, music plays an important role in the interpretation and understanding of Arthurian legend in Lerner and Loewe's musical. While numerous changes are made to the source material, the decision to turn certain dramatic moments into musical ones lends a particular tone to the story, offering a new perspective to this mid-twentieth-century retelling. Indeed, the music enhances both the magical and sensual qualities of Arthurian legend, attributes which have made the tale an enduring one.

Unlike the musical adaptations of Mark Twain's novel, *Camelot* represents a different type of engagement with ideas of nation. While Twain's novel and subsequent productions insert an explicitly American character and American ideals, Lerner and Loewe's musical displays an American

From Camelot *to* Spamalot. Megan Woller, Oxford University Press (2021). © Oxford University Press.
DOI: 10.1093/oso/9780197511022.003.0004

fascination with British culture. Although this is a more nebulous connection, it is one with a long history, including that specific to the American musical. As exemplified by the lasting popularity of Arthurian legend, Lerner and Loewe's musical version "reveals the extent to which definitions of modern American culture continue to negotiate within a strong awareness of a British social and cultural legacy."[1] The eventual association of Camelot as emblematic of American political idealism vis-à-vis the Kennedy administration strengthens this relationship. If the comparison represents an "incredible distortion of reality," it also helped the nation cope with the president's assassination as well as look back at his shortened administration as one of hope in light of later political strife.[2] Given the history of American engagement with Britain's mythology and Lerner and Loewe's own particular propensity towards British stories, Camelot offers the perfect example of the relationship between Britishness and Americanism in popular culture.[3]

Alan Jay Lerner and Frederick Loewe's musical Camelot takes T. H. White's popular version of Arthurian legend, The Once and Future King (1958), as its source material. Premiering in 1960, the stage musical concentrates on the famous love triangle between King Arthur, Queen Guenevere, and Sir Lancelot. In 1967, the release of a film version of Lerner and Loewe's stage musical inserted another interpretive layer. On one hand, the film remains fairly close to the original Broadway stage production. However, the changes made by the filmmakers provide an important reference point for understanding the continued musical adaptation of The Once and Future King.

The original Broadway production and later film adaptation of Camelot streamline Arthurian legend as presented in The Once and Future King. The layers of adaptation and intertextuality inherent in the Lerner and Loewe musical add to the richness of this popular legend. Adaptation from novel to stage to screen involves a direct reference to the existing works and a fair amount of creative interpretation. In translating White's literary work into a musical on stage and screen, the creators altered the original sources in such a way that highlights the change in medium, reflects the relevant industries, and intersects with the socio-cultural aura of the time period in which they were made. Camelot, in its film incarnation, illustrates nostalgia for the supposed political ideal of the Kennedy administration while strongly intersecting with conventional musical tropes. Lerner and Loewe shaped the tale of King Arthur through song, yet White's writing continues to inform the musical.

T. H. White and Fidelity

The 1958 work entitled *The Once and Future King* includes four distinct parts: *The Sword in the Stone*, *The Queen of Air and Darkness*, *The Ill-Made Knight*, and *The Candle in the Wind*. The 1958 collection includes both new material and shorter works that had been published earlier. T. H. White first published *The Sword in the Stone*, which deals with Arthur's child-hood, in 1938. *The Witch in the Wood* (later revised into *The Queen of Air and Darkness*) was released in 1939, and *The Ill-Made Knight* was published in 1941. By the time Alan Jay Lerner expressed interest in adapting T. H. White's version of Arthurian legend, White had been writing and revising the story into its final form for over twenty years. White's interpretation of the well-known legend through characterization and expansion enters into a centuries-long tradition, which accentuates the "remarkable flexibility and infinite expandability of the central story."[4] Of course, various aspects of the tale of King Arthur and related stories had populated literature and other forms of media throughout England, France, and Germany as early as the twelfth century.

White relies on Thomas Malory's *La Morte d'Arthur* (published 1485) as the basis for his twentieth-century retelling, often explicitly referring the reader to Malory's earlier text for more detail or a "truer" account.[5] Scholars observe that Malory's version tends to be the most familiar for English-speaking audiences. Moreover, Norris J. Lacy claims that "most readers first become acquainted with the Arthurian legend through Malory's version as retold by modern authors."[6] As the most popular of these modern retellings, White's novelization offers an entertaining read that encapsulates the sprawling, complex legend. Alice Grellner goes so far as to claim that *The Once and Future King* is "the one book more responsible than any other for the twentieth century revival of the popularity of the legend."[7] White updates the unwieldy legend for a post–World War II audience, presenting the readers with humor and numerous anachronisms that often comment on Malory's rendering and contemporary issues. White also provides detailed descriptions and intricate character development of Arthur, Guenevere, and Lancelot, which form the basis for Lerner and Loewe's characters.

The Once and Future King introduces Arthur as the young Wart, ward of Sir Ector. The reader witnesses the protagonist grow up, become king, and develop his political ideals—much of which occurs well before Lancelot or Guenever even appear as characters. Arthur is the center of White's tetralogy, even when he seems sidelined by other characters in certain books. The reader sees Arthur's ideas and personality cultivated throughout the decades. Elisabeth Brewer observes that the aging king is "both a symbolic figure and an individual growing in wisdom as in maturity."[8] While White's Arthur is not without serious flaws, his honesty, caring nature, and pure ideals allow his followers to love him wholeheartedly. Guenever loves him for his kindness and goodness, whereas Lancelot admires and loves him for his vision as well as his person. White's highly complex characterization creates the foundation for Lerner and Loewe's version of King Arthur. Yet as this chapter will discuss in further detail, *Camelot* smooths out a number of Arthur's flaws in order to emphasize his idealism. While the intricacies of language and characterization in a novel allow for an extremely complex, flawed, nuanced version of Arthur, the demands of the stage and screen necessitate an easily likeable king in order for the audience to quickly understand his appeal.

While Arthur evolves through decades of character growth, the Guenever of *The Once and Future King* quickly emerges as a tempestuous woman with a jealous streak when it comes to Lancelot's affections. Yet her characterization is more complicated than this. In his typical tongue-and-cheek manner, White describes her thus:

> She was beautiful, sanguine, hot-tempered, demanding, impulsive, acquisitive, charming—she had all the proper qualities for a maneater. But the rock on which these easy explanations founder, is that she was not promiscuous. There was never anybody in her life except Lancelot and Arthur. She never ate anybody except these. And even these she did not eat in the full sense of the word. People who have been digested by a man-eating lioncelle tend to become nonentities—to live no life except within the vitals of the devourer. Yet both Arthur and Lancelot, the people whom she apparently devoured, lived full lives, and accomplished things of their own.[9]

As this passage indicates, White attempts to show that Guenever is not what she appears to be. However, scholars have noted White's difficulties creating her and the problems with her characterization throughout the novel.[10] Guenever remains a remarkably selfish woman throughout the decades. However, Brewer contends that she is nevertheless "a real-life figure, as someone known but not known intimately."[11] White rarely narrates the story from Guenever's perspective but reveals aspects of her inner thoughts and character through others' experiences. As such, Guenever does not appear as well drawn as her male counterparts, and her characterization (along with other female characters in the novel) carries misogynistic undertones. For this reason, the ability of Guenever to express herself through song in *Camelot* proves an important shift from White's version of her.

As the final member of the love triangle, White's Lancelot provides another crucial reference point for Lerner and Loewe. In *The Once and Future King*, White portrays Lancelot as a fundamentally imperfect human being, and his illicit affair with Arthur's wife is merely a symptom of his character flaws. White notes Lancelot's failings and the resulting insecurities multiple times. White states that "his Word was valuable to him not only because he was good, but also because he was bad. It is the bad people who need to have principles to restrain them," and "he felt in his heart cruelty and cowardice, the things which made him brave and kind."[12] Lancelot's proclivity towards cruelty even causes him to fall in love with Guenever; only when he treats her poorly does he recognize her personhood.

Lancelot's aspiration to become the perfect knight both stems from his attempt to overcome his faults and a love for Arthur, whom he met as a young boy. As a youth, Lancelot hero-worships King Arthur and spends his teenage years striving to become worthy of Arthur's Round Table.[13] Upon first meeting Guenever, Lancelot is jealous of her and the obvious affection Arthur has for his wife. White's writings even posit Lancelot's potential bisexuality in reference to his deep feelings for both Arthur and Guenever.[14] Lancelot is the dominant figure in *The Ill-Made Knight*, and he constantly struggles with his religion in conjunction with his earthly love and desires. As a well-drawn, multifaceted character, White's version of Lancelot is a fascinating individual who shares his hero's ideals and continually attempts to be a better person.

For their musical *Camelot*, Lerner and Loewe drew primarily from the final two books of White's tetralogy, *The Ill-Made Knight* and *The Candle in the Wind*. Lerner also cut many integral story elements from the books. For example, the musical completely omits the quest for the Holy Grail, which has not only become one of the key tenets of the Knights of the Round Table but figures heavily in *The Once and Future King*. While earlier versions of Arthurian legend displayed a fascination with the Grail, White was initially reluctant to include this overtly Christian aspect. In May 1939, he wrote in his journal, "the Grail. I had meant to leave it out."[15] Nevertheless, White did include the quest prominently. The search for the cup apparently used by Jesus Christ at the last supper inserts a strong Christian element into Arthur's reign. Unlike in many previous versions, including Malory's, White makes the Grail Quest Arthur's idea rather than simply a plan made by the knights. King Arthur acknowledges the crisis surrounding his Round Table, which happens when the knights simply turn to Might (i.e., fighting). Brewer states that Arthur "decides that what is wrong with the Table is based on a temporal ideal, and only by changing that to a spiritual one, can the Table be saved."[16] White uses descriptions of the questing knights' experiences once they return to Camelot to explore the level of spirituality found in Arthur, Lancelot, and various other knights. The removal of the Holy Grail and accompanying quest not only takes away any explicit connection to Christianity but keeps Sir Lancelot firmly ensconced in Camelot, close to his illicit love Guenevere.

Lerner also eliminates the character Elaine, which eradicates Lancelot's complicated relationship with her. In *The Ill-Made Knight*, Lancelot rescues Elaine, who promptly falls in love with him. Elaine disguises herself as Guenever in order to seduce Lancelot, who had heretofore remained a virgin. White depicts the unfortunate Elaine as a needy, undesirable woman, making her an unreasonable choice when compared to Guenever.[17] White's Elaine is not a viable romantic partner for Lancelot, yet Lerner removes her entirely. In doing so, Lerner simplifies the star-crossed love affair. Furthermore, the deceitful union between Elaine and Lancelot results in a son, Galahad. Since the almost too-perfect Galahad ultimately finds the Holy Grail and ascends into Heaven, Lerner's decision to ignore the quest makes additional sense. Even though Arthur's idealism and vision of the Knights of the Round Table remain intact, the musical narrows its focus significantly and emphasizes the infamous love triangle between the king, his queen, and the most-favored knight. Arguably, this focus causes many of the issues surrounding the second act since this love triangle was always going to end in tragedy. The result is a distinct—potentially jarring—shift in tone from Act I to Act II.

This concentration on the love triangle also makes it the primary cause of the fall of Camelot and, by extension, Arthur's utopian ideal. This represents a modification away from the more intricate, highly difficult situation in White's version. Arthur's illegitimate son, Mordred, plays a key role in the downfall of Camelot in both White's and Lerner and Loewe's tellings, but the particulars of his parentage are glossed over somewhat in the musical. White details Arthur's unwitting act of incest when Morgause (Arthur's half-sister on his mother's side) seduces the young king. The handling of magic in *The*

Once and Future King, as I will discuss further, leaves the reasons behind the seduction open to reader interpretation since Morgause uses magic with questionable effectiveness in the process.

Regardless of whether Arthur sleeps with his half-sister due to her beauty or her witchcraft, the act transpires and comes to represent Arthur's greatest sin. Although Arthur did not know that Morgause was his sister at the time of consummation, he finds out and eventually attempts to drown Mordred as a baby. He fails but tragically kills other babies of the same age. White's Mordred grows to adulthood with this knowledge and gains Morgause's own poisonous hatred of not only Arthur but also what he represents. Although Mordred's hatred stems from legitimate grievances, scholar John K. Crane interprets him as more than simply a fleshed out character but a symbolic figure who represents the complexity of evil.[18] Both Mordred's animosity towards his father and Arthur's own complicity due to his highly unsavory actions as a young man become a major source of the tragedy in White, even more than the love triangle.

The magical fantasy quality of Arthurian legend, particularly as manifested in the wizard Merlyn, separates the source material from the musical versions on stage and screen. *The Sword in the Stone* emphasizes Merlyn's magical abilities and Arthur's experience with them. Merlyn teaches young Arthur, called the Wart, life lessons by turning him into various animals. Interestingly, White treats magic as something not for everyone. Some characters do not really believe in magic, whereas others are unable to experience it. Furthermore, Merlyn's magical teachings are reserved for Arthur's childhood. As Arthur grows up, Merlyn no longer transforms Arthur but simply remains an advisor until such time as his fickle love Nimue locks him away in a cave.

As the remainder of this chapter further explores, T. H. White's interpretation of King Arthur's tale lies behind the musical *Camelot* in both its original stage and film forms. Lerner and Loewe not only nominally but also obviously used *The Once and Future King* as the basis for their musical. At the same time, the team made distinct changes and specifically chose to emphasize the love triangle to a greater degree. In doing so, the use of song to delineate certain character traits of Arthur, Guenevere, and Lancelot, as well as their intertwined relationships, is an essential ingredient to this adaptation. As such, much of my analysis similarly focuses on the portrayal of these three characters and their songs. However, other elements represent significant factors in the adaptation of White's novel as well, including the handling of magic and politics, and I treat them according to how they are dealt with in each production of the musical.

Original Broadway Production

The Broadway production of *Camelot* opened at the Majestic Theatre on December 3, 1960. Richard Burton starred as King Arthur, Julie Andrews as Guenevere, and Robert Goulet as Lancelot. Coming on the heels of the critically acclaimed and enormously popular *My Fair Lady* (1956), *Camelot* invited comparison, especially in terms of casting. The musical engages not only with Arthurian legend but also with theatrical conventions and its status as a "Lerner and Loewe musical." In creating a cast with striking similarities to *My Fair Lady*, director Moss Hart and other collaborators cultivated this musical as part of a Broadway brand and capitalized on the success of that earlier show.

Julie Andrews, who had previously played Eliza Doolittle, originated the role of Guenevere. Andrews began her career in England as a child, able to sing with a mature, clear tone and high range. In 1954, she made her Broadway debut as Polly Browne in *The Boy Friend*, but it was *My Fair Lady* that would make her a Broadway star. In a documentary, Andrews later tells a story about her audition for Rodgers and Hammerstein's *Pipe Dream*. She admits that Rodgers generously advised her to take the Lerner and Loewe opportunity if offered but to let Rodgers and Hammerstein know if she was free so that they could use her.[19] Although she ultimately chose *My Fair Lady* over *Pipe Dream*, Andrews soon had another opportunity to sing a Rodgers and Hammerstein musical. The team wrote the television musical *Cinderella* (1957) for her. 107 million viewers tuned in to the broadcast of Rodgers and Hammerstein's *Cinderella*, turning the Broadway darling into a household name. Similar to Rex Harrison's Professor Higgins, Richard Burton brought his acting abilities and increasing renown to the part of King Arthur. Burton had appeared in a number of plays and films prior to *Camelot*, from Shakespearean works to the historical epic film *The Robe* (1953). Already nominated for two Academy Awards as well as garnering a Tony nomination for his performance in *Time Remembered* (1957), the thirty-five-year-old Welsh actor would win the Tony Award for Best Actor in a Musical for *Camelot*. Pairing Andrews's crystal-clear voice with a non-singer of considerable acting clout once again worked well for a Lerner and Loewe musical.

A young Robert Goulet rounded out the primary cast in his Broadway debut, providing his own strong baritone to complement Andrews's soprano.

These casting choices are significant in the understanding of the intertextual nature of the original production of *Camelot*. Despite the ephemerality of live theater, later audiences can access concrete evidence through cast recordings. Therefore, my analysis includes discussion of the performance choices and vocal quality of the original Broadway cast as represented on the cast recording in conjunction with other musical features. In part, this provides a foundation for considering the impact of differing interpretations, particularly when compared to the 1967 film adaptation. While actors in later productions vary their interpretative choices and have their own skills and abilities, the original Broadway cast provides a powerful model for characterization. They also reveal how Lerner and Loewe envisioned these roles throughout the lengthy production process.

Despite its eventual success, *Camelot* had a troubled writing, revision, and rehearsal process. From the outset, Lerner had more enthusiasm for the project than Frederick Loewe did. When approached to adapt Arthurian legend, Loewe reportedly exclaimed, "you must be crazy. That king is a cuckold. Who the hell cares about a cuckold?" and dismissed the longevity of the legend as "English and American romanticism."[20] Although Lerner eventually got his way, Dominic McHugh stresses that the show "turned out to be the most troubled of the Lerner-Loewe relationship and effectively brought it to an end."[21] The troubled adaptation and production processes likely have much to do with the less exalted place that *Camelot* holds in Broadway history in relation to the earlier *My Fair Lady*.

Unlike *My Fair Lady*'s source material provided by George Bernard Shaw's *Pygmalion*, the final books of White's tetralogy problematically presented Lerner with a "tremendous saga filled with elements of satire, playful anachronism, and complex motivations and characters."[22] The resulting show lasted over four hours long at the Toronto tryout. In a letter to J. W. Fisher in 1979, Lerner recalls that "in *Camelot*, with Moss Hart, our director, in the hospital, I rewrote the entire play from scene two to the penultimate scene in the second act."[23] Hart's serious illness coupled with Lerner's own health problems led "tremendous strain of the creation of the show," according to Miles Kreuger.[24] Additionally, Kreuger feels that the director Moss Hart's illness sorely hurt the show, and it led to a show with "too much material for a conventional evening of musical theater."[25] Even with the extensive revising and cutting, which necessarily occurred before the premiere, the show initially received a mixed critical response. The general audience seemed to agree with critics, despite an enormous amount of presold tickets based on the previous success of *My Fair Lady*.[26] After a brief lag in ticket sales, the show's attendance was boosted by a performance of several songs by the cast on *The Ed Sullivan Show*.[27] The musical went on to win four Tony Awards, including Burton's Best Actor, and ran for 873 performances.[28]

Critics and scholars agree that Lerner's Herculean task of turning Arthurian legend, even one modern version of the overarching story, contained many pitfalls. Despite Lerner's simplification of Arthurian legend, many still felt that the attempt proved too ambitious. Harold Taubman praises several aspects of the show but laments that "unfortunately, *Camelot* is weighed down by the burden of its book. The storytelling is inconsistent."[29] Joseph Swain calls the book "fatally defective in several ways. Much of the dialogue, though inspiring in theme, is badly overwritten."[30] Similarly, author Gene Lees cites problems with Lerner's libretto for *Camelot* as a primary reason why *My Fair Lady* works better, claiming that Lerner's lyric writing skills topped his book writing. In particular, he notes that "the very effort to put White's fantasy on stage presented a series of problems that were never solved."[31] Lees criticizes the handling of the love triangle and especially Lerner's treatment of Lancelot, both of which change significantly from White's original and will be explored in more depth later in this chapter.

In its stage incarnation, *Camelot* attempts to extend the increasing seriousness and ambition in musical theater as realized by Rodgers and Hammerstein, and of course Lerner and Loewe themselves in *My Fair Lady*. *Camelot* follows in the tradition of the so-called integrated musical.[32] Although the impulse to create stage musicals in which song and dance serve the plot and characterization had been part of American musical theater for decades, the realization of this type of approach in shows such as *My Fair Lady* and *Camelot* was, as Elizabeth Wollman observes, "perceived as artistically superior for it cohesion."[33] The stage version of *Camelot* also draws on tropes from the musical subgenre operetta. As Raymond Knapp establishes, it is Guenevere who inhabits the world of operetta, particularly before her emotional affair with Lancelot.[34] Guenevere's vocal virtuosity, as well as her tendency towards risqué desires and behaviors, dovetails with operetta tropes. Casting Julie Andrews certainly reinforced the ties to operetta through her strong, clear singing abilities. As a whole, the musical remains firmly rooted in long-established musical theater types. Several of the changes made from the source material indeed reflect the change in medium in different ways, both in terms of plot and musicality.

The portrayal of Arthur's illegitimate son exemplifies this shift in medium and tone. Lerner retains the character Mordred, yet the character becomes the illegitimate child of Arthur with a mother who is never openly acknowledged to be related to the king. Audience members familiar with the legend recognize Queen Morguase as Arthur's unsavory half-sister, but many experience Mordred's hatred of his father differently without explicit discussion of the apparent incest. Lerner preserves Arthur's purity and honor and highlights the role of adultery in the collapse. In the original Broadway production, Mordred (played by Roddy McDowall) sang two songs in Act II, "The Seven Deadly Virtues" and "The Persuasion." In "The Seven Deadly Virtues," Mordred sings about his disdain for the basic virtues, from courage to fidelity. Mordred's vocal line has a limited range and is quite repetitive, and in fact, McDowall talk-sings through much of the verses. The clever rhymes and bouncy tune in $\frac{2}{4}$ accompanied by generally light orchestration replete with staccato articulation during the refrains all emphasize his glee. In the verses, longer durations in the bassoon and trombones give Mordred's disgust for courage, purity, and humility a comic heaviness as they move through a stepwise pattern with tenuto markings. This amusing song exposes Mordred as an almost cartoonish evil figure.

In "The Persuasion," Mordred convinces his aunt, the sorceress Morgan le Fay, to help him, despite her fondness for King Arthur, by bribing her with candy. Often omitted from later productions, the score for this song shows that none of the vocal lines are actually sung but marked in the *Sprechstimme* style with "x's" rather than traditional note-heads. In true musical theater fashion, the villainous Mordred can barely sing.[35] Mordred's songs provide comedic relief as the second half of the show becomes increasingly serious, and he emerges as joyfully evil.

Although Mordred is "not acknowledged" by Arthur throughout most of his life, Lerner's Arthur does not attempt infanticide. Mordred's appearance at Camelot as well as his intent to destroy his father's dream seems more overblown, and his songs further set him up as doing evil for evil's sake. Notably, the 1967 film cuts Mordred's songs, considerably reducing his role and over-the-top persona. This change downplays Mordred's insidious part in the downfall of Camelot in favor of other characters. Regardless, Mordred acts as a leader in the demise of his kingly father, but the musical in both its stage and screen versions focus the blame on the adulterous love between Lancelot and

Guenevere as the primary reason. Mordred may instigate the fall of Camelot, but the actions of the lovers lead to his ability to exploit this weakness.

Musical Characterization and the Arthurian Love Triangle

The musical's characterization offers a unique depiction of each of the primary roles, giving them a specific voice through song. The songs sung by Arthur, Guenevere, and Lancelot, respectively, reveal how Lerner either draws or departs from White's characterization of the three lovers. Though Lerner uses White's version of these figures as inspiration, he changes crucial aspects of each, which Loewe's music further emphasizes. As Raymond Knapp dexterously illustrates, the opening sequence of songs builds off one another harmonically and melodically.[36] Knapp observes that "the series of songs unfolds almost as in a logical syllogism, with each song extending something of the previous song."[37] Music then subtly weaves these characters together from the outset, revealing their connection to each other. Arthur, Guenevere, and Lancelot's opening songs are both utterly their own and intrinsically linked—even developing specifically from Arthur. The king's music unites the trio and brings Guenevere and Lancelot together. In the following discussion, I further tease out the characterization of the three primary characters through their songs, considering how not only their introductory musical numbers but also all of their solo numbers define them.

In Lerner and Loewe's musical, the action begins directly before King Arthur meets his betrothed. Unlike White's decades-long depiction of Arthur's coming-of-age, *Camelot* begins with an adult King Arthur. He almost immediately sings the lively "I Wonder What the King Is Doing Tonight." This song exposes his anxiety and naiveté regarding women. "I Wonder" highlights Arthur's inexperience. As Dominic McHugh and Amy Asch succinctly comment, "our first impression of Arthur is one where the masculinity associated with him in the legends is shattered by his apprehension about marrying Guenevere."[38] The music and performance in the original Broadway production enhance this impression greatly.

Frederick Loewe's handwritten piano-vocal score from January 24, 1959, reveals that he initially conceived of Arthur as fully singing; in other words, Loewe did not use the *Sprechstimme* notation style which was used in "The Persuasion."[39] Once cast, Burton leans toward talk-singing throughout much of the show in a similar manner as Rex Harrison's Henry Higgins. Burton/Arthur, however, is not entirely unmusical—rather he shifts between a pleasant, if not always fully sustained singing style, and actual "talk-singing." The "tranquillo" opening section of "I Wonder" begins spoken then smoothly transitions to singing on the lyrics "whenever the wind blows this way, you can almost hear everyone say." Accompanied by gentle strings and a clarinet, the opening verse moves effortlessly from Arthur's monologue to the song. Throughout the rest of the song, now "allegretto" and including fuller orchestration, Burton resorts to talk-singing in the moments that most convey his state of mind. For example, the line "I'll tell you what the king is doing tonight—he scared! He's scared!" is incredibly speech-like in performance. This leads into patter sections where Arthur juxtaposes instances of his past bravery with his current fear. At the same time, Burton maintains a resonance that bridges the seemingly disparate vocal styles fluidly. All in all, Burton's energetic performance, coupled with the frequent harmonic shifts of the song, emphasizes the king's insecurity. This represents a telling difference from Arthur in *The Once and Future King*.

   White's version of Arthur conceives of the "Might for Right" ideal and the Knights of the Round Table before marrying Guenevere. Lerner's script delays the beginning of Arthur's ideology until well after the couple's marriage. In fact, the song "I Wonder," and the show in general, further intimates that the noble King does not truly come into his own until meeting and falling in love with Guenevere. Arthur's uses his next song, "Camelot," in order to convince Guenevere to stay and honor their arranged marriage. The optimistic song reveals Arthur's love for his city as well as his idealism in his most memorable tune, which becomes its own political symbol. Suggestively, Burton sings more in this song than during "I Wonder" (though he still tends to clip the ends of phrases). After meeting Guenevere, Arthur's insecurities immediately recede to a noticeable degree. The octave leaps which characterize the beginning of the refrain's phrases effectively illustrate Arthur's feeling of confidence and idealism as he woos Guenevere. While Arthur never matches the vocal virtuosity of Guenevere, he has an appealing clarity and resonance to his vocality, which convinces her to stay and marry him. The orchestration reinforces the vocal line with a light texture supported by frequent use of staccato. The careful use of brass punctuates rather than overwhelms, creating emphasis and regal associations without being overbearing. The sense of grandeur and even wonder created in this song weaves Arthur's spell around Guenevere.

As mentioned in the opening of the chapter, the music of "Camelot" threads throughout the show. In the first two reprises, Guenevere takes up Arthur's "Camelot" theme. Her first iteration repeats not only his melody but the lyrics as well. However, the character of the orchestration matches her opening song (as discussed later in this chapter). Guenevere does not adopt Arthur's music wholesale. She has become convinced by his charm but retains her own identity. The second reprise occurs at the end of the study scene in which Arthur develops the idea for the Knights of the Round Table. In this brief vocal line, Guenevere now claims that the greatest aspect of Camelot is its "resplendent king." In fact, this reprise leads directly into the fanfare of "C'est Moi." Given that Lancelot's introductory number, "C'est Moi," musically builds from Arthur's ode to Camelot, the reprise of this song represents an important ideological moment that brings the three together.[40] More than that, Arthur himself represents the source of their connection.

Arthur's final solo song enhances the portrayal of his honesty and displays the purity of his love for Guenevere. When frustrated by his queen, Arthur begins a forceful introduction but soon shifts into the verse of the gentle "How to Handle a Woman." The opening of the verse employs Loewe's ranting style, made famous by *My Fair Lady*'s Henry Higgins and similarly used for Gaston Lachaille in *Gigi* (1958). Unlike both his predecessors, however, Arthur's musical style changes, and Loewe never returns to the upheaval of the beginning. By the end of the verse, Arthur has a revelation, and Loewe highlights this by marking the score "tranquillo" and shifting from a quick cut time to a gentle common time while harmonically leading into the chorus's D-major tonality (in the published piano-vocal score). While Higgins and Gaston vacillate—arguing with themselves in their respective songs—Arthur quickly forms a resolution. Unsurprisingly, Arthur's final solo is firmly tonal; both the question of "handling a woman" and the answer of love stay within a strong dominant-to-tonic harmonic profile. At the same time, Loewe infuses the chorus with more harmonic richness than was present the king's earlier songs at strategic moments. For example, when considering options, such as whether to "brood or play the gay romancer," Loewe centers the chord progression around F♯ major and includes a thirteenth in the dominant chord of that key. Arthur is more reflective and perhaps a bit ironic at times, yet he retains his steadfast love and optimistic nature, even as he recognizes something is wrong in his marriage.

While not a difficult melody, "How to Handle a Woman" requires more vocal control than do Arthur's previous songs. From the outset of the chorus,

Loewe writes a fairly disjunct melodic contour. The lyrics "how to handle a woman" sit on a rising fourth, descend a third, and go back up a fourth. Although not particularly large or difficult leaps, the gentleness required for the song necessitates a smooth delivery in order to do justice to the characterization provided by Lerner and Loewe. Both Richard Burton and the film's Richard Harris sing this song more fully than their previous talk-singing styles, though Burton's tone is clearer. Arthur seemingly cannot understand the change in their loving marriage but has faith that his love will prevail. The gentle orchestration, which relies heavily on the string instruments, enhances this interpretation. The instrumentation here has a marked similarity to Guenevere's songs (discussed later in the chapter), representing Arthur's deep love for his wife. Unlike the earlier Henry Higgins, Arthur's ode to women and his love in particular, lacks the misogynistic tone. The king muses about "handling" women, quickly coming to the conclusion that loved ones simply require love rather than coercion or manipulation. In Arthur's estimation, women are not to be "handled" at all.

Taken together, these songs depict a considerably less emotionally complex version of Arthur than White presents in *The Once and Future King* yet a compelling one all the same. Arthur's solo numbers show an increasing maturity and ability to overcome his insecurities. Furthermore, these songs highlight Arthur's idealism, especially in light of the fact that Lerner removed the most grievous of Arthur's flaws (his unsuspecting act of incest and subsequent appalling actions). In many ways, Arthur emerges as a much more desirable romantic partner than Lancelot. Others, however, have noted that Arthur's inability to fully sing in the way that both Guenevere and Lancelot do displays a deficiency. As William Everett puts it, "he lacks something— that very thing which Guenevere desires but cannot find—that thing which Guenevere finds in Lancelot and sacrifices everything to obtain."[41] Arthur is not wholly unmusical, however, and arguably, his songs sow the seed for and even grow into that "something" identified by Everett. In fact, both Guenevere and Lancelot recognize this to some extent and are drawn to Arthur for this very reason. Lerner and Loewe's Arthur is a fundamentally good man with an incredible capacity for love and potential for greatness as a king. His love for Guenevere helps him realize much of this potential; Arthur overcomes his insecurities and develops his ideals even as this very love leads to his ultimate ruin.

The musicalization of *Camelot* does the most for Guenevere's character, giving her a perspective not present in White's novel. Lerner and Loewe's character displays more agency than the one in the novel, particularly through song. On her way to meet Arthur on the eve of their wedding, Guenevere runs off and sings "The Simple Joys of Maidenhood." The orchestration in this song sets up a particular sound for Guenevere; it contains a decided focus on the string instruments with occasional reinforcement from the woodwinds. As Raymond Knapp discusses, this song, along with "The Lusty Month of May," draws from tropes of fairy-tale operetta, particularly in terms of sexual innuendo and the treatment of romance.[42] After a harmonically and metrically shifting opening verse, the song settles into a lilting chorus, which amusingly (if troublingly) details Guenevere's courtship expectations. After rejecting the patronage of St. Genevieve, Guenevere relates her desires for knights to rescue and fight over her. In contrast to Arthur's speech-like opening verse for "I Wonder," Guenevere's frantic prayer to St. Genevieve is not particularly speech-like—though neither is it remarkably difficult vocally. The entire song sits in a medium-high range well suited to a strong soprano such as Andrews but never goes above the staff. Despite a few leaps (never more than an octave) in the melody, "Simple Joys" does not require an inordinate amount of vocal virtuosity. Instead, the lyricism of the song humorously contrasts with the sentiment. "Simple Joys" immediately reveals Guenevere's rebellious, slightly naughty streak in addition to her potential to become restless in an uneventful, if happy, marital situation.

"The Lusty Month of May" continues to develop Guenevere as a heroine of operetta in a lighthearted song, which is both naïve and highly suggestive. With the abundance of "tra-las" and an up-tempo chorus joining in the fun, Knapp's parallels to operetta are more than apt. The clarity, wide range, and versatility of Andrews's voice only enhance the effect. Andrews never sacrifices vocal precision or tone despite the focus on clever wordplay and a bouncy, allegretto tune. This tune is more virtuosic than "Simple Joys" with additional melodic leaps and the possibility for displays in a higher range. Loewe uses a C♯ diminished chord to denote Guenevere's lustful feelings, often punctuating lyrics such as "lusty" or "libelous," in the otherwise carefree milieu of C major. The generally light orchestration favors the string section, similar to "Simple Joys," and also features a harp. When woodwinds enter, clarinets tend to dominate. At this point, this instrumentation characterizes Guenevere's musical self and augments her connection to operetta as it reinforces the sense of frivolity. The call-and-response with the chorus further heightens the sense of abandon, which increases throughout the song. Guenevere has not lost her youthful taste for ribaldry during her marriage with Arthur.

While White's Guenever tries to get to know the newcomer knight for Arthur's sake, Lerner and Loewe's Guenevere shows obvious distaste for the Frenchman when her husband introduces him. Prolific author Ethan Mordden claims that Guenevere's attitude smacks of protesting too much since "she has in fact fallen in love with him at sight and is trying to exorcise her feelings."[43] Given Lancelot's handsomeness in the musical, an immediate physical attraction certainly seems probable. However, Guenevere's adverse reaction to Lancelot might also be read as a form of jealousy toward the knight who instantaneously obtains her husband's affections. While Guenevere takes an immediate disliking to Lancelot in *Camelot*, the reverse is true in *The Once and Future King*: Lancelot feels the jealousy due to his obsessive worship of Arthur. Shifting the onus of dislike to Guenevere fleshes out her character somewhat and certainly opens up varying levels of interpretation.

No song exemplifies the fraught creative process of *Camelot* more than "Then You May Take Me to the Fair." Eventually cut from the Broadway production when it ran longer than four hours, "Take Me to the Fair" shows Guenevere's spiteful scheming against Lancelot. Stylistically, "Then You May Take Me to the Fair" resembles elements of Guenevere's earlier songs. As she connives to persuade three knights to best Lancelot in the jousts, she sings a jaunty repetitive tune that ends on a literal high note. Although cut from the original run, the song does appear on the 1960 Broadway cast recording. As such, a record of Andrews's version is easily accessible. Her vocal performance delightfully matches her first two songs with the addition of moments of intense speaking as her knights promise to "thrash" newcomer Lancelot du Lac. Guenevere's solo numbers before falling with love with Lancelot reveal frivolousness and a naïve interest in sex. At the same time, a propensity for vindictiveness emerges in Guenevere's early characterization in *Camelot*. Collectively, these attributes alter her from White's version of the queen. The novel's Guenever is most certainly not oversexed, and this trait seems to stem from her operetta-like characterization in the musical. Although White's Guenever is far from perfect, periodically flying into jealous rages and perennially selfish, she also does not demonstrate the type of calculating spite on display in "Then You May Take Me to the Fair."

On the other hand, the songs "Before I Gaze at You Again" and "I Loved You Once in Silence" reveal Guenevere's character growth. Everett claims, "her transformation from a young maiden to a mature woman is evident in her music. It becomes increasingly refined and cultured as the show progresses."[44] Similarly, both songs have more reflective lyrics as Guenevere muses on her feelings for Lancelot, first before he is about to depart on quests then when finally openly vocalizing her love.[45] The music, too, becomes more harmonically complex and lyrical with slower tempos and longer drawn-out melodies. By the end of the first act, Guenevere matures into a more contemplative woman, moving away from the innuendo and lighthearted songs of her youth. Initially, Guenevere's final Act I number was the song "Face to Face," which was replaced with "Before I Gaze at You Again" after the tryouts, and McHugh and Asch believe the lyrics for this original song to be lost.[46]

Guenevere's more sedate, medium-range melody in "Before I Gaze" is accompanied by her signature strings and woodwinds. However, the woodwinds, especially the clarinets along with the flute, have more prominence. The accompaniment sounds warmer due to the move away from busier, shorter notes towards longer durations and a narrower range. Loewe combines simplicity with a sense of sophistication not present in Guenevere's earlier songs. Due to the moderate tempo and lilting $\frac{3}{4}$ meter with a strong emphasis on the downbeat, the song takes on the character of an expansive waltz. This enhances the sense of romance while moving away from the lighter, more playful notions indicated in Guenevere's earlier Act I songs. The melodic construction is motivic, centered around a leap (typically a fifth or sixth) and largely diatonic stepwise motion (typically a stepwise turn except at the end of four measure phrases). On the lyrics "I have so much forgetting to do" and the later "stay far away," Guenevere sings a flat seventh scale degree. The use of the blue note in these strategic moments, coming in the first four bars of the second eight measure section, emphasizes the longing and despair created by Guenevere and Lancelot's illicit love affair. While the sixteen-measure sections that bookend the song remain squarely in F major, the bridge passes through the dominant key to the relative minor. Although the lyrics at this point mention a time when their love might fade, the harmonic movement illustrates that thinking of Lancelot "barely once a day" is not the current reality. All in all, Loewe develops Guenevere's musical characterization in such a way that drives the development of her character.

"I Loved You Once in Silence" continues Guenevere's musical progression. An undated manuscript of the song in Frederick Loewe's papers reveals that "I Loved You" originally began with a verse that uses the melody from "The Simple Joys of Maidenhood." The lyrics to this cut verse are as follows:

Where are the simple joys of maidenhood?
When the world was so eas'ly understood,
Good was good, bad was bad for me,
And joy was never sad for me,
But here you are unhappy that you came,
And had you not you still would feel the same.[47]
Lyrics By Alan Jay Lerner
The Alan Jay Lerner Testamentary Trust (ASCAP) and
     The Frederick Loewe Foundation (ASCAP)
All rights administered by WB Music Corp.

Guenevere references her and Lancelot's complicated situation as well as the simplicity of her youth. Musically, the verse blends seamlessly with the beginning of the chorus for "I Loved You" with a modulation from E major to G major in the early piano-vocal score. The addition of the original verse would have changed Guenevere's musical progression, alluding to her earlier carefree nature as told through her Act 1 songs. Without this added verse, the song begins in a statelier manner without the explicit reference to Guenevere's earlier musical self and whimsical disposition. Instead, the increasingly somber lyricism of "Before I Gaze" is extended in "I Loved You." With longer held notes and descending stepwise patterns, the ABAC chorus of "I Loved You" completes Guenevere's shift from clever wordplay and vocal virtuosity to mature reflection. The bridge's modulation from D-flat major through F minor before landing back into the F major of the published piano-vocal score stresses the turmoil Guenevere feels at the revelation of her and Lancelot's love. Furthermore, the song contains more textural complexity than Guenevere's earlier songs—although her characteristic instrumentation remains largely intact. While Guenevere's vocal line is more sedate, the richness of the orchestration underneath her singing indicates the depth of her feeling. Although the musical does not explicitly span the decades as White's novel does, these songs disclose Guenevere's emerging solemnity, if not her age.

Lerner and Loewe alter the character of Lancelot quite a bit from his depiction in *The Once and Future King*. First of all, White constantly describes Lancelot as ugly yet the musical's directors cast Robert Goulet in the stage production and Franco Nero in the film. This casting indicates a more superficial attraction on the part of Guenevere to the now conventionally good-looking knight. In *Camelot*, Lancelot hears accounts of the Knights of the

Round Table from France and travels to the castle in the belief that no one is more worthy to sit at Arthur's table than he is. Lancelot sings the incredibly pompous "C'est Moi"—a much showier tune than any of Arthur's songs, dripping with bravado. The song begins with a regal call in the woodwinds and brass before Robert Goulet opens with the rising "Camelot" triad, which has no trace of "talk-singing" in his tone (Example 3.1). Instead, he lengthens the horn-like call, savoring the triumphant motive. As Knapp discusses, this opening directly parallels the bridge of "Camelot," complete with the harmonic shift from D major to F major.[48] Unlike the earlier statement, Lancelot's lengthening of the foundational motive is punctuated by brass or woodwind calls each time. As such, Lancelot's version heightens the heroic sense of the "Camelot" motive, forming the foundation for his ode to his own perfection.

Throughout the opening verse and during the beginning of the chorus, the orchestration makes way for Goulet's strong baritone. By the end of the chorus, the instrumentation gains in intensity, highlighting Lancelot's self-congratulation. Knapp describes the song's conceit through use of meter changes, "moving from a broadly heroic $\frac{4}{4}$ of its 'Camelot' calling card to a sense of emphatic resolution 'alla marcia' . . . as Lancelot details what a knight ought to be, to a rollicking $\frac{6}{8}$ as he himself lays claim to those

Example 3.1a 1st 3 measures of Trumpets in "C'est Moi". Alan Jay Lerner and Frederick Loewe. *Camelot*. Warner-Chappell Full Orchestral Score. Box 1, Folder 10. Library of Congress.

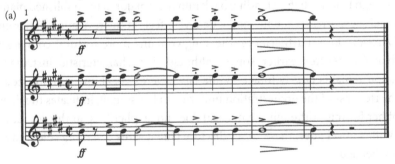

Example 3.1b "Camelot" Motive. Alan Jay Lerner and Frederick Loewe. *Camelot*. Vocal Score. New York: Chappell Music, 1962.

virtues."[49] These sections are marked not only by meter changes but also by key changes which parallel the D major to F major move first made by Arthur in "Camelot." In addition to enhancing the connection to Arthur, "C'est Moi" gives the modulation its meaning. Lancelot's perfection as a knight embodies the very heroic ideal for which Arthur strives. Moreover, the reliance on dotted rhythms and eighth- and sixteenth-note patterns infuses vitality into Lancelot's character. Melodically, "C'est Moi" is no more difficult to sing than any of Arthur's songs.

The rhythmic vitality coupled with the expectation that Lancelot will not talk-sing, however, brings Lancelot's vocality closer to Guenevere's in the stage show. Young Robert Goulet's clear tone and over-the-top (yet not ridiculous) relish of his own vocal prowess emphasizes his perceived perfection. Knapp further notes, "Lancelot, as a character, does not swagger (or at least should not swagger) for he lacks sufficient perspective on himself for that."[50] This represents a significant change from White's insecure and remarkably self-aware Lancelot. Through this song, Lancelot's initial characterization has more in common with his son Galahad (cut from the musical), who White represents as so unbearably perfect as to be almost inhuman. Lancelot's over-sincerity and general sense of cluelessness, as first shown in "C'est Moi," affects his relationship with both Arthur and Guenevere.

Lancelot's big romantic song, "If Ever I Would Leave You" illustrates the nature of the love between Guenevere and Lancelot. As I have noted elsewhere, "the original script emphasizes Lancelot's persisting selfishness and feelings of courtly love. He has just written a poem about himself, claiming he cannot write about Jenny because 'he loves her too much' to put into writing."[51] The opening "madrigal" is sung within a relatively limited range while "If Ever I Would Leave You" shows off Loewe's full melodic gift. Similar to My Fair Lady's "On the Street Where You Live," "If Ever" is a lovely romantic ballad with lush orchestral accompaniment and sung by a young, good-looking male. Lacking the bluster and self-importance of "C'est Moi," "If Ever" provides a chance for a singer, like the young Robert Goulet, to truly sing the beautiful tune. Although they have admitted their feelings for one another, the relationship remains chaste. Lerner uses the medieval ideals of courtly love in reference to Guenevere and Lancelot's relationship in order to highlight the fundamental goodness of the pair and the ensuing tragedy, which Loewe's romantic ballad supports.

The solo songs of the three members of Camelot's love triangle illustrate the myriad ways in which Lerner and Loewe adapted T. H. White's The Once *and Future King*. Throughout this chapter, I focus largely on individual numbers in my musical discussion, particularly those of the main characters, rather than choruses or duets as a means of exploring characterization in more depth. While clearly inspired by White's version of these characters and their situation, the musicalization reinterprets aspects of the story, creating an intertextuality that continues in the Hollywood film adaptation.

Film Version

The 1967 film adaptation of *Camelot* stays relatively true to Lerner's original script. In fact, Lerner penned the screenplay and remained actively involved in the filmmaking process. At the same time, the musical and cinematic decisions made during the process of adapting the Broadway musical greatly impact both the Arthurian interpretation and the audience's experience of the Lerner and Loewe musical. Despite the relative fidelity, notable changes affect characterization in such a way that once again correlates to White's version of the tale. In fact, the stage and screen versions of *Camelot* intersect with *The Once and Future King* in distinct ways. This palimpsestuous relationship makes the 1967 film an interesting case study in adaptation. Yet the Hollywood adaptation, directed by Joshua Logan, has an even more troubled history—particularly in terms of reception and legacy—than its stage counterpart does.

During the production process, a number of issues plagued the film's creation. Richard Harris rather famously lobbied hard for the role of Arthur, badgering director Joshua Logan until he received it.[52] After winning the role of Arthur, his investment continued. Knowing of Harris's temperament and extreme dedication to playing King Arthur, the filmmakers were careful to avoid rocking the boat. In a letter dated January 28, 1967, Logan writes:

> And there is another person to be considered, and that is Richard Harris. He is passionately involved in the character of Arthur and if I should present him with a cut version without properly conditioning him for it, it might put him in a state of depression that would delay us by lots of discussion, or, if he is given an ultimatum, by a disgruntled performance.[53]

Joshua Logan's papers also reveal a lengthy discussion among varying parties regarding the role of Pellinore.[54] Harris, too, had an opinion, suggesting

Jack Hulbert for the role. Logan initially had difficulty casting Merlyn, and Harris again offered a suggestion—himself. Although Harris did not get his way, the possibility is an interesting one given the handling of magic in the film. Harris playing Arthur's mentor, as well as the king himself, would certainly strengthen the interpretation of magic as imaginative. As producer Joel Freeman's letter demonstrates, however, Logan and others never seriously considered the possibility: "I agree about Richard Harris not playing Merlyn. It would be confusing to an audience and I have spoken to Warner and MacEwen who concur."[55] Along with Harris's (over)investment, the filmmakers had to negotiate rising star Vanessa Redgrave's busy schedule, particularly coming off of her filming Michelangelo Antonioni's Blow-Up.

It was financial considerations, however, which most afflicted Camelot's production. An itemized budget from April 22, 1967, illustrates that the film was over budget by $1,223,019.[56] At this point in time, not only was Logan eleven days behind schedule but wardrobe and prop manufacture also accounted for tens of thousands of dollars in excess of the budget. John Truscott's enormously elaborate production and costume design played no small part in the financial extravagance of the film. These issues have consistently plagued the reception and legacy of the film. As Matthew Kennedy puts it, "fifteen million dollars just sits there on the screen, proud, gauzy, and inert."[57]

Major contemporary critics generally panned Hollywood's version of Camelot, and often those reviewers who enjoyed the film still found elements to criticize. For example, Bosley Crowther of the New York Times laments that the problematic aspects of the stage version were not corrected but emphasized in the film adaptation.[58] And Los Angeles Times critic Charlie Champlin gives a laundry list of the film's deficiencies:

A slow static pace, a lack of style, the pinched and artificial quality of the proceedings, the jumpy and inconsistent cuts, the incessant overuse of close-ups, the failure to sustain emotional momentum, the fatal wavering between reality and fantasy, the inability to exploit the resources of the film medium.[59]

The Washington Post's Richard L. Coe outright states, "besides being hopelessly, needlessly lavish, this misses the point squarely on the nail: what was so hot about King Arthur? We never really are told."[60] Coe identifies the film as a missed opportunity, particularly in terms of the possibility to reinsert some of the magic lost in the translation from White to Lerner and Loewe's stage musical (literally—Coe laments that the cinema's ability to show Arthur changing into animals, for instance, is never truly realized). However, a number of critics, from Roger Ebert to the reviewer for *Variety*, quite enjoyed the performances of the lead actors—especially Vanessa Redgrave's.[61] And for those who enjoy the lavish spectacle, which arose from the highly expensive sets and costuming, those (quite apt) deficiencies noted by Champlin were easily forgiven. Despite the handful of decent reviews from regional papers, Hollywood's *Camelot* seems to miss the mark for many people and for understandable reasons.

Lerner leaves the major plot structure and much of the dialogue intact in the film adaptation. However, a new opening scene produces a darker tone from the outset. Rather than beginning with the introduction of Guenevere and Arthur, the film opens with a scene that shows Arthur readying for impending war. The bulk of the action, then, is a flashback recounting the events that led to the destruction of everything Arthur believes in. This upfront reminder that the story of Camelot ends in tragedy casts a pall on the more lighthearted tenor of the musical's first half. The film version of *Camelot* cuts only five songs entirely. The omission of certain songs accommodates adjustments made in the name of "cinematic realism." For example, "The Jousts" at the end of Act 1 moves from a musical number to an actual filmed joust. Others, such as the removal of Mordred's musical numbers, alter the telling of the Camelot's downfall. Without his songs, Mordred's role in the capture of Guenevere and Lancelot, as well as his reasoning, is downplayed greatly. While his spiteful nature persists, the full weight of the tragedy (and perhaps the blame) falls more squarely on the shoulders of the love triangle. Without the modicum of comic relief provided by "Seven Deadly Virtues," and even "The Persuasion," the second half of the musical feels even heavier in tone.[62] The perceived realism of film may have had an impact on the decision to remove Mordred's more lighthearted, even cartoonish, songs in order to focus on the impending tragedy of the situation.

Overall, Logan exploits the medium of film in a manner both detrimental and beneficial to the film. Similar to many critics contemporary to the film, later scholars have often censured Logan for using the resources at his disposal ineffectively. Raymond Knapp specifically considers the tension between an attempt at cinematic realism and the musical's idealism.[63] Taking this view, the replacement of the song "The Jousts" with an actual onscreen joust might be seen as undesirable. However, the change makes filmic sense.

Yet—as Knapp argues—the overall Renaissance Fair sequence's "sense of authenticity is further undermined by a number of close-ups, disrupting continuity through being obviously filmed separately, and showing us as much make-up as they do sweat, tears, blood, or other tokens of the 'real.'"[64] This "realistic" impetus affects a number of elements of the film, from casting and the setting to the treatment of magic and characterization.

The film version builds on the stage musical by playing on the features of British heritage and legend inherent in *Camelot*. The choice of two leading actors, Richard Harris and Vanessa Redgrave, with backgrounds in Shakespearean theater brings a sense of gravitas and pride in the theatrical traditions of the country. Prior to *Camelot*, Redgrave had appeared in various Shakespeare productions, including the Royal Shakespeare Company's *As You Like It*. In 1966, she created the title character in a London production of *The Prime of Miss Jean Brodie*. At the time of *Camelot*'s production, Redgrave's film credits included Michelangelo Antonioni's *Blow-Up* and *Morgan: A Suitable Case for Treatment* (1966) in a performance that earned the actress her first Academy Award nomination. Thus, Redgrave had already garnered a reputation for serious acting abilities. Irish actor Richard Harris also began his career on the English stage. He began appearing in films in the late 1950s and received an Academy Award nomination for his leading role in *This Sporting Life* (1963).

Certain cinematic choices enhance the medieval setting, in an attempt to represent the mythical status of the story. While most of the film was shot on a Warner backlot, Logan did manage to secure some time in Spain for location shooting. Here, the filmmakers utilized medieval castles meant to evoke the lost or since modernized castles from England's past. The film draws on the conventions of the cinematic epic spectacle. Sheldon Hall and Steve Neale observe that these terms have had fluid or loose meanings throughout their use. Nonetheless, the epic "was as indicative of size and expense as it was of particular kinds of historical setting, of protagonists who are caught up in large-scale events as it was of those who sway the course of history or fate of nations," while spectacle refers more to the "presence of spectacular settings, action, and scenes."[65] *Camelot* contains all these elements. With its $13 million budget, the film employed forty-five highly detailed sets plus the aforementioned location shooting.

In an interview, Logan stated that he worked with John Truscott to create a unique look to represent a period out of time for the film.[66] The wedding of Arthur and Guenevere provides a prime example with a great candlelit hall and Redgrave wearing a $12 thousand gown for the short scene (Figure 3.1). A promotional write-up on Truscott describes the wedding dress as "made by a dozen women who crocheted the overdress and eight-foot train over a period of twelve months, then decorated the panels with pumpkin seeds and the gown, itself, with tiny pearl seeds."[67] The focus on lavish visuals in the knighting of Lancelot provides yet another example. The jousts and fighting during the dissolution of Arthur's dream also conform to ideas of the epic. Furthermore, the legendary content of the film in which lust affects the state of an entire kingdom fits one definition of the epic. As such, *Camelot* combines elements of various genres or types of filmmaking to produce an epic musical with a focus on the spectacular.

The film reduces the role of magic in the story of *Camelot*, even implying that it might not be real. This represents a significant shift from both the original Broadway production and T. H. White's novel. As mentioned before, White includes magical characters and spells, though at times dubiously. Merlyn changes Wart into animals and sends him on magical adventures, but these adventures are specifically couched as manifestations of childhood and cease once Arthur grows up. Arthur's half-sister Morgause may or may not have seduced the young king via magic. Lerner and Loewe introduce magic as a tangible presence that helps to shape the events of the play. Both Merlyn and Morgan Le Fay are magicians. The stage version includes scenes in which Merlyn interacts with other characters, talking with Sir Dinadan in Act I, Scene 2 for example. Early in the plot, Nimue sings a song that calls Merlyn away from Camelot. And at the end of the action, Morgan Le Fay's magic prevents Arthur from protecting Lancelot and

Figure 3.1 Guenevere's Wedding Gown. Alan Jay Lerner. *Camelot*. Directed by Joshua Logan. Burbank, CA: Warner Home Video, 1967. DVD.

Guenevere from discovery. Mordred convinces Morgan Le Fay to surround Arthur with a magic circle that binds him to that spot in the forest. Knapp recognizes that "magic stands behind and informs Arthur's idealism"; however, he contends that eventually "idealism displaces it."[68] Although magic is a concrete presence (as much as magic can be), the musical largely moves away from its influence. Scott Miller perceives, "in Act II, the real world collides with Arthur's ideal and we see that no one can live in an ideal world."[69] Despite the use of magic at the climax of the play, it is ultimately the clash between earthy concerns and idealism that causes the destruction of Arthur's dreams.

In the film, Merlyn left Arthur to his own devices long before he meets Guenevere. Although this always seems to have been the idea for the film adaptation, earlier drafts include a scene in which knights acknowledge Merlyn's existence and influence on Arthur before leaving Camelot.[70] Additional notes further indicate that the filmmakers had an idea that Merlyn's castle in the forest would be shown at some point in the film, and T. H. White's description of the magician's home provided a template.[71] In development, the conception of magic differs from the final film; although Nimue traps Merlyn before the events of the film, concrete traces of his presence and impact remain. Importantly, these materials demonstrate that the filmmakers consulted *The Once and Future King* in addition to Lerner and Loewe's treatment of White. In the final film, Lerner leaves open the very plausible possibility that the film incarnation of Merlyn exists only in the struggling king's mind. Scenes that feature the wizard are set off using Vaseline on the camera lens to frame the image with hazy edges—a device long used to denote memory or fantasy. In calling on Merlyn, Arthur blends memory of the past with events in the present.

Furthermore, Arthur explains the childhood practice of changing into animals in order to learn new ways of thinking as imaginative rather than an enchantment. When Arthur describes his lessons to Guenevere, he states that he did not physically change into animals but simply pretended to do so—a caveat not present in the stage script or in White's original. This change seems to have been gradually implemented as the filmmakers slowly decided to undermine the presence of magic. Arthur still contends that the animal transformations really happened in an earlier undated draft, but he admits that it was simply a thought exercise by the June 1966 final screenplay.[72] Although the film includes a scene toward the end in which Arthur presumably morphs into both a fish and a bird, the audience never actually sees the transformation. Mordred interrupts the king's reveries. Arthur seems to float down, but neither acknowledges anything out of the ordinary.

The film also eliminates Morgan le Fay as a character, discarding her magic circle by association. Lerner replaces this scene with a more mundane yet insidious device. Mordred simply asks Arthur to remain in the forest for the night in order to prove the virtue of his loved ones. This shift is actually closer to the events as depicted in *The Once and Future King*. In White's telling, Arthur's considerable failings combined with his goodness and trust have a bearing on the final action. In the film version of the musical, Arthur remains for a time of his own free will before realizing his horrible mistake. His love, coupled with the belief that Lancelot and Guenevere will be cautious for his sake, leads to their discovery.

The film score reinforces the ambiguous nature of magic. In the stage production, an offstage voice, acknowledged by Merlyn as Nimue, calls the wizard away with the song "Follow Me." The film cuts this scene but not the music. Pieces of "Follow Me" can be heard in the orchestral background music. In fact, music directors Alfred Newman and Ken Darby wanted to use this tune for the main title music in order to "create an aura of mysticism and enchantment."[73] If used, this music would have set up a more prominent place for magic within the world of the film. In the end, however, the filmmakers settled on a treatment of "Camelot" instead, placing the focus on idealism. The opening motive of "Follow Me" does later accompany Arthur's description of Merlyn's lessons. Non-diegetic voices finally sing the song when Arthur talks to Merlyn alone in the forest before Mordred's unwelcome intrusion. For the choral statement of the song, Lerner wrote new lyrics, which begin:

> Through the clouds gray with years;
> Over hills wet with tears;
> To a world young and free
> We shall fly. Follow me.[74]

Rather than Nimue's call to lure Merlyn into enchantment, the new lyrics represent Arthur's nostalgia for his carefree youth. The treatment of magic may represent a need to adhere to some form of cinematic realism as explored by Knapp—a perception which does not plague literature or theater in the same way.[75]

The changes made for the film also affect the characterization of the three lead characters to varying degrees. Casting in congress with other considerations has much to do with the representation. Richard Harris, like Burton, talk-sings through the majority of Arthur's songs. Harris, however, does not have the same vocal resonance that bridges Burton's singing and speaking in the original Broadway production. For example, in "I Wonder What the King is Doing Tonight," Harris's over-the-top performance begins with a breathy, almost whispery, timbre. Harris does manipulate his voice quite a bit, but the result is that his performance of Arthur moves past insecurity into camp. Harris almost whines at many points throughout the song. In the film, the lead-in to "Camelot" enhances the fact that Arthur tends to see life through rose-colored glasses by adding a line about everything being "pink." Harris's performance interprets Arthur as less forceful and more whimsical while retaining the optimism inherent in the song. Furthermore, his rant before "How to Handle a Woman" has a higher-pitched tantrum-like quality, which once again fades into a near-whisper. Harris's performance of these songs portrays Arthur as outwardly contemplative with a weaker, gentle vocal quality. This interpretation changes not only the audience's view of King Arthur but also the character's relationship with Guenevere and Lancelot.

Once again, the characterization of Guenevere alters quite a bit in further adaptation. The film version slows down both of Guenevere's opening songs significantly. Additionally, Redgrave's voice lacks the clarity of tone and stylistic similarities to operetta singing inherent in Andrews's versions. Given the fact that Redgrave does not have Andrews's vocal prowess, Guenevere's vocal virtuosity disappears. In fact, the lush orchestration of the film version often overpowers Redgrave's limited singing voice. "Lusty Month" especially becomes much more over-the-top in its ribaldry than the stage version had been, particularly through the opening section of the song until the chorus takes over and the tempo speeds up. Redgrave injects a sensual breathiness, which emphasizes sexual awareness more than innocence and fun—a mode that Knapp identifies as a "brooding sexual discontent."[76] Logan repeatedly indicated his choice to cast Vanessa Redgrave for her overt sex appeal, which is brought out in her performance of Guenevere's songs.[77]

Several screenplay drafts in Alan Jay Lerner's papers show that Lerner continued to have trouble with the song "Take Me to the Fair." An undated screenplay remains very close to the original script but does reinsert the song, which had been omitted from the original Broadway production. While the "final screenplay" from June 20, 1966, skips the song, the revised version from July 14 of that year once again reinstates it. Similar to the stage production, length may have been a consideration in whether to use the song or not. However, its presence also makes a clear statement about Guenevere's character. Ultimately, the film includes "Take Me to the Fair," confirming Miller's declaration that Guenevere is both "more oversexed than your average musical theatre ingénue" and "quite bitchy from time to time."[78] She schemes and manipulates the three knights into challenging Lancelot by both playing on their existing aversion to the French newcomer and offering her favor. The film's version of Guenevere, as portrayed by Vanessa Redgrave, revels in her own sex appeal in a way that is quite different from both White and the Broadway stage production.

Additionally, the second half of the film cuts "Before I Gaze at You Again" completely and adds Lancelot to "I Loved You Once in Silence." While the undated draft retained "Before I Gaze," the omission of the song by June 1966 shows a change in how the filmmakers were thinking about Guenevere's character. "I Loved You Once" shows the extramarital couple to have a clandestine passion that culminates in a feeling of martyrdom in choosing to give one another up for duty. While the stage directions prior to the song indicate that Lancelot "puts his arms around her [Guenevere] tenderly," the film shows them kissing before and after the song plus a number of intimate caresses.[79] The scene focuses on close-ups of the actors' faces, either with both in the frame or concentrating Redgrave's passionate expressions as the two touch. This simple presentation nevertheless further establishes the love between Guenevere and Lancelot. At the same time, Guenevere's personal growth becomes less complex than it had been in the original stage production.

While "C'est Moi" changes very little from the original score, its placement and performance differ significantly from the stage production. In the film version, a lengthy proclamation scene intercedes between the reprise of "Camelot" as sung by Guenevere and Lancelot's opening verse, which picks up on the "Camelot" triadic figure. The proclamation music does include some treatment of "Camelot" but is more militaristic in nature and emphasizes other musical themes. As such, the way the opening songs weave together—while still present—is lost somewhat in the intervening music.

Significantly, Franco Nero was the only actor dubbed for the film adaptation with Gene Merlino providing the singing voice. The discrepancy between Lancelot's voice and body is apparent. Nero's lip-synching leaves something to be desired, and Merlino does not quite land the actor's Italian accent. While Merlino easily out-sings both Harris and Redgrave, his tone does not have the flexibility and clarity of young Robert Goulet. Furthermore, Nero's physical performance contains an over-the-top expressiveness of over-sincerity that Merlino's vocal performance does not match. As a result, the tension between the humor of the song and Lancelot's entirely earnest demeanor becomes lost in translation.

The original stage production of *Camelot* shows a chaste, courtly love between the two adulterers so that a sense of physically unfulfilled longing permeates the looming tragedy. In Lerner's screenplay drafts, he toyed with the representation of love and potential physical distance between Guenevere and Lancelot. When realizing her feelings for Lancelot after his miracle at the joust, Guenevere makes plans with her friend/maid Clarinda to go visit her father for an undetermined amount of time. Lancelot, however, announces that he is leaving to go questing for anywhere between one and three years in order to earn his knighthood. Both lovers express a desire to get away so that they do not act on their feelings and betray Arthur. In drafts up to at least July 14, 1966, Lancelot actually leaves Camelot in order to go questing (but really as a means to escape his feelings for the queen).

In the 1966 screenplay drafts, then, Lerner actually adhered more to White's version of events. Lancelot leaves after realizing his love for Jenny (Arthur and Lancelot's nickname for Guenevere) to go on quests—ostensibly for the "good of Camelot and the Round Table." He rides through Britain either routing enemies or converting them to Arthur's cause. Like White's version, the version of Guenevere in the drafts awaits Lancelot's return and acts very vain directly before he does. Guenevere's desire to leave for the same reason, however, represents a departure from White. Suggestively, this situation does not occur in the final film. Instead, Guenevere and Lancelot both remain in Camelot, indulging in their forbidden love much more than the stage production on which the film is based. Ultimately, Lerner and Loewe's version of Lancelot cannot bear to leave Guenevere.

Unlike the original stage production, the film strongly implies a consummated sexual relationship between Guenevere and Lancelot (not to mention Guenevere and Arthur). The screenplay drafts in the Library of Congress reveal that Lerner gradually developed the potential for physical love between Guenevere and Lancelot. As I have described elsewhere, the montage shown during "If Ever I Would Leave You" visually chronicles the physical relationship between the couple.[80] While the undated screenplay draft does not feature any indication of the montage, Lerner was certainly thinking in this direction by June of 1966.[81] Lerner specifically notes, "we see them as their physical love develops."[82] Additionally, Lerner envisioned Guenevere singing a statement of the melody at the end of the song, joining her voice with Lancelot's earlier than what actually occurs in the film. Joshua Logan's interpretation presents the adulterers' relationship as carnal rather than courtly, particularly through the use of this song throughout the film.[83] The two versions of *Camelot* interpret the illicit love affair quite differently.[84]

The film's reinsertion of sex into the love triangle actually brings the musical closer to White's version of the tale. Brewer claims, "White was not interested in so-called courtly love."[85] At the same time, he was cautious in over-sexualizing the love affair. White remains fairly oblique regarding much of their physical relationship while making it clear that they do share a bed off and on throughout the years. While the original stage production emphasizes longing and guilt, both White's novel and Logan's film tell a slightly different tale. Logan shared none of White's hesitancy in implying the consummation of the adulterous love affair, instead reveling in the visual possibilities of physical intimacy.[86] In White's novel, losing his virginity mars Lancelot's perfection. He can no longer perform miracles. While many other knights love him, his perceived betrayal corrupts Arthur's vision, allowing for its downfall. In the film *Camelot*, the Knights of the Round Table often correctly accuse the pair of adultery, which sows discontent among Arthur's knights. The fact that Arthur deliberately chooses to ignore the affair aids in the ultimate demise that occurs in all of the versions. Certainly, the consummation of Guenevere and Lancelot's love lends a different understanding to the end of Arthur's utopian dream.

These distinct treatments alter how each version connects to White's book. Elizabeth Archibald observes that the main source for T. H. White's *The Once and Future King*, Thomas Malory's *La Morte d'Arthur*, "was unusual in the English tradition in making the love affair a central theme."[87] While White draws from and comments on Malory's text, he complicates the role of the love triangle quite a bit through characterization and themes. As mentioned earlier in this chapter, incest and Arthur's own failings figure into his downfall as much as, if not more than, the adultery. The Lerner and Loewe musical, in both its original stage version and film adaptation, streamline White's treatment of the love triangle and ensuing collapse of Camelot. Furthermore, the role of magic and characterization represent their own interpretive layer to the legend.

Conclusion: Political Idealism and the Legacy of *Camelot*

The Once and Future King reflects White's own political leanings during the post-war years. Arthurian scholars note how the influences of White's pacifism, as well as the events of World War II, inform much of the approach.[88] Lerner and Loewe's musical, on the other hand, espoused a type of political idealism that quickly became associated with President John F. Kennedy's short time in the White House. Several musical theater scholars comment on the relationship between contemporary politics and Arthur's utopian ideal.[89] Mark Steyn details how the musical became so connected with the Kennedy administration in American culture, pinpointing a *Life* magazine interview with Jacqueline Kennedy rather than any indication from the president himself as integral to the close ties between the two. Specifically, the widowed first lady quoted from the title song:

> Don't let it be forgot
> That once there was a spot
> For One Brief Shining Moment that was
> Known as Camelot.[90]

The link between the musical and Kennedy grew after his assassination. Steyn relays Lerner's account from a touring production of the show, in which he claims everyone, audience, cast members, and crew alike, began to cry. As Lerner poetically put it, *Camelot* became "suddenly the symbol of those thousand days when people the world over saw a bright new light of hope shining from the White House."[91]

Even without the association with Kennedy administration, Lerner and Loewe's *Camelot* inherently promotes an idealistic or utopian vision through King Arthur's principles and actions. While Knapp explores the various manifestations of idealism in the musical, Jones compares *Camelot* to the team's earlier musical that depicted an "isolationist utopia," *Brigadoon* (1947).[92] Jones asserts that *Camelot* "laments a utopia failed, lost, or destroyed."[93] Lerner fleshes out this utopia by adding scenes and dialogue to the film version's screenplay, enhancing the significance of Arthur's idealism in Act II and reflecting the deeper political meaning that the accumulated associations about Kennedy had given the musical. At the time of *Camelot*'s high-profile film premiere, four years after the assassination of President John F. Kennedy, the musical's relationship to Kennedy and his presidential term had solidified. The film version plays up this association. Matthew Kennedy observes that there are "moments when Harris's kingly voice and bearing nearly elevate *Camelot* into the zone of moving drama and do justice to the powerful associations for a recently slain and newly mythologized president," yet for many viewers, the naïve political idealism did not connect with the current times.[94] Nonetheless, the film adds scenes which engage in a sense of nostalgia for the perceived political ideal.

The first scene directly after the Intermission demonstrates this emphasis. Rather than opening the second act with a scene between Lancelot and Guenevere in which Lancelot, egotistical as ever, writes a poem about himself that leads into "If Ever I Would Leave You," the film shows Arthur moving among his people. A subject offers the king the keys to his town because his "Might for Right" policy has rendered them unnecessary. The background music reinforces the utopian possibilities of Arthur's England. A trumpet fanfare accompanies Arthur's ride through his subjects, then transitions to the chorus theme from "Camelot." During the ensuing dialogue, the flute and other woodwinds continue to play "Camelot" extremely softly. The brief exchange ends with another triumphant sounding fanfare. The addition of this scene shows the potential of Arthur's ideas as well as the safety that resulted from putting them into action. However, this vision of utopian society does not last long. The subsequent scene shatters the illusion as the camera cuts to a duel between Lancelot and a knight of the Round Table. The knight has accused Lancelot and Guenevere of treasonous infidelity. Ever powerful, Lancelot defeats his accuser and demands a repeal. Before being banished, the knight states that the adulterous couple is a "poison in the court": a poison that will eat away at Arthur's perfect England. The remainder of the film adds scenes that underscore Arthur's political acumen while fostering a sense of nostalgia for that better time.

In order to safeguard Lancelot and Guenevere's secret, Arthur puts a new law into place that requires a civil court rather than dueling in order to decide the verdict of an accused crime. Of course, this law, with malicious help from Mordred, ultimately causes the downfall of the tragic lovers and Arthur's perfect kingdom. Arthur discusses his newest idea in Act II, Scene 2 of the book. In addition, the film continually brings up the need for evidence and a trial in order to resolve a proposed crime. Lancelot apprises Guenevere of the imminent change. He lets her know that in making sure no evidence can be found against them, Arthur will surely never give the couple the opportunity to be alone again. Arthur further explains the process of the court twice more to his friend, Pellinore. In an extended scene dealing with the law, the old man humorously fails to grasp the purpose or method of a court rather than simply fighting and killing a challenger.

These added scenes about Arthur's innovative way of dealing with crime and accusations stress his prescience in matters of state as well as his continued idealism. Both the original Broadway run and the film also cut the knights' song "Fie on Goodness," which removes the restlessness of Arthur's subjects and further highlights nostalgia for the hoped-for perfection.[95] Of course, the king cannot maintain his forward-thinking politics while his queen and trusted knight attempt to deceive him. His tolerance of the "poison" that exists in the form of the betrayal from the two people he loves the most, in fact the very thing that makes Arthur an exemplary ruler, proves to kill his vision of perfection. Camelot, which David Walsh and Len Platt read as an analog for America, eventually falls, and the film highlights the tragedy of that fall.[96]

The original cast, their recordings, and other elements haunt the subsequent versions of the musical, inviting comparison. The original Broadway cast of *Camelot*, featuring Richard Burton, Julie Andrews, and Robert Goulet, offers a compelling case for seeing and hearing characters in relation to the actors that first portray them. As the original stage version informs both the creation and reception of a film, so does the film version (which becomes a fixed, widely available product) present the possibility of influencing later stagings. Subsequent productions of *Camelot*, in particular, provide an illustration of this intertextual relationship. After appearing as Arthur in the film, Richard Harris later reprised his role in touring productions that were more closely aligned with the film version than they were with Lerner and Loewe's original conception of the work. Furthermore, Lerner continued to tinker with the book well after the film's screenplay was completed. Not only did Harris reprise his role as Arthur, but Richard Burton too played the ancient king again in a 1980 revival. When Lerner learned of Burton's interest, he wrote the actor a letter that states "in perusing the script after all these years, I found several places where, with a little bit of work, I could strengthen some of the scenes."[97] While Loewe had left the partnership, Lerner expressed a desire to keep perfecting his earlier work.

Arthurian legend then and now populates popular consciousness. The versions explored throughout this study, including Disney's *The Sword in the Stone* (1963), develop a rich intertextual relationship with *Camelot*. These tellings and retellings of the well-known story of King Arthur and his

Knights of the Round Table offer a background for understanding and engaging with the stage version and the 1967 film musical. *Camelot* has not had the type of lasting mainstream cultural impact that musicals such as *West Side Story* (1957) and *The Sound of Music* (1959) continue to enjoy. The musical does, however, illustrate the continued fascination with Arthurian legend, representing a now familiar interpretation of the love triangle.

4

Naiveté and the Depiction of Arthur's Childhood in Disney's *The Sword in the Stone*

A boy miraculously pulls a sword from a large stone: this image has become one of the most famous scenes associated with the legend of King Arthur. Sometimes explicitly linked with the renowned Excalibur, a young Arthur's ability to remove the sword firmly stuck in stone marks his destiny as king of all England. While this element has formed a foundational part of Arthurian legend since the twelfth century, T. H. White is responsible for expounding on the childhood development of the future king and events that led up to his ascent. In 1963, Disney's Animation Studios released a feature film adaptation of White's book. Similar to Lerner and Loewe's musical and the earlier Twain retellings, Disney's filmmakers instill an American perspective into the Arthurian legend. With six songs written by Richard M. Sherman and Robert B. Sherman, the animated musical fantasy inserts a different interpretation of Arthur's childhood—one which dovetails with Disney's own cultural agenda.

White's Novel

As the first book in T. H. White's eventual tetralogy *The Once and Future King*, *The Sword in the Stone* holds a special place in regard to the author's approach to Arthurian legend. White first published the story in 1938 as a stand-alone novel; then he revised it into its final form, which was published with the remaining books in 1958. As such, the genesis of *Sword* was complicated with both English and American versions before its last iteration as part of the larger whole.[1] Of all of White's forays into Arthurian legend, *The Sword in the Stone* is unique, displaying not simply his idiosyncratic retelling but an entire newly imagined segment of Arthur's life. Although the details

From Camelot *to* Spamalot. Megan Woller, Oxford University Press (2021). © Oxford University Press.
DOI: 10.1093/oso/9780197511022.003.0005

of Arthur's parentage, along with the fact that Uther hid the boy away, and the eventual retrieval of the sword from stone all have antecedents in the annals of the myth, a thorough exploration of the future king's childhood had never been written.

Young Arthur—called the Wart—and his adventures in magic, the description of his lessons from the wizard Merlyn, as well as his emotional and moral growth are all creations of T. H. White. Elisabeth Brewer observes that White displays a "depth of understanding of children, and especially of young boys" throughout his depiction of Arthur's childhood.[2] Not only the language used by the Wart but his worries, fears, and desires emerge through the narrative as remarkably insightful. Brewer picks up on the Wart's insecurities based on his parentage and the fact that he is not Sir Ector's true son as indicative of White's perception. At the same time, White peppers the so-called children's story with historical and literary allusions entirely appropriate for a knowledgeable adult audience.

The episodic novel details various adventures and lessons that the Wart experiences during his childhood. White's treatment of well-established characters throughout *Sword* reveals the author's attitudes and priorities in significant ways. As mentioned in the previous chapter, scholars grapple with White's generally negative depiction of women throughout *The Once and Future King*. Kurth Sprague posits that the women in *Sword* create a "kind of moral attitude toward women in general and women of responsibility and power in particular."[3] Sprague cites the undesirable and even damaging teaching methods of the female governess as well as Morgan le Fay's ugly, wicked witch persona as representative of White's overall attitude toward women as evidenced in the first book.

Although a comedy, *The Sword in the Stone* explores the role of upbringing and education in the development of a person's life as well as its lasting influence. C. M. Adderley identifies education as a common thread in White's fictional works. He suggests that White's own troubled childhood and educational history led him to explore educational ideals. Adderley and Sprague note the extremes of age that White excels at depicting, particularly in terms of the teacher-student relationship. Merlyn and the Wart represent the ideal because "the very young were open to new ways of thinking and the very old carried the authority of experience."[4] Adderley further states that "the purpose of education, for White himself, was to learn to be self-sufficient."[5] Arthur thus epitomizes this ultimate goal because he uses Merlyn's lessons to become an idealist ruler and formulate his Might for Right philosophy.

The Sword in the Stone contains five animal transformations, which serve as the main thrust of the Wart's education. Throughout the course of the book, Merlyn turns his young pupil into a fish, a hawk, an ant, a goose, and a badger. During each of these transformations, Arthur learns about the animals, and nature more broadly, via lived experience with representatives of each species. As Adderley discusses, the main goal of Arthur's education is to learn to think for himself. White's own pacifist tendencies surface as an important topic, explored through the Wart's naïve ideas regarding war, which are constantly tested in his lessons. This particularly comes through when the Wart transforms and joins the ants, the geese, and finally the wise, old badger. In the ant episode, Arthur encounters a highly militaristic and "belligerent" species of ants, in which any form of deviation is viewed as insane and war is upheld as glorious.[6] By contrast, the geese display no concept of war; indeed, Lyo-lyok is appalled at Arthur's description. When the Wart innocently claims "I like fighting . . . It is knightly," Lyo-lyok only answers "because you're a baby."[7] The badger confirms this particular lesson, incidentally the Wart's final one, when he states, "well, it is true that man has the Order of Dominion and is the mightiest of the animals—if you mean the most terrible one—but I have sometimes doubted lately whether he is the most blessed."[8] The badger laments man's propensity for war, a trait otherwise extraordinarily rare in the natural world. When the Wart seems to have learned nothing as of yet, the badger simply asks, "which did you like best, the ants or the wild geese?"[9] White's post-war grappling with the very existence of war shines through each of the books in The Once and Future King, and it proves to be the most important lesson Merlyn teaches the Wart in Sword. Although a children's book, Sword sets up a number of the larger, serious subjects explored throughout the entire novel. In the hands of the Disney Company, the complexity inherent even in White's first book diminishes in favor of a more straightforward children's story.

Walt Disney Animation Studios

Both lauded and censured by scholars over the last twenty-five years, Disney—in its various meanings—has been a rich source of scholarship. Several monographs, in particular, are devoted to interrogating Disney and the company's vast influence on American (and global) culture.[10] As many scholars have noted, Disney has taken on the role of moral educator and the production of childhood innocence and values.[11] Yet a number of these scholarly works focus on the so-called Disney Renaissance era. Easily the most well-known company and creator of children's entertainment as well as the "biggest name" in this book, Disney has long been synonymous with children's entertainment.

Since the Disney Company's first foray into full-length animated film with *Snow White and the Seven Dwarfs*, familiar fairy tales and folk stories have provided the basis for many of their feature animations. As with any form of adaptation, Disney changes aspects of the tales for a multitude of purposes. Annalee Ward writes, "Disney rewrites the original tales for its particular version of American values."[12] This approach allows Walt Disney, and subsequently the company more broadly, to promote a defined type of morality, teaching children according to their brand of these American values. Jack Zipes goes even further, stating:

> He robs the literary tale of its voice and changes its form and meaning. Since the cinematic medium is a popular form of expression and accessible to the public at large, Disney actually returns the fairy tale to the majority of people. The images (scenes, frames, characters, gestures, jokes) are readily comprehensible by young and old alike from different social classes. In fact, the fairy tale is practically infantilized, just as the jokes are infantile.[13]

Though specifically discussing Walt Disney's treatment of *Puss in Boots* in this excerpt, Zipes's point is wide ranging as he contends that in some way Disney returns the fairy tale writ large to the masses when the genre has effectively moved from aural to literary tradition. The use of fairy tales in this way allows Disney to engage with cultural traditions, building upon the morals and meanings within the stories in order to contribute to American culture. Although Arthurian legend is not a fairy tale, or even a folk tale, due to its lengthy literary tradition, much of what Disney scholars observe in their discussions holds true for *The Sword in the Stone*. The Disney Company similarly uses T. H. White and the legend of King Arthur more generally to further its own twin goals of mass production and educational ideals. Furthermore, the Disney Company draws on a white British heritage in order to promote its American "edutainment" agenda in its use of Camelot as utopian past. As will be explored in the next section of this chapter, *Sword* undergoes the process of simplification and Americanization identified by Janet Wasko.[14]

Although the Disney Company had produced twenty animated feature films by 1963, the focus of Walt Disney, and the Company in general, had broadened into other areas. The creation and development of the Disney Theme Parks, for instance, took a great deal of Walt Disney's time and creative energies. California's Disneyland had opened in 1955, and while Disney World would not open until after Walt's death, he was deeply involved in the planning of the Florida location.[15] The Company's production of several live-action television shows in the 1950s, including *The Mickey Mouse Club* and *Zorro*, similarly split the corporation's focus. In the realm of film, *Treasure Island* from 1950 marked the beginning of a period of live-action productions for theatrical release. In fact, over thirty live-action films were released by Walt Disney Pictures by the time *The Sword in the Stone* premiered. Following on the heels of *One Hundred and One Dalmatians* (1961), *Sword* represented an animated film from a company renowned for animation at a time when animated film was not the main focus.

Due to the Walt Disney Company's branching out, the animation studios had been undergoing a fair amount of change. Although Walt Disney traditionally exercised a certain amount of control, he no longer had the time to do so in the same way by the early 1960s.[16] Chris Pallant contends that Wolfgang Reitherman "arguably held the greatest authorial claim over the Studio's animation" during this period.[17] One of Disney's so-called Nine Old Men, Reitherman began as an animator for *Snow White* and had moved into directing by the 1950s. Michael J. Barrier notes that Reitherman was known more for his action sequences as an animator and seemed an odd choice to lead the animated features.[18] Nevertheless, he co-directed *One Hundred and One Dalmatians* with Ham Luske and Gerry Geronimi and became the sole director of *Sword*. Barrier further posits that Reitherman's directorial shortcomings impacted the final film, stating

Compared with Bill Peet's fifty-one-page treatment for *Sword* from 2 October 1961, Reitherman's film is broad and careless . . . Honestly felt emotion—so much a part of the early Disney features—does not figure much in *Sword*, and Reitherman was plainly uncomfortable with it, as he was with irony or anything else that required delicate shading to be effective.[19]

The issues addressed by Barrier are representative of other criticisms against *Sword* throughout the scholarship on Disney animation.

Contemporary critics, however, found much to like in the lighthearted film. Bosley Crowther of the *New York Times* enjoyed the film as a silly bit of Christmas fun.[20] Familiarity with White's novel seems to have impacted responses in different ways. Crowther notes, "adapting T. H. White's beloved novel of King Arthur's boyhood, the Disney unit has shaped a warm, wise and amusing film version. The unorthodox source, with its artful earthiness, was certainly no snap undertaking as a movie cartoon."[21] On the other hand, the *Variety* reviewer complains, "one might wish for a script which stayed more with the basic story line rather than taking so many twists and turns which have little bearing on the tale about King Arthur as a lad," while still calling the film a "tasty confection."[22] Although willing to point out its flaws, many contemporary critics seemed disposed to experience the film as a piece of fun, children's movie fluff.

Despite a number of positive critical reactions, *The Sword in the Stone* does not have the same staying power as other Arthurian interpretations. Yet the film's intertextuality certainly extends to the Disney Company's canon of animated features. James Bohn asserts that *Sword* "has never entered the pantheon of classic animated Disney features. Perhaps the reason is that the film lacks an emotional center."[23] As discussed later in this chapter, other scholars have advanced other such issues, including an overabundance of repetition and the lackluster underscoring, as additional shortcomings of the film. As an adaptation of Arthurian legend via White, *The Sword in the Stone* inherently invites intertextual analysis. Another level of intertextuality permeates the animated feature, however, as it constantly references earlier Disney films. In the limited scholarship on the 1963 *Sword*, the role of this film as a Disney product looms large. Bohn's discussion of *Sword* details the opening book sequence, considering it as an extension of a technique used in numerous other films since *Snow White and the Seven Dwarfs* (1937).[24] He also notes the connection of "Higitus Figitus" as a magical nonsense word with *Cinderella*'s highly successful "Bibbiti-Bobbidi-Boo."

Additionally, "Higitus Figitus" and subsequent dancing dish scenes, strongly suggest "The Sorcerer's Apprentice" sequence from *Fantasia* (1940). Douglas Brode goes so far as to refer to *Sword* as the "unofficial sequel" to the magical sequence featuring Mickey Mouse and dancing brooms.[25] Of course, both "The Sorcerer's Apprentice" and Merlin's unique packing and washing techniques share the visual spectacle of animated inanimate objects.[26] The very idea and image of brooms sweeping the floor or dishes cleaning themselves invites the comparison. Musically, the later film also seems to reference

Example 4.1 "Higitus Figitus" Theme. Transcribed from Bill Peet. *The Sword in the Stone*. Directed by Wolfgang Reitherman. Burbank, CA: Disney, 1963. DVD.

Example 4.2. "The Sorcerer's Apprentice" Theme. Short motive transcribed from Paul Dukas, *The Sorceror's Apprentice*, 1897.

Paul Dukas's orchestral work. The main melodic theme with its bounce and running eighth notes resembles a simpler version of Dukas's main theme (compare Examples 4.1 and 4.2).

The stepwise turns on the magical nonsense words add interest to the walking feel of the short tune. The use of the bassoon in the orchestration to indicate the motion of the various objects at key points represents another likeness. While not directly based on the Dukas, the character of "Higitus Figitus" bears striking similarities to the piece.

The Sherman Brothers

Robert and Richard Sherman wrote the songs for *The Sword in the Stone*, thus impacting the interpretation as discussed in more detail later in this chapter. In fact, the brothers' songs would quickly become the sound of Disney in the 1960s. Bohn comments that the "Sherman brothers' collaboration bore rich fruit, yielding over two hundred songs, many of which are both memorable and popular."[27] These songs appeared on television, in theme parks (including "It's a Small World"), and in both live-action and animated films. The songwriting team would gain a massive amount of critical and popular success with their contributions to *Mary Poppins* (1964). In a 1966 radio interview, Walt Disney called the Sherman brothers "a very important part of our organization here. They're wonderful. Well, they go for the 'team play,' you know. That's the way we work here. It's the team that gets together and builds these things. The Sherman Brothers are not only very talented, but very cooperative."[28] *Sword*, however, was the pair's first animated feature and relatively early in their working relationship with Disney.

In 1960, the Sherman brothers became the first staff songwriters for Disney. Previous to the sibling team, the Disney Company had contracted a variety of outside songwriters for the many projects since *Snow White*. Before *Sword*, the Shermans had primarily written stand-alone songs, even when working on live-action films. These include the title song as well as "Let's Get Together" for *The Parent Trap* (1961) and the infectious "Enjoy It," written for Maurice Chevalier in *In Search of the Castaways* (1962), among several others for film and television. *Sword* represented the duo's first foray into writing for character and plot, which Robert Sherman said they greatly enjoyed "because with animated films the songs seem so much more important to the entire story line of the film. For example, the song 'Higitus Figitus' was written to both establish Merlin's rather bumbling character and to advance the story line of the film. That's something you don't get to do when just writing popular songs."[29] Of course, the Shermans would have ample opportunity to write story songs for films to an even greater degree after *Sword*, but this film represents their first opportunity to approach songwriting in this way. At the same time, they often referred to *Sword* as a lesson in songwriting and storytelling, namely to not "just turn in our songs and walk away from the picture."[30] The team claimed that they had "neither the experience nor the clout" to insist on more involvement but learned that "a tight interaction between song and story is the secret to achieving the *real* magic in a musical motion picture."[31]

Disney's Version of White

Unsurprisingly, the animated version of *The Sword in the Stone* vastly simplifies White's tale of childhood adventure. The reasons for this are manifold and, in some ways, obvious. First and foremost, the Disney film is a mere seventy-nine minutes long, whereas the first book in White's tetralogy is over three hundred pages. Streamlining the novel is an adaptation necessity in this case. Additionally, the intended audience of each version is quite disparate. While White's book is an entertaining fantasy full of adventures for young readers, the whimsy offers an equal measure of entertainment for an adult audience. Furthermore, White writes a story replete with deeper political meaning. The Disney film, on the other hand, avoids the qualities of the original that cater to an older audience. Similar to the earlier animated feature *Bambi* (1942), *The Sword in the Stone* aims for a very young audience.

The cuts made from the novel give the animated film a much more repetitive narrative, and even the shared themes—such as the value of education—feel more heavy-handed than even White's not entirely subtle style. As Douglas Brode asserts, "to effectively transform the Arthur legend into a work of personal expression, Disney took considerable liberties not only with T. H. White's highly regarded children's book, but the legend as it dates back through Tennyson to Malory."[32] Indeed, the animated version of *The Sword in the Stone* simplifies in a way typical for the Disney Company's approach to telling familiar tales. Simply put, *Sword* undergoes the "process of Disneyfication" described by Janet Wasko, "which involves sanitization and Americanization."[33] The removal of White's political engagement, more complicated versions of characters like Morgan le Fay, and the sheer scale of the cuts all speak to this process. Many of the changes discussed throughout the rest of the chapter affect interpretation and the experience of Arthurian legend as promoted by Disney.

Although Disney gained the rights to *Sword* prior to the creation of Lerner and Loewe's musical, *Camelot* nonetheless provides another frame of reference. At the time of the film's release in December 1963, the Broadway production had finished its run, but the subsequent touring production was well under way. Although each musical telling deals with a different stage in the life of King Arthur, they both specifically adapt T. H. White's version of the tale. As such, the treatments of characters—namely Arthur himself, Merlin, and even Pellinore—represent interpretations based on White's descriptions. The potential for overlapping audiences for the stage musical and animated film is likely, perhaps even more so than with the readership of White's novel given the media involved and the fact that *Camelot* was on tour at the time. As such, the parallel potential for knowing audiences to relate *Sword* to *Camelot* seems equally possible in considering the palimpsestuous quality of the work.

Additionally, the association of President John F. Kennedy's administration with Camelot had recently been made by Jacqueline Kennedy, specifically referencing Lerner and Loewe's musical. James Bohn observes that the premiere of *Sword* benefited from an "inadvertent timeliness" based on the tragedy of Kennedy's assassination and the high profile association of the legend with his administration.[34] Given these circumstances, even audience members who had not seen Lerner and Loewe's stage musical had a frame of reference for understanding the Disney film. Owing to the idealism expressed in Jacqueline Kennedy's connection of her husband's administration with Camelot, the ideas of American values and education as foundational for *Sword*'s expression of utopian reign would resonate with audiences still reeling from the President's recent assassination. The concept of the British Arthur's reign being cut short had become an analog for an optimistic American administration, which was similarly ended before its time. Since the Disney version also explicitly uses Arthur's childhood as its basis, the film dovetails with the connection to the Kennedy administration without presenting an overly nostalgic vision of Arthur's adulthood.

While White utilizes the long-held assertions that Arthur was the secret child of King Uther and Igraine of Cornwall, Disney brushes past Arthur's parentage entirely. The film simply presents Arthur as an orphan with an unusual destiny. The special edition bonus features reveal that this was not always the intended opening explanation for the film. The feature acknowledges multiple versions of this legend and that specific choices were made in making the Disney version. In this proposed opening, the narration states outright that Arthur is Uther's long-lost son.[35] In the final version, however, this logical explanation for Arthur's ability to pull the sword from the stone is never given or acknowledged. As such, Arthur—known as Wart—becomes a normal young boy, and the film frames the poor boy's rise to kinghood as remarkably similar to the ideal of the American dream. Arthur may be destined for greatness, but education and hard work ultimately get him there.

In White's book, Merlyn uses various adventures and devices to teach the young Wart. He not only turns the boy into several animals but also arranges for escapades involving Robin "Wood" (i.e., Robin Hood) and the witch Morgan le Fay. All of Merlyn's lessons—magical or not—are meant to instill specific lessons for Arthur's eventual kingship. In the Disney version, three animal transformations make up the bulk of Merlin's magical teaching: a fish, a squirrel, and a bird. In White's story, Merlyn does not always change forms alongside Arthur and tends to appoint a mentor from the actual species in order to convey their unique perspective and wisdom. In the animated film, Merlin does change into the animals (with the exception of the bird since talking owl Archimedes already fills that role). The wizard and Archimedes then act as Arthur's sole educators.

Both White's novelization and the Disney film contain a focus on education. Merlin specifically enters Arthur's life in order to teach him, imparting the skills and knowledge he needs to become the king of England. For White, the evils of war represent a foundational part of this education. This reflects White's own stance as a pacifist, especially (though not exclusively) in the post-war revision of the book as explored in a previous section of this chapter. Disney's version removes the pacifist stance to some degree, though Merlin continues to show disdain for knightly occupations like jousting. The single-minded focus on education, particularly with the less complex plot, feels more Disney than White. In his analysis, Raymond H. Thomson notes that the film ultimately "offers little beyond the one basic message and through repetition it grows tiresome, despite the charm of individual scenes."[36] By 1963, the role of Disney films in promoting education, and especially moral education, had solidified. Already, as Henry Giroux and Grace Pollock put it, "generations of children [had] learned from Disney films."[37] George Rodosthenous further observes that the Disney Company takes advantage of the fact that "musicals can develop and shape young children's understanding of society and life around them."[38] Disney films strive to set a standard for "edutainment," as evidenced in their version of *The Sword in the Stone*.

Similar to many other Disney animated features, *The Sword in the Stone* opens with the image of a book. Brode notes that these images are used to "employ the film medium not as an alternative to, but a means of hooking children on, reading."[39] Not only is *Sword* explicitly presented as a story that can be found in a book, but Merlin and Archimedes also stress the importance of reading to the illiterate Wart. In a short feature, the Sherman brothers discuss their initial hope that the music would further enhance the educational theme.[40] The cut song "The Magic Key" aligns magic and knowledge. The lyrics underscore the importance of "using your brains" and acts as more of a "story" song than the song used in the film ("Higitus Figitus"). The Shermans later posited that "songs like this one ['The Magic Key'], which give more meaning to the story, might have made the difference between a good film and a great one."[41] The melody and structure for "The Magic Key" are simple. The straightforward and repetitive song focuses on the message that education is "the magic key" to success.

Furthermore, the film's treatment of Sir Ector communicates the position that ignorance breeds fear. The meaning is clear: education alleviates fear of the unknown. Since *Sword* associates magic and imagination with education, the uneducated Sir Ector fears magic. When Merlin first appears at Ector's castle, Arthur's guardian scoffs at the old man's claim to magic. In order to prove his magical prowess, Merlin makes it snow indoors. While Ector capitulates to the existence of magic once shown, he quickly displays a terror of "black magic." Merlin, however, distinguishes his magic, which is "used for education purposes," from any black magic. After being persuaded to let

Merlin stay and teach Wart, Ector gives the magician a dilapidated tower to live in—clearly hoping that he will leave. Throughout the film, Ector shows nothing but disdain and alarm toward Merlin's powers, even punishing young Arthur for putting his lessons above his page duties. Thus, Sir Ector represents ignorance and fear, and his uneducated perspective makes him an obstacle for the future king to overcome.

While the overall theme of the importance of education has primacy in the film, *Sword* also contains other themes common to the Disney brand. Janet Wasko lays out a number of these themes and values in her discussion of so-called classic Disney films. Wasko identifies the following as prominent: "individualism and optimism; escape, fantasy, magic, imagination; innocence; romance and happiness; and good triumphing over evil."[42] Although several of these themes are present in White's original novel, the changes made for the film stress these typical Disney values. Of course, Arthurian legend invites imaginative fantasy and includes magic, especially through Merlin as a character. The film's Merlin connects the aforementioned ideas for Arthur explicitly, implying that magic needs imagination. When first changing Wart into an animal, Merlin asks if he can imagine himself as a fish. Once the boy answers in the affirmative, Merlin appears pleased and states, "magic can do the rest." The Disney version also highlights morality, aligning goodness with intelligence and the main theme of education. Wasko observes that Disney "moralism is clear and overt" with "little ambiguity or complexity."[43] The character Madame Mim, discussed in further detail later in this chapter, and her "battle" ' with Merlin highlights the moral component in a clear-cut manner.

While ostensibly taken from White's novel, several minor characters alter significantly, becoming "Disneyfied" in various ways. Sir Ector and his son Kay have personality traits that are changed or magnified from earlier versions of their characters. In White's novel, Sir Ector is the consummate knight. He believes in "might" for its own sake, takes delight in jousting and hunting, and is skeptical of magic. While depicted as a representative of the status quo and backward to Merlin's eyes, Ector is ultimately kind to Arthur and clearly cares for his ward. As discussed earlier, the film version Ector becomes an exaggerated symbol of ignorance, shown through his irrational fear of all things magical. More than that, his quick-to-punish treatment of Wart gives the orphaned boy a Cinderella-type childhood. A number of scholars, including Alice Grellner and Raymond Thomson, have noted the similarity and make another connection to Disney's penchant for reimagining fairy tales.[44] Sir Ector constantly assigns Wart "demerits," which result in extra kitchen chores. As such, images of the future king washing dishes in the kitchen certainly recall Disney's depiction of Cinderella's toiling in the earlier film (Figure 4.1). Although Ector truly worries for Wart's safety when he goes missing and displays immediate—perhaps opportunistic—remorse

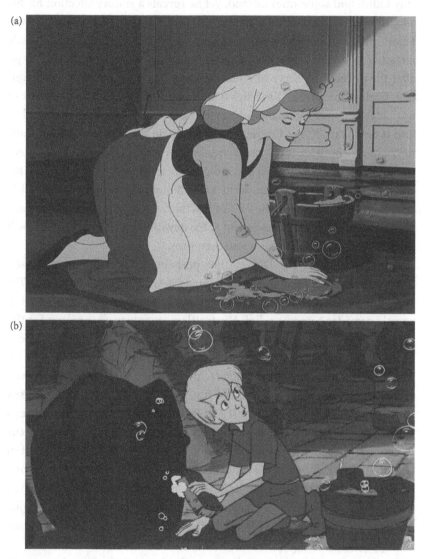

Figure 4.1 Cinderella vs. Wart Cleaning. a) Bill Peet, et al. *Cinderella*. Directed by Clyde Geronimi, et al. Burbank, CA: Disney, 1950. DVD. b) Bill Peet. *The Sword in the Stone*. Directed by Wolfgang Reitherman. Burbank, CA: Disney, 1963. DVD.

for his treatment after his ward proves himself king, Ector rarely shows any compassion or understanding toward him.

Disney's treatment of Kay is even worse than their portrayal of his father, removing any of his redeeming qualities. In the novel, Kay is remarkably selfish and sometimes unkind, yet he reveals a sincere affection for his adoptive brother in moments throughout their youth (and importantly, well before Arthur fulfills his destiny as king). Episodes, such as Kay callously releasing a hawk into the wild which prompts the thoughtful Arthur to go after the prized bird, serve to make the older boy a foil to White's protagonist. Grellner observes, "Kay's behavior demonstrates his petulance, lack of responsibility, and habitual tendency to assert his privilege of birth and to lord it over Wart."[45] The Disney film picks up on and enhances these qualities, ignoring both Kay's envy of Wart's lessons with Merlin (and subsequent adventures arranged by Wart) and moments of fondness peeking through his abrasive exterior. Notably, the adult Kay—though never a particularly likeable character—becomes one of King Arthur's most stalwart companions. However, the filmmakers never hint at the devotion and loyalty that Kay will show his brother-figure throughout their lives.

Pellinore's role in the Disney film perhaps changes the most drastically from White's version. While comedy appears throughout all of *The Once and Future King* to some extent and in various guises, Pellinore often overtly provides comedic relief. His fruitless seventeen-year search for the Questing Beast, his anachronistic behaviors and language, general eccentricities, and eventual marriage with "Piggy," all lead toward a highly idiosyncratic and amusing character. As Elisabeth Brewer notes, White emphasizes Pellinore as a "figure of fun."[46] While Alan Jay Lerner grasps this characterization while simplifying Pellinore's role in the story, Disney's version merely makes him superfluously innocuous. Pellinore only seems to exist in order to bring news of the tournament and add another adult to help train Kay. He shows little interest in Wart until suggesting that the boy be able to demonstrate his ability to pull the sword from the stone when no one believes him. The Disney version of Pellinore shifts from a lighthearted side character that infuses Arthur's childhood and later life to an unimportant minor figure.

Similar to many cartoons of the time, *The Sword in the Stone* has a great deal of underscoring. The film was scored by George Bruns, whose style is remarkably typical of animation to the point of cliché. In his article on Disney's animation music, Ross Care observes, "the previously interesting Disney background scores slipped into a kind of sameness, mostly due to the some-what bland sound of George Bruns."[47] Beyond making room for some di-alogue and select dramatic moments, the underscoring closely follows the "wall-to-wall" style typical of early cartoons. The orchestral music follows the action extremely closely, even using mickey-mousing, a technique that directly mirrors the physical action onscreen, throughout the course of the film. In their interview short, the Sherman brothers lament the fact that the underscoring did not pull any of the musical themes from their songs in order to delineate character.[48] The songwriting team states that once they gained Disney's confidence, they attended the spotting sessions for their films, which enabled them to have some input on how their songs might be used in the context of the underscoring. In the minds of this influential team, the general lack of connection between the songs and the underscoring af-fected the end product to its detriment.

In the most interesting moments of instrumental music, the connection with song does exist. Merlin's song "Higitus Figitus" (discussed in the fol-lowing section) provides the basis for the instrumental music played when the magician enchants the dishes to clean themselves so that Wart may evade his chores. The scene is *almost* a reprise, placing the tune in a jazzy setting with Merlin interjecting magical words here and there. He does not fully sing but rhythmically speaks lines and treats the few magical phrases as scat singing. The arrangement features syncopated piano with countermelodies on the saxophone. After a brief interval, the music returns once Sir Ector discovers the magic. The "Higitus Figitus" tune is no longer easily discernible, however, once Ector begins a fight with the dishes. A more frantic bebop-influenced treatment takes over in the trumpet and saxophone playing style, punctuated by mickey-mousing instrumental effects. In these scenes, the music takes on a more songlike character and function, differing from the character-istic cartoon underscoring of Bruns apparent throughout the majority of the film. Significantly, the cue sheet published in James Bohn's book on Disney music identifies George Bruns as the composer for all of the dancing dishes scenes.[49] While the Sherman brothers lamented the lack of their tunes in the underscoring, this technique does occur during this key sequence.

The jazzy setting of "Higitus Figitus" also epitomizes one of the major criticisms of *The Sword in the Stone*, as pointed out by Leonard Maltin, that the film is too much of its time.[50] Moreover, much of the musical pro-file is specifically rooted in American popular styles. Unlike T. H. White's source novel or the later Monty Python treatment, the Disney film's use of anachronism somehow did not work as well for audiences. Similar to White's story, the character of Merlin justifies anachronistic language or descriptions because he lives "backwards in time," and thus has already experienced the twentieth century. As such, he can reference later historical figures or inventions with impunity. Although Bohn notes that the animated feature certainly uses White's anachronisms, and especially Merlin, as "justifications for stylistic inconsistency," he claims, "the film does suffer a bit from disparity."[51] More specifically, the discrepancy arises from the jazz and popular music influence from the 1960s coupled with animation style underscoring and even attempts at vaguely medieval sounding music at times (almost entirely through the use of trumpet calls). The manipulation of the legend itself in order to adjust to American values is mirrored by the use of American popular styles. While the Americanization of the story works on a deeper level, the musical influences are overt.

Again, the instrumental setting of "Higitus Figitus" provides a good example. It begs the question: why would Merlin's magical antics be accompanied by jazz? Other than the fact that the musical accompaniment is fun and slightly chaotic in nature, there is little to warrant the stylistic influence in context with the rest of the film's musical approach. Certainly, the Sherman brothers' songs themselves, written largely to be sung by Merlin himself, do not allude to this style in the same way. Therefore, I would posit that for many viewers, the use of contemporary styles in select scenes feels forced. The lack of stylistic consistency—particularly as it relates to the use of contemporary American music—has an impact on the reception.

The opening and ending songs (not accompanying the credits) represent the only songs that do not delineate character within the film. In the limited musical scholarship on Sword, authors note the 1960s character of the song "The Legend of the Sword in the Stone." Bohn, in addition to considering the connection to earlier Disney animated features, perceives an incongruity with the title music and the opening ballad. Due to the guitar accompaniment, William Everett considers the song a " '60s-style folk ballad."[52] A muted brass fanfare fades into the solo guitar with singer Fred Darian. Darian's career as a popular music singer with the minor hits "Johnny Willow" and "The Battle of Gettysburg" in an early 1960s folk style strongly supports both Bohn and Everett's assertions. However, Darian's vocal style draws more on a light operatic singing in timbre and use of vibrato in "The Legend of the Sword in the Stone." As such, his vocal style shares similarities to mid-twentieth-century interpretations of John Dowland songs. The possibility of considering the guitar as a sort of modern lute casts the ballad as more in line with a 1960s interpretation of troubadours than the folk music genre. To be sure, the ballad shares elements with popular folk of the time, and the storytelling aspect makes the genre a logical influence for the opening book sequence. The supporting choir, which enters when the miracle of the sword in stone is referenced, thickens the texture, adding a majesty to the song and further removing the style from a typical 1960s folk ballad.

The "final" song is a short snippet of melody featuring a celebratory choir. Merlin notes that Arthur's story will become so famous that "they'll be writing books about you for centuries to come—why they might even make a motion picture about you." After inadequately attempting to explain motion pictures to a confused Arthur, a brass fanfare precedes a choral statement that proclaims "Hail to King Arthur. Long Live the King!" as the end card appears and zooms out before the final fade. Shorter than any other song in the film (which contains only short songs), this final musical declaration alludes to the majesty and wonder implied by Merlin regarding Arthur's reign once he grows into adulthood.

The songs that occur during the main action of the film are entirely character songs. Throughout the film, the song are quite short and interspersed with Brun's underscoring so that the musical styles flow in and out of one another—some more seamlessly than others. Significantly, Merlin emerges as the most musical character in *Sword*. The magician sings three songs written by the Sherman brothers during the film, all of which deal with magic and/or Wart's education. In fact, Merlin imparts this musicality as part of his lessons to Wart. Merlin's first song, "Higitus Figitus," occurs after the magician decides to become young Arthur's tutor and packs his belongings for the move to the castle. As discussed earlier in this chapter, "Higitus Figitus" lacks the explicit connection to education that the cut song "The Magic Key" addresses. Instead, "Higitus Figitus" does its own narrative and intertextual work. Again, the connection to both the earlier animation for "The Sorcerer's Apprentice" in *Fantasia* and even "Bibbiti-Bobbiti-Boo" from *Cinderella* represents important reference points. This understanding perhaps alludes to the studio's acclaimed history of animation at a time when television, live action, and theme parks seemed to be the main focus of the Disney Company.

With its bouncy tune and descending melodic lines that accompany the nonsense words, the song also portrays Merlin in a specific way; he appears whimsical and even a little ridiculous. The Shermans' music combines simplicity with whimsy in an appropriate manner for a children's song. The moderate tempo and $\frac{6}{8}$ time signature provide a dancelike structure for the simple melody, which focuses on repeated notes and stepwise motion. Moments of chromaticism and the choice to begin the song with F minor in an otherwise solidly F major song add a slight, easily resolved sense of mystery. These musical decisions dovetail with the nonsensical, magical atmosphere that characterizes Disney's Merlin.

While the made-up magical words are characteristic of earlier Disney magical figures as well as the Sherman brothers' writing style (e.g., "Super califragilisticexpialidocious"), Richard Sherman notes that the language was created to reflect Merlin's character.[53] Since Merlin is in many ways the quintessential British magician, the Shermans wanted his magical language to sound British. At the same time, they thought it should be reminiscent of Latin due to Merlin's level of education. Sherman thus claims that the resulting "higitus figitus" draws from the surname Higginbottom with a Latin flavor.[54] In this way, Merlin's brand of magic becomes entirely nonthreatening and fun in much the same way as Cinderella's fairy godmother. Although Merlin states that magic cannot solve all of your problems, "Higitus Figitus," both in its original iteration and the subsequent instrumental versions, emphasizes magic.

Merlin's second song, "That's What Makes the World Go 'Round," accompanies Merlin's first transformation lesson and proves to be the most educational song. In fact, Bohn asserts that "World Go 'Round" represents the "movie's central song" due to its moral message.[55] The message, however, is a simplistic one, representing the world as a construction of binaries (e.g., left and right, day and night, in and out, thin and stout, up and down . . . the list continues). Like all of the songs in *Sword*, dialogue and unrelated underscoring interrupt the song itself. At the beginning, the left and right fin movements, which Merlin uses to teach Wart to swim as a fish, create the rhythmic basis of the subsequent song. "World Go 'Round" has a strong duple meter, giving emphasis to the binary pairs throughout the tune. The primary motive is similarly simple with a triad moving up the third from the tonic before descending to the lower fifth. Merlin's singing, in this song as in his others, is highly declamatory. An off-screen women's choir adopts this style but sings the tune in a quicker tempo. This adjustment makes the plodding melody lilt more in their iteration. Finally, Wart takes up the final phrase of the song, signaling his learning process. In fact, Wart will sing a brief reprise of "World Go 'Round" while doing his chores back at the castle. Music acts as a teaching tool, and Wart's ability to adopt Merlin's song displays his absorption of the lessons.

"The Most Befuddling Thing" accompanies Merlin and Wart's transformation into squirrels when Arthur encounters an infatuated female squirrel. Again, Bruns's underscoring is interspersed with "The Most Befuddling Thing." Merlin's song teaches Wart about the mysteries of love, albeit without offering any concrete advice. And as Merlin's own missteps with an older female squirrel reveal, the experienced tutor is ill-equipped to teach this particular lesson. For those audience members familiar with Arthur's marital troubles as an adult, the ineffectiveness of the lesson is significant. The song itself is more lyrical than Merlin's other tunes but nevertheless contains its own brand of silliness. Merlin's propensity for making up words does not seem to be relegated to magical language. Merlin sings of the "discomboomeration" that accompanies romantic feelings. This song represents Merlin's final lesson, since Archimedes assumes more leadership in later educational scenes. While Merlin does transform Arthur into a bird, Archimedes teaches Wart how to fly due to his status as an actual bird. Significantly, this transformation does not have a song; although, the underscoring is more tuneful than most of the other non-singing sequences in the film. Within the action of the film, song signifies magical practice.

Other than Merlin, the only other character to have her own song is Madam Mim, another magic user. The American edition of White's novel cut this character; however, an earlier version did include Madam Mim.[56] Since Disney acquired the rights to *The Sword in the Stone* as early as 1939, the earlier iteration of White's book provides the source here rather than the 1958 collection that comprises *The Once and Future King*. The inclusion of Mim allows an antagonist for both Wart and Merlin without resorting to the complexities of story and character inherent in another magical woman, such as Morgan le Fay.

Mim's song revels in her "evil" ways, and she shows off by changing her form throughout it. Mim's vocal performance includes even less sustained singing than Merlin's does. While neither magician displays virtuosic singing or clarity of tone, Mim's reliance on talk-singing (or simply gleeful shrieks) sets her apart from the gentler Merlin. She does sing more when turning into a "beautiful" version of herself and claiming to have a "silvery voice," though the change is not particularly stark. In contrast to her rough vocality, the instrumental accompaniment to Madam Mim's song includes harp flourishes and an emphasis on violins. The light, enchanting orchestration of the song softens Mim's status as an "evil" sorceress. While she delights in mischief and aims to destroy Wart for no other reason than to thwart Merlin, Mim is still magical and musically portrayed as not *too* threatening. Ultimately, Merlin will beat her in their (overlong) wizards' duel.

Other than Madam Mim, *Sword*'s minor characters prove to be entirely unmusical. The Sherman brothers wrote a song for the knights called "The Blue Oak Tree." While the song itself was cut, the final film does allude to it. The simple tune, which Richard Sherman plays and sings in the documentary short, highlights the blind focus on "might" and empty symbols that exemplifies the knights of the film. While Merlin stresses the importance of education, the portrayal of knighthood is one of utter ignorance. The inclusion of the song in its entirety would have emphasized this point. Even still, Arthur's impending reign—bolstered by Merlin's teaching—is set up as diametrically opposed to the coarse behavior of the knights. Additionally, song remains specifically within the realm of magic, enhancing the positive influence that Merlin has on Wart. Although the future king is not magical, his learned musicality represents his absorption of the magician's lessons and further sets him apart from the typical knight during the proclaimed "dark time" of the film's setting.[57]

Conclusion

In many ways, Disney's *The Sword in the Stone* represents the simplest version of Arthurian legend included in my study. Unsurprisingly, the animated feature takes on Arthur's childhood—a portion of the future king's life relatively unexplored until T. H. White. *Sword* is a highly mediated and resoundingly twentieth-century version of the legend. The songs are short and woven together with largely (but not entirely) unrelated underscoring. Throughout the film, the musical styles included delineate an American character to the legend, and specifically Merlin as the most musical character. Although the quintessential British magician, Merlin's musical profile and outlook read as distinctly American in the film. As such, Disney's adaptation of T. H. White's first Arthurian book becomes not only simplified but Americanized in various ways—including musically. Despite any perceived weaknesses of the film itself, Disney's version of Merlin remains familiar territory, representing the whimsical wizard for a number of children across the decades since its release. For many audiences, the legend of King Arthur and the sword in the stone is as much Disney as White, if not more so. While this retelling might not be the most critically acclaimed, popular, musically complicated, or rich in characterization, it nevertheless adds to the American popular consciousness of Arthuriana.

PART 3
MONTY PYTHON AS ADAPTERS

5

Parody and the Role of Song in
Monty Python and the Holy Grail

In the 1975 film *Monty Python and the Holy Grail*, King Arthur gravely states, "On second thought, let's not go to Camelot. It is a silly place," directly after the audience has witnessed knights capering throughout their "Camelot Song." As a goofy send-up of the musical as related to Arthurian legend, the song indeed constructs Camelot and its knights as ridiculous in direct contrast to the idealistic depiction of Lerner and Loewe's *Camelot*. In this parody of Arthurian legend, the British comedy troupe plays with ideas of mythical place and idealism in the long-standing story. As explored in earlier chapters, King Arthur's court is emblematic of a utopian British past as well as a more general metaphor for political idealism. The comedic retelling by Monty Python turns this ideal on its head in a number of ways. Similar to the literary versions by Mark Twain and T. H. White, Monty Python manages to lampoon the apparent medieval time period of the tale alongside contemporary viewpoints.

The quest for the Holy Grail provides the ostensible narrative framework for the troupe's early feature film. The Grail, typically understood to be associated with Jesus Christ and the Last Supper in modern times, has become one of the most enduring tales of Arthurian legend. The Grail reference appears in a romance by Chrétien de Troyes in the twelfth century, developing from that point to include various descriptions of both the Grail itself and the questers. The earliest quester identified as attaining the coveted Grail, Perceval, does not figure into *Monty Python and the Holy Grail*. Instead, the film focuses on King Arthur and select Knights of the Round Table, including Lancelot, Galahad (Grail finder in later versions), and Robin (a Python creation). In Monty Python's rendering, the Grail remains unattainable—at least by Arthur and his knights.

The familiar background provides a unifying element for the film while allowing individual sketches and characters to shine. The loose plot structure of *Monty Python and the Holy Grail* is twofold. The film begins with

From Camelot to Spamalot. Megan Woller, Oxford University Press (2021). © Oxford University Press.
DOI: 10.1093/oso/9780197511022.003.0006

Arthur, self-proclaimed King of the Britons, in search of knights to join his Round Table. After a few hilarious misses, including his encounter with the peasant Dennis, King Arthur finds knights to join his cause. The final assemblage includes Sir Bedevere, Sir Lancelot, Sir Galahad, and Sir Robin. After rejecting Camelot as a "silly place," Arthur and his knights begin a search for the Holy Grail at the behest of God. The group decides to split up in order to cover more ground in their quest, and the adventures of each knight occupy the next section of the film. The knights eventually reunite, ending their quest with a number of final encounters, including with Tim the Enchanter, the killer bunny, and belligerent Frenchmen, before modern British police interrupt the proceedings.

Monty Python, Arthurian Legend, and Film

Monty Python uses familiar aspects of the Arthurian legend without adhering to any one version. Raymond H. Thomson observes that *Holy Grail* is "based upon the general romance tradition rather than any one account," mocking the conventions that have come to surround Arthurian retellings.[1] As several scholars have observed, however, Thomas Malory, T. H. White, and even Mark Twain certainly exert an influence. The Pythons draw on these influential texts only to critique them, using parody to highlight the absurdity of the notions of chivalry and divine providence inherent in many versions of Arthurian legend. Susan Aronstein states, "in its deconstruction of history, tradition, and multiple genres, [*Holy Grail*] offers both apocalypse and parody, exposing the absurd at the core of the Arthurian legends and the authoritative social and political structures that had appropriated them."[2] She further claims that this deconstruction works to disrupt the existing texts by emphasizing aspects such as the violence of Malory's version and the high-mindedness of Tennyson's account through its mockery. Rebecca A. Umland and Samuel J. Umland discuss *Holy Grail* in the context of "intertextual collage," in which they note that Monty Python layers references to a number of Arthurian stories.[3] Umland and Umland claim that, among the dense web of allusions within the film, Twain's description of the grail quest is the "distant intertext" for Monty Python.[4] Twain's particular use of comedy as a means of social criticism provides a model for the troupe.

As these scholars affirm, Monty Python uses Arthurian legend in a sustained yet loose way, never using specific stories from past versions.

Comparisons have been made to Chrètien de Troyes's *Perceval* due to the focus on the Grail quest. In particular, Elizabeth Murrell calls *Holy Grail* a "surprisingly accurate cultural 'translation'" of *Perceval*.[5] While there are important resonances with multiple versions, the film has more in common with later British retellings than with the French cycle. Indeed, Daniel L. Hoffman asserts that Malory represents "the most direct Arthurian source for the film."[6] In a comparison that further considers T. H. White's modern retelling of the Malory, Andrew Lynch describes Monty Python as "White's natural inheritors" in their smart use of comedy as well as the troupe's similar background as products of the British educational system.[7] The characters chosen for the film, including Bedevere, Lancelot, and Galahad, indicate knowledge of the Malory (perhaps through White's more recent novel). Furthermore, *Holy Grail* appends Galahad with the honorific "the Pure." In *The Once and Future King*, White characterizes Galahad as too good for this world, constantly annoying the other knights with his impossible purity and self-righteousness, before ultimately obtaining the Grail and ascending into heaven. Without employing these specifics, the casual reference of Galahad's untainted nature, which becomes a joke when he nearly succumbs to sexual desire, takes Malory by way of White's version of the character as standard.

As much as *Holy Grail* relies on the literary Arthurian tradition, the film also engages with previous retellings in popular culture. Kevin J. Harty posits that, in fact, "what the troupe lampoons is not the legend of Arthur but rather earlier treatments."[8] Furthermore, Darl Larsen chronicles all of the references included throughout the entire film. Going scene by scene, Larsen discusses allusions acknowledged by the Pythons or implied in the finished film or published script.[9] He illustrates how *Holy Grail* dovetails with the myth and medieval history in addition to the myriad other references. The intertextuality of *Holy Grail* is dense, underpinning the humor with an intellectual foundation. While not the focus of this chapter, a few allusions are noteworthy enough to merit further discussion. Ingmar Bergman's *The Seventh Seal* (1957) and Robert Bresson's nearly contemporary film *Lancelot du Lac* (1974) are each parodied mercilessly in *Monty Python and the Holy Grail*.

Contemporary critics and scholars alike have noted the influence of Robert Bresson's stark 1974 Arthurian film *Lancelot du Lac*. Vincent Canby observes that both the look and sound of Bresson's film provide fodder for the Pythons' film. Unlike *Holy Grail*, the overall soundtrack of Bresson's film strives for sense of realism. *Lancelot du Lac* does not include underscoring. Instead, all the music (apart from the opening text sequence and the credits) is source music: bagpipes accompany a jousting sequence; a horn signals people's arrival to Camelot; Mass includes chant; and so forth. The ever-present clanking of the knights' armor and the sounds of riding horses dominate. While Monty Python does not resort to the constant sound of jangling armor, the opening parody of the sound of a horse's hooves draws attention to the "realistic" soundscape of the French film. More than that, the look of *Holy Grail* is incredibly similar to Bresson's severe film, as illustrated in Figure 5.1.

The lighting, types of landscapes shown (especially in forest scenes), and the emphasis on grime all evoke Bresson's style. The stylization of the gore at the very beginning of *Lancelot du Lac* bears striking similarities to the Black Knight sketch in *Holy Grail* (though obviously, sans black humor). Hoffman states that the "too easily lopped off limbs comically echo Bresson's treatment of battle, particularly in the mass quantities of blood that issue from cavernous wounds."[10] Canby claims that the "comparison, which may never have been intended, is nevertheless lethal to the work of the great French director."[11] Despite Canby's statement, the likenesses are too prominent to be coincidental, and given the film's intense use of cinematic references, it seems likely that at least one of the directors, Terry Gilliam and Terry Jones—if not more Pythons—were familiar with *Lancelot du Lac*.

Even more pronounced than the parody of *Lancelot du Lac* is *Holy Grail*'s consistent engagement with Ingmar Bergman, especially *The Seventh Seal*. Unlike the obvious but more oblique use of Bresson's nearly contemporary film, Monty Python explicitly spoofs Bergman from the outset. The nonsensical "Swedish" titles, which open the film, herald the caricature of Bergman's work. Several of the Pythons, including the directors and Michael Palin, have acknowledged the satire of Bergman.[12] Gilliam and Jones openly discuss sending up Ingmar Bergman in their directors' commentary, particularly in the use of pseudo-"Swedish" titles during the opening.[13] Since *The Seventh Seal* represents one of the most famous uses of medieval setting in film, as epitomized by the iconic chess game with Death, Monty Python using this film as a reference point makes sense. As I will discuss later in the chapter, the flagellants' scene in *Holy Grail* is a direct allusion to the corresponding scene in *The Seventh Seal*.

While no other sequence in the film offers as direct of a parody as the flagellants' march through town, several key elements of Bergman's film resonate with Monty Python's depiction of the Middle Ages. The backdrop of the plague sets the stage for Bergman's film and its serious interrogation

Figure 5.1 *Holy Grail* vs. Bresson Visual Aesthetic. a and b) Robert Bresson. *Lancelot Du Lac*. New York: New Yorker Video, 1974. DVD. c and d) Terry Gilliam and Terry Jones, dirs. *Monty Python and the Holy Grail*. Culver City, CA: Sony Pictures, 1974. DVD.

of concepts of faith and religion—aspects which certainly play a role in *Holy Grail*. *The Seventh Seal* begins with the medieval trope of a knight riding through the countryside with his squire. Unsurprisingly, *Holy Grail*'s opening scene parallels this image with a humorous twist (Figure 5.2).

Figure 5.2 Two Tropes of Knight and Squire. a) Ingmar Bergman, dir. *The Seventh Seal*. New York: The Criterion Collection, 1957. DVD.
b) Terry Gilliam and Terry Jones, dirs. *Monty Python and the Holy Grail*. Culver City, CA: Sony Pictures, 1974. DVD.

In fact, the entire loose structure of a knight and his companions traveling through a troubled countryside and encountering various people and adventures represents a marked resemblance. Larsen further examines the similarities through contemporary reviews of Bergman's work that easily could apply to Monty Python's film.[14] In their travels, both Antonius Block of *Seventh Seal* and King Arthur encounter a girl being accused of witchcraft/encounters with the devil, for example. The parallels are manifest and purposeful. Each in their own way, these films tackle the tropes of medieval atmosphere, storytelling, and morals in order to expose their problematic aspects as well as comment on contemporary issues.

Similar to the "meta" approach used in *Monty Python's Flying Circus*, which scholars note sends up the very medium it uses, *Holy Grail* engages in pointed satire of not only cinematic genres but also the medium itself.[15] From the outset, *Holy Grail* mocks cinematic convention as Arthur grandly "rides" across the stunning Scotland location accompanied by his squire banging coconuts together (Figure 5.2). As a running gag that also happened to save money, King Arthur and his knights pretending to ride, with their squires providing sound effects, evokes earlier medieval epics while employing overt artifice. Additional examples include the intermission that occurs before the final sequence of the film as well as the modern police physically covering the camera as a concluding device. Both of these moments destroy the illusion of cinema as realistic, pointing out the conventions and mechanisms of the medium in funny ways. Throughout the film, the Pythons reference the historical epic, swashbuckling adventure film and the musical as genres. The result is a film awash with what Umland and Umland identify as a "dense assemblage of heterogeneous elements and allusions."[16]

Most of the film takes place squarely in the medieval era. A title card at the beginning claims that the film takes place in "932 A.D.," yet the actual look of the setting is later. Hoffman posits that the arbitrary date, signifying nothing in Arthuriana, "reveals a certain perverse intelligence for the Pythons to have arrived at a date so completely certain to reverberate soundlessly, to evoke so clearly associations with absolutely nothing."[17] The Pythons obviously found the highly specific date amusing, and Terry Jones acknowledges that the actual time period being represented is in the fourteenth century.[18] The co-director cites the codification of the legend around this time as the reason for the actual setting; early literary tellings of Arthurian legend deal with the earlier time period, but the Pythons are approaching their take from the time of the literature's writing. From Jones's commentary, the actual Arthuriana that forms the basis for *Monty Python and the Holy Grail* is unclear. While the elements used have an affinity with Thomas Malory's *La Morte d'Arthur*, the look of the setting is roughly one hundred years prior to that work. However, Jones remarks that he was immersed in the work of Geoffrey Chaucer at the time. As such, the fourteenth century setting makes sense. Although Chaucer does not tell the story of King Arthur and his Knights of the Round Table, *The Canterbury Tales* absolutely represents an idea of British medievalism.

"Authenticity" is a word that gets thrown around in relation to the look of this film a lot; however, as the time period discrepancy illustrates, Monty Python was more concerned with an *appearance* of authenticity. The troupe utilizes various cinematic tropes in order to aid in the audience's suspension of disbelief and directly contrast with the contemporary elements. In his 1976 article on Monty Python's legal battle with American Broadcasting Companies, Inc., Hendrik Hertzberg casually refers to *Holy Grail* as "one of the most authentic-looking films ever made about the Arthurian legend."[19] Darl Larsen points to the filth and location settings as the probable causes for Hertzberg's statement.[20] Indeed, the location settings in Scotland for the landscapes and castles are responsible for a great deal of *Holy Grail*'s visual presentation. As shot, the open fields and forests of Scotland fit in with a stereotype of untamed natural beauty as medieval knights roam the country on quests. While Monty Python hoped to use a number of castles in Scotland, the Scottish Department of the Environment denied their request to use several of them. Therefore, many of the exterior and interior castle scenes used Doune Castle from different angles to represent several different castles that Arthur and the Knights of the Round Table come across in their travels (Figure 5.3).

Although visual authenticity has become part of the discourse surrounding *Monty Python and the Holy Grail*, the film both conforms to and upends potential viewer expectations regarding the Middle Ages on film. Jones states outright that they were going for "*ideas* of authenticity."[21] He cites the constant filthiness and especially the bad teeth, both of which permeate the film, as markers of popular concepts related to the medieval past. Jones goes on to discuss the fact that likely people during this era did not have terrible teeth due to the lack of sugar in the diet.[22] Regarding the look, a mythical medieval era is evoked. As Martha W. Driver remarks, film "[reveals] not only historical aspects of the Middle Ages but perceptions of the Middle Ages in various times and places, and also in popular culture."[23] To put it even more

(a)

(b)

Figure 5.3 Doune Castle. Terry Gilliam and Terry Jones, dirs. *Monty Python and the Holy Grail.* Culver City, CA: Sony Pictures, 1974. DVD.

explicitly, William Woods states, "the stereotypes found on film—medieval life was dirty, dangerous, sexy, ignorant, passionate, doomed, and so on—are important."[24] These stereotypes have cultural significance, helping audiences to accept potential inconsistencies or even experience a feeling of authenticity. The "bad teeth" of Monty Python's medieval peasants as well as numerous other details function in this exact way, supporting perceptions of medievalism as created by earlier films.

When discussing a sense of authenticity or realism in film, the sheer length of time involved and its effect on any sort of knowledge or interpretation must be taken into account. When Monty Python places *Holy Grail* in 932 A.D. yet draws on costuming and other features from hundreds of years later, the troupe is both playing with time and stretching the audience's suspension of disbelief. Indeed, Woods claims that films set in the Middle Ages are "vitalized by *what we can accept* as authentic features of medieval reality."[25] Obviously, the level of audience acceptance varies based on a number of factors. In an absurd comedy, we can accept quite a bit of nonsense and anachronism. Yet *Holy Grail* also works as a medieval film—a fact which makes the modern intrusions and sensibilities funnier. Woods posits, "the most compelling medieval films have this kind of power because they invite their audience to collaborate with them in what could be called a shared cinematic medievalism."[26] For many, Monty Python taps into this idea of shared cinematic realism, and they use particular means to do so.

The interpretation of Arthur and his knights not only adapts Arthurian legend but makes use of cinematic signifiers for Arthuriana and the medieval in general. Film scholars on the medieval film have noted the importance of the knight as a symbol for the Middle Ages.[27] In David Day's discussion of *Holy Grail*, he notes how Monty Python plays with notions of authenticity from the beginning of the film. He describes the post-credit opening scene as "cryptic, but nonetheless, it feeds our preconceptions... [while it] may not be authentic, the scene achieves its intended effect."[28] Significantly, Day observes the juxtaposition of the "authentic" *sound* of a horse's hooves with the obvious *visual* artifice with the coconuts. He states that the film "impudently insists on getting the sound of a medieval icon right," even as it withholds the proper visual representation of the knight.[29] As the film moves forward, Graham Chapman's performance as Arthur provides the touchstone for traditional ideas of the medieval knight. The remaining Pythons comment on his use of heightened language and the sustained seriousness of his performance, even stating that Chapman was "actually in a different film" from the rest of them in terms of approach.[30] The contrast between Chapman's cinematically "authentic" performance of the medieval knight ideal and the absurdity of the situations and even other knights fuels the film's humor.

The music also evokes popularized ideas of the medieval, and as I discuss further, specifically Hollywood notions of the Middles Ages. The musical approach in *Holy Grail* plays on these very perceptions. In fact, the relative dearth of knowledge regarding medieval musical practice—especially instrumental music—makes reliance on later concepts or recreations of period music a necessity. As the coconut example illustrates, sound has an important role to play throughout *Monty Python and the Holy Grail*. Indeed, music represents a significant element in the troupe's comedic style in this film and throughout all of their output. In *Holy Grail* specifically, the ways in which music intersects with or departs from varying notions of authenticity represents a key aspect of the film's interpretation of Arthurian legend, and the Middle Ages more broadly.

Modern Comedy in the Middle Ages

Even as the specter of authenticity haunts *Monty Python and the Holy Grail*, contemporary touches abound. The most overt blending of pseudo-historical with modern Britain occurs through the historian and subsequent events surrounding his death. The travels of King Arthur and his companions are interrupted by a historian attempting to lecture on the events. The modern scholar nonsensically enters the world of the film and gets brutally killed by a passing knight. The investigation into his death becomes a recurring anachronism, which eventually serves as a way to end the film without any resolution to the Grail quest (ostensibly, the entire plot thread). Beyond the intrusion of contemporary characters into Arthurian legend, other twentieth-century allusions permeate the film. In a particularly hilarious scene, a peasant named Dennis angrily challenges Arthur's kingship, expounding upon issues of class and collective government. This persistent blending of historical atmosphere with abundant anachronisms follows in the literary tradition of Mark Twain and T. H. White. Indeed, the film maintains a strong balance between period atmosphere and twentieth-century sensibilities.

The musical approach, particularly as evidenced in the songs, highlights this balance. Sprinkled throughout *Holy Grail*, three songs and brief reprises as well as an "almost-song" enhance the story, character representation, and satire in various ways. The musical style of these short songs varies between an attempt at cinematic authenticity and entirely anachronistic, according to their purpose. At times, the period atmosphere created visually is mirrored by the onscreen songs' attempt at a sense of medieval sound. However, the Pythons also take advantage of music to engage in the genre parody that permeates the comedic approach. Regardless, these musical moments provide an additional unifying force, guiding the audience to understand Arthurian legend through the lens of Monty Python.

Given the popularity of *Monty Python and Holy Grail*, an abundance of popular literature, commentaries, and interviews detail the creation of this film. Additionally, Terry Jones put together *Monty Python and the Holy Grail (Book)*, which includes the published screenplay along with an earlier draft and notes for the film.[31] In short, there is no shortage of information regarding the writing and filming of *Holy Grail*.[32] For the purposes of analyzing *Monty Python and the Holy Grail* as an Arthurian adaptation, one particular aspect of the film's genesis becomes salient: the medieval setting. In the original screenplay draft, the Pythons conceived of the Grail quest as even more anachronistic by playing with time periods beyond what occurs in the final version. Initially, the film's setting was to move back and forth between the past and present. The Grail quest even ended in a modern-day department store. Terry Jones and Michael Palin take the most credit for insisting that the film be set entirely in the Middle Ages (with the aforementioned anachronisms intruding on the medieval setting).[33] As such, the final film becomes a more sustained interpretation of Arthurian legend in a way that the original conception would not have been.

As Monty Python's first full-length, (sort of) narrative film, *Monty Python and the Holy Grail* was filmed on a tight budget. Interestingly, rock musicians helped finance the film. The troupe approached Led Zeppelin and Pink Floyd, among other investors.[34] Existing Pythons, Terry Gilliam and Terry Jones, co-directed—the first film for both directors. The lack of directorial experience and funds affected the filming while providing a learning experience for the entire troupe.[35] As fit their working style for *Monty Python's Flying Circus*, the troupe each wrote segments of the film. While more work on setting and structure was necessary to provide the (still loose) narrative, the sketch model remained the norm throughout the creation of *Holy Grail*.

Another common aspect incorporated into the film was the established practice of each Python playing the characters that they wrote.[36] For example, Eric Idle wrote the material for Sir Robin as well as playing him onscreen. Similarly, Michael Palin wrote the Prince Herbert and father sketch, playing the disapproving king. In its basic make-up and process, *Holy Grail* had much in common with the British troupe's earlier television work. The larger scale and filming process, however, were new experiences. In particular, stories abound regarding the frustrations between the "two Terrys" in addition to the rest of the troupe's exasperation with Terry Gilliam's fixation on the look of the film. John Cleese, especially, has repeatedly aired his personal aggravation during the filming of *Holy Grail*.[37] Even the normally temperate Michael Palin apparently lost his cool after wallowing in the mud for a significant amount of time without actually being filmed.[38]

Stories such as these pervade popular literature and commentary due to the fact that *Monty Python and the Holy Grail* has become a cultural institution not only in the United Kingdom but in the United States as well. Indeed, the comedy troupe began to gain popularity in the United States in the mid-1970s through television airings of *Monty Python's Flying Circus* and comedy album sales in addition to the film releases. Promoter Nancy Lewis notes that the albums began to generate some buzz early on in the forays into the US market, and though the "albums never sold in enormous numbers . . . they provided a wonderful base."[39] She goes on to describe that they "really promoted the Pythons more as a rock band in a funny way, going through radio channels, because that was their audience, rather than going straight to a TV audience."[40] Given the fact that *Holy Grail* was financially backed by famous rock bands, the Python's apparent affinity with the music business and rock musicians holds significance. The irreverence of the group coupled with the musical sensibilities displayed in their television programs and films affects their popularity to no small degree.

In fact, Monty Python's US fan base proved to be extremely devoted to the group. Jeffrey Miller observes that *Flying Circus* "would claim a fanatically devoted audience in the United States with sketches that avoided topicality in favor of multi-layered attacks on all manner of institutional authority."[41] Although not initially concerned with translating to an American audience, the Pythons would eventually embrace their US following and even cultivate it well beyond the 1970s. The promotional efforts, television releases on PBS and the controversial ABC versions of *Flying Circus*, film releases, and tours all worked to enhance Monty Python's cultural imprint in America.[42] Terry Gilliam reminisces:

> It was fantastic; we were like rock stars. What's so weird about it, it was a time when becoming a rock star was the dream—*everybody* wanted to be a rock star. And we did it in kind of a different way. It wasn't like we set out to do it; but we ended up on those American tours, and it was like that. Having the Hollywood Bowl with fifteen thousand people sitting out there doing the lines with you, it was good fun.[43]

The building enthusiasm of the American audience, which would ultimately lead to the 1980 Hollywood Bowl performance Gilliam mentions (released as a film in 1982), certainly involved *Holy Grail*'s US release in late April of 1975.

The US release of *Holy Grail* had a modicum of popular success as well as a number of positive reviews. At the time of its release, the fan base for Monty Python was still limited, though devoted. John Cleese notes that Monty Python "never made any real money until the *Holy Grail* came out in America."[44] Eventually, *Monty Python and the Holy Grail* would gross $1,827,696 in the United States; this total, however, includes the 2001 limited release.[45] Indeed, the success of the film has been cumulative, gaining a cult following on the back of the troupe's growing popularity throughout the 1980s and 1990s and lasting into the twenty-first century. Vincent Canby of *The New York Times* summarizes well when he states that the film "has some low spots but that anyone at all fond of the members of this brilliant British comedy group—which more or less justifies Sunday night television in New York—shouldn't care less"; he goes on to describe the film as "a marvelously particular kind of lunatic endeavor."[46] Like Canby, most contemporary critics found *Holy Grail* uneven. While some willingly forgave this flaw, others could not look past it. Gene Siskel admitted, "I guess I prefer Monty Python in chunks, in its original television review format."[47] Although reviews were somewhat mixed, a familiarity with Monty Python is apparent. Whether audiences preferred *Flying Circus* or *Holy Grail*, the resoundingly British comedy troupe was beginning to make its mark on American culture.

Indeed, Monty Python's brand of humor is unapologetically British in style and sensibility, yet the troupe's comedy has made an impact on American popular culture (and indeed, elsewhere in the world). In his study of the relationship between British television and American culture, Jeffrey Miller examines the influence and history surrounding this association. He posits, "comedy can indeed travel when the norms of the culture producing the comedic text are recognizable to the culture receiving it."[48] The long-standing, historical affiliation between the United Kingdom and the United States plays a considerable role in this type of cultural exchange. In the case of Monty Python, the references to specific British figures or language may not translate but the general customs do. This type of comedic translation from England to America has a long history. The operettas of Gilbert and Sullivan, particularly *H.M.S. Pinafore* and *The Pirates of Penzance*, represent a nineteenth-century precedent. Miller also observes that Monty Python "focused on institutions of authority familiar to both national cultures" in their keen parody.[49] In *Flying Circus*, television itself represented one of the major institutions under comedic scrutiny. In *Holy Grail*, it is the film industry, and indeed, Hollywood—the dominant, and of course American, film industry—in particular that receives the brunt of the mockery. Monty Python, then, is both eminently British and somehow universal in its humor.

As "Oxbridge" educated men, the members of Monty Python consistently use an effective blend of intelligent humor and sheer foolishness. The Pythons can refer to major historical or political figures and events while simply walking and talking funny or applying scatological humor at the same time. Both clever and idiotic, the comedy of Monty Python continues to resonate with audiences. Gary Hardcastle and George Reisch claim that Monty Python "wiggled into the collective consciousness, and [has] become one of the most successful and influential comedy institutions of the twentieth century."[50] A number of American comedians, including the likes of Jim Carrey and Seth MacFarlane, have acknowledged the influence; one needs only look at the parody of the *Flying Circus* opening in the *Family Guy* episode "Space Cadet" to encounter a concrete example of the inspiration on MacFarlane. From countless pop culture references to the evolution of sketch comedy and the unique postmodern style of the troupe, Monty Python's brand of humor has had an impact on popular culture in the United States and beyond. Although *Monty Python and the Holy Grail* plays fast and loose with Arthurian legend, the film represents one of the most culturally resonant versions considered in this book.

Monty Python's Musical Approach

As illustrated in *Holy Grail*, Monty Python shows a proclivity toward music in their comedic approach. As a sketch comedy show, *Flying Circus* included all sorts of scenes throughout its run. While many are not particularly musical, a number of songs have had lasting impact. From the television show, for instance, "The Lumberjack Song" was released as a single and produced by George Harrison. The comedic song is typical of Monty Python in its juxtaposition of a highly stereotyped masculine profession with lyrics about a lumberjack cross-dressing. True to form, the Pythons also make a joke about the experience of musical performance in certain sketches. Giorgio Biancorosso opens his exploration of the listening experience with an analysis of the well-known "Cheese Shop Sketch." In the sketch, John Cleese walks into a cheese shop that frustratingly does not contain any cheese. When he first enters, we (as well as he) are struck by Greek dancers accompanied by a bouzouki. Although he seemingly ignores them throughout much of the sketch, he finally yells out for the performers to stop as he becomes increasingly irritated at the lack of cheese. Biancorosso observes that the "reason Cleese's sudden and unexpected charge at the bouzouki player is so funny is that, engrossed by the absurd gag playing at the counter, we are no longer paying attention to the music—and believe he is not either."[51] Biancorosso uses this scene as a jumping off point to discuss the nature of listening in the cinema, and the use of Monty Python here is particularly apt as the troupe specializes in emphasizing the nature of the media they use—whether television or film.

The musical approach of Monty Python throughout their career impacts the understanding of *Holy Grail*. While select sketches in *Flying Circus* highlight music, the existence of a number of Monty Python albums, which include both songs and audio sketches, attests to the troupe's musical inclinations. Additionally, the troupe includes songs in their films. It is clear that music, and especially the strategic use of song, plays an important role in Monty Python's comedy. As such, it comes as no surprise that both the orchestral score and the short songs of *Holy Grail* are so important in this telling of Arthurian legend. Although not technically a musical, the Pythons consistently engage with the conventions and ideas of the genre throughout the course of the film. Furthermore, the orchestral score for *Holy Grail* contributes to the overall tone of the film.

The final orchestral score for Monty Python almost entirely comes from pre-existing music licensed from De Wolfe Music library. Since the early twentieth century, De Wolfe had been providing stock music for film and was a common choice for production music by 1975.[52] Monty Python's musical collaborator Neil Innes initially composed an instrumental score for *Holy Grail*. In audio commentary and in print, Eric Idle often discusses the change from Innes's original score to the pre-existing pieces. Idle states that the purpose of Innes's original score dovetailed with Terry Gilliam's goal of visual authenticity. He reveals that the original soundtrack contained "sackbuts and other period instruments," but they ultimately chose to replace Innes's score with classic film music that used "regular instruments."[53] As such, the background score became one of the "early victims of various screenings."[54]

Due to their inexperience in filmmaking, the preview screenings became especially important for Gilliam and Jones, as well as the other Pythons, to see what worked in the film. While Innes's instrumental music provided a more pseudo-historical soundscape, the period style did not land with audiences. In his commentary, Terry Jones refers to Innes's original scoring as "quaint" several times due to the use of period instruments.[55] Given Innes's approach to "The Tale of Sir Robin" and the monk chant, it seems likely that early music ensembles and stereotypes influenced his original score. Since the budget did not allow them to compose and record additional original music, Jones went to De Wolfe and spent several weeks choosing pieces from the library.[56]

The shift to stock music from De Wolfe results in a change to the soundtrack's purpose. Idle identifies the parody inherent in the final soundtrack, stating that it is "sort of a classic bad Hollywood soundtrack."[57] Indeed, both the chosen De Wolfe library pieces and the songs by Neil Innes work as parody on a number of levels. In his work on the creation of a cinematic sound for the Middle Ages, John Haines identifies six sonic tropes in films from the twentieth and twenty-first centuries. These aural "medieval" signifiers include: the bell, the horn call and trumpet fanfare, court and dance music, the singing minstrel, chant, and the riding warrior.[58] In his discussion of each of these musical stereotypes, Haines considers how film music does or does not mesh with actual medieval music.

Collectively, the music in *Monty Python and the Holy Grail* hits the majority of Haines's identified tropes. Despite the extreme importance Haines's analysis gives to the sound of the church tower bell, not only in history but onscreen, Monty Python does not draw on this particular trope. Although the film parodies religion in a number of ways, *Holy Grail* never features a physical church. From the appearance of God to the chanting monks and the presentation of the Holy Hand Grenade of Antioch, the religious figures in *Holy Grail* are all mobile. Therefore, no bell tower ever provides the context for a ringing church bell. Instead, the film's soundscape employs other cinematic medieval aural signifiers.

Given the dissatisfaction with Innes's more "authentic" score and the prevalence of Haines's tropes in earlier films, it seems clear that Terry Jones's choices reflect Hollywood's version of medieval music rather than that of the actual era. Due to the relative lack of knowledge regarding performance practice or any written sources for certain types of music, Haines observes that "by the 1950s, the American medieval epic and its grandiose orchestral accompaniment had become an iconic Hollywood genre."[59] The De Wolfe orchestral selections follow the expectations of a medieval epic, providing all of the grandiosity one could wish for in a parody. The way the final soundtrack uses these tropes feels cliché in a way that underscores Idle's identification of the score as a bad Hollywood soundtrack. More than that, it is a classic bad Hollywood *medieval* soundtrack.

King Arthur's theme, which recurs throughout the film, provides a prime example of how the library pieces act as an integral part of the parody. The recurring theme is drawn from De Wolfe's "Homeward Bound" by Jack Trombey. It features a brass fanfare, which builds to include the full orchestra. This theme tracks with John Haines's identification of the "riding warrior" in medieval film. Haines claims that "when the central figure of the Middle Ages appears, the riding warrior, nothing other than classical underscore will do."[60] Haines discusses the opening scene of *Holy Grail* as subverting the image and sound of the riding warrior (i.e., the banging coconuts replacing a horse and no musical accompaniment). Later instances of King Arthur pretend-riding throughout the countryside utilize a more typical grandiose score, sending up the stereotype in a different way. The trumpet call, accompanied by snare drums, delivers a vaguely military feel (Example 5.1). The short opening figures in the brass increase in length and majesty, creating the "mock heroic" atmosphere that the directors tried to create through the stock pieces used in the film.

Terry Gilliam calls the musical choices "pretentious" when discussing the orchestral score, alluding to the way it enhances the film's parody.[61] Like Arthur himself, the sound of "Homeward Bound" feels as if it belongs in a different movie. The over-the-top drama of the music underscores the silliness of Arthur pretending to ride through Great Britain accompanied by a servant banging coconuts together and a band of inept knights. The King Arthur theme, in fact, represents a prime example of cinematic medieval stereotyping. In its use of a brass fanfare, "Homeward Bound" follows the fact that "filmmakers have drawn on medievalist, rather than medieval, traditions for actualizing the trumpet fanfare and horn call."[62] In this case, the orchestral scoring based in the Romantic tradition hearkens to these cinematic ideas of chivalry and heroism.

Example 5.1 Brass Call from Arthur's Theme. Transcribed from Terry Gilliam and Terry Jones, dirs. *Monty Python and the Holy Grail*. Culver City, CA: Sony Pictures, 1974. DVD.

From chant to the singing minstrel, *Monty Python and the Holy Grail* draws heavily on the signifiers that Haines recognizes in his work. While I will explore the songs in the final section of the chapter, additional onscreen music and moments of the orchestral score further illustrate the use of these aural tropes in significant ways. In Terry Gilliam's animated sequence that introduces the Quest for the Holy Grail, trumpets are featured prominently. The animation heralds God's request that Arthur and his knights find the Holy Grail with an irreverent depiction of a trumpet call-and-response. A grouping of trumpets appears from the heavens with an answer from another grouping, now being played through people's butts. The short, animated scene visually lampoons the trumpet call cliché, which Haines claims is the most common onscreen, even as it uses it aurally. The opening call is produced by higher pitched trumpets, while the answering one is sounded by lower pitched horns. This discrepancy matches with the visual disconnect: heavenly trumpets are irreverently answered by lower pitched instruments vaguely emulating farts, drawing on scatological humor in order to parody the quest for the Holy Grail and its religious significance.

"The Tale of Sir Lancelot" further provides a crucial example of these Hollywood medieval sounds at work. The wedding music for Prince Herbert's forthcoming nuptials draws on ideas of court and dance music. Light dance music, featuring recorders and other wind instruments as well as a tambourine, can be heard as the wedding preparations appear onscreen. The camera then cuts to four musicians playing outdoors under a small awning during the festivities. The onscreen instruments include a fiddle, recorder, lute, and bagpipes. In his discussion of court and dance music in medieval films, Haines observes that both the Early Music movement and "the use of contemporary folk traditions enhances the feeling of authenticity in a medieval film."[63] The visual and aural components of the wedding music in this scene draw on both with a mixture of bagpipes from the Celtic folk tradition and instruments such as recorder from the Early Music movement. The music heard does not match the onscreen ensemble; most strikingly, no string instruments are discernible in the soundtrack. Clearly, one is not meant to listen too carefully or watch the onscreen musicians playing. Rather, showing the musicians and some brief accompanying dancing serves to enhance the medieval, festive atmosphere.

Once Lancelot arrives on the scene, robust orchestral scoring supplants the onscreen dance music. Lancelot's dramatic arrival is accompanied by drums as he runs up the field to the castle (amusingly never seeming to make any headway). The drum rolls are intercut with the onscreen courtly dance music before he finally bursts onto the scene. Lancelot shouts "ah ha" as he mercilessly kills one of the castle guards, and the dramatic orchestral score completely takes over. Michael Palin describes Lancelot's erratic, violent behavior as "Errol Flynn gone berserk," even as Eric Idle refers to the score as "classic swashbuckling music."[64] The reference here is clear: Sir Lancelot's wanton violence parodies the swashbuckler in general, and likely the 1938 film *The Adventures of Robin Hood* specifically. Erich Korngold's highly regarded score, based in the Romantic tradition, provides the model for this type of dramatic orchestral scoring. Korngold's score contains plenty of large-scale orchestral dramatization for fight scenes. "The Flying Messenger" by Oliver Armstrong from the De Wolfe Music library supplies the appropriately overdramatic, heroic music to accompany Lancelot's ill-advised slaughter. Musically, this scene offers a number of filmic interpretations of the Middle Ages as well as an amusing take on the musical as genre through Prince Herbert's desire to break out into song.

The Songs of *Holy Grail*

Though brief, the songs in *Monty Python and the Holy Grail* are nevertheless integral to the style, humor, storytelling, and characterization of the film. As discussed earlier in this chapter, the film sends up more than Arthurian legend. It draws from several cinematic genres in its multitude of parodies crammed into the hour and a half film. Packed with references from swashbuckling adventure films to Ingmar Bergman, it should be no surprise that musicals get their turn as well. In the commentary provided by John Cleese, Eric Idle, and Michael Palin for the fortieth anniversary edition of *Holy Grail*, Palin notes that "it wasn't just Bergman we brought up, it was also the Hollywood musicals."[65] Indeed, Terry Gilliam states, "we always wanted to do musicals."[66] While the "Camelot Song" and Prince Herbert's song that never materializes represent the most obvious examples of satirizing the musical as genre, song permeates the film in ways which frequently reference the musical. Indeed, the style of music used in these varying moments of song underscores their means of enhancing the humor and telling the story of the Grail. From some degree of verisimilitude to complete musical non-sequiturs, *Holy Grail*'s songs help to shape the film's Arthurian retelling.

Given the approach and humor attached to the "Camelot Song," the probable parodic nod toward Lerner and Loewe's *Camelot*, particularly the film adaptation, seems likely. Susan Aronstein refers to the line "we eat ham, and jam, and spam a lot" in passing as indicating familiarity with the Lerner and Loewe musical (it rhymes).[67] Of course, the mention of spam, as Darl Larsen observes, is "certainly just fun for rhyming purposes, yes, but the inclusion of that 'mystery' pork meat harks back to both episodes 20 and 25" of *Monty Python's Flying Circus*.[68] For audiences familiar with the sketch comedy show, the spam reference is an in-joke as it figures quite prominently in the aforementioned episodes. Larsen does not discount the influence of the well-known Lerner and Loewe musical and its film adaptation, noting the fact that "the formerly sober denizens of Camelot had been singing and dancing for about thirteen years when the Pythons came to write their own version, with perhaps expected results," namely the earlier musical sets up the foundation for Camelot's silly behavior.[69]

At the same time, the musical number does not follow Lerner and Loewe's style, neither compositionally nor in performance practice. An opening musical cliché leads the audience into the interior of Camelot to witness the singing knights (Example 5.2). In a brisk common time, a male chorus sings a short, repetitive tune almost entirely in unison. The catchy melody is simple with many repeated notes. While not complicated, the quick tempo and use of eighth and sixteenth notes creates rhythmic interest within the very clear duple framework—not to mention the percussion break using knights' helmets. Harmonically, also, the song follows familiar paths with the most complex progression simply alluding to the relative minor of the song's key (C major in the published piano-vocal score). Similarly, Monty Python's Arthurian undertaking purposefully avoids the seriousness and romanticism of *Camelot*. Notably, *Holy Grail* removes Guinevere from the narrative entirely. Moreover, Sir Lancelot emerges as one of Arthur's many loyal knights rather than a particularly privileged friend. While the "Camelot

Example 5.2 Opening Cliché for "Camelot Song." Transcribed from Terry Gilliam and Terry Jones, dirs. *Monty Python and the Holy Grail*. Culver City, CA: Sony Pictures, 1974. DVD.

Song" brings to mind the 1960s musical, the performance has a richer place within the context of the film itself.

The Knights of the Round Table's "Camelot Song" represents the most obvious starting point for considering the interpretive work that song does within *Monty Python and the Holy Grail*. The performance of this song leads Arthur to turn away from Camelot with his newly gathered knights, stating that "it is a silly place." And indeed, the representation of Camelot via this song is absolutely silly. Inserting an almost vaudevillian musical number into the film as a way to represent the legendary seat of King Arthur turns the mythos of Camelot on its head. Monty Python's Camelot is not an ideal utopian place but ridiculous. The overtly anachronistic musical style further emphasizes this impression. Michael Palin has commented of the scene that this is the part where they "go into a rather corny Hollywood musical."[70]

The rousing male chorus number certainly evokes a number of musical theater types, including operetta and musical comedy of the twentieth century. The printed script identifies "If My Friends Could See Me Now" from *Sweet Charity* as the stated model.[71] The style of the Knights of the Round Table's song, however, more closely sits somewhere between a British musical comedy number and operetta. The use of drum kit and bright brass instruments, along with the melodic simplicity and rhythmic vitality described earlier, emphasize the musical comedy style of the song. Indeed, Larsen notes, "the style of the song and the more rambunctious, less-refined choreography (likely for non-dancers primarily) is less like a Verdon/Fosse number and more like the opening and closing numbers from the Marx Brothers' 1933 film *Duck Soup*."[72] Since the Marx Brothers' film is in itself a comedy utilizing all of the musical styles at its disposal for their satirical songs, the comparison is apt.

Trained male voices with humorous mock operatic portions complete the send-up. For instance, the held note and only use of vocal harmonization (singing in thirds), which punctuates the line "we sing from the diaphragm a lot," playfully suggests the vocal training evident in the professional male chorus used for the recording. The silly bass solo on the lyrics "I have to push the pram a lot," accompanied by a visual gag of "proper" singing stance with clasped hands, similarly spoofs the trained singing needed for genres like operetta. Indeed, a number of the visual gags, such as a kick line and tap routine, absolutely suggest Hollywood musicals (really American musicals more broadly).

Of course, the anachronistic and often ridiculous lyrics are a key aspect of the "Camelot Song." In his commentary to the film, John Cleese recalls that the Knights of the Round Table number is the "only song that I can remember Graham Chapman and I trying to write."[73] He remembers encountering particular problems when attempting to rhyme Camelot, resulting in absurd lines such as "we eat spam a lot" and "push the pram a lot." Furthermore, the song delights in the silliness of rhyming the word "table." Coupled with the musical style, the lyrics turn Camelot into such an outlandish place that Arthur decides to turn around even before the Grail quest begins. The newly recruited knights never sit at the legendary Round Table. Camelot is simply too silly for their ever-serious king.

The only other overt reference to the musical as genre occurs through a song that never fully materializes. During the chapter of the film identified as "The Tale of Sir Lancelot," young Prince Herbert longs to escape his arranged marriage and overbearing father. Lancelot receives Herbert's plea for rescue and responds by hacking his way through the castle to find a supposed damsel in distress. This sequence mocks not only the adventure film but the musical mercilessly. The scenes that feature Prince Herbert contain no less than four aborted song attempts, signaled by an orchestral swell. Like the rest of the orchestral music used in *Holy Grail*, these brief snippets of instrumental introductions were drawn from the De Wolfe Music library. The opening portions of "Starlet in the Starlight" by Kenneth Essex and "Love Theme" by Peter Knight provide the set-up for songs that will never take place. The king stops his son from singing each time, clearly viewing singing as effeminate and, therefore, improper for his male offspring.

While Herbert is never allowed to sing, this sequence represents the most sustained allusion to the musical as genre. Interestingly, each instance of "almost-song" dovetails with familiar musical theater song types. Forty-eight minutes into *Holy Grail*, Prince Herbert appears and gears up to sing an "I Want" song in order to differentiate his own desires from those of his land and money-grubbing father. Within the next minute, Herbert tries to sing again— this time a song about his ideal love. The crux of the recurring joke throughout this sequence hinges upon the fact that the song attempts are acknowledged by the characters, specifically the king. Once Lancelot affects his rescue, another orchestral swell accompanies Herbert's rapturous exclamation of "I knew someone would come!" At this point, the king not only halts the orchestra but a sound effect as if a tape is slowing and being stopped occurs. The scene amusingly erases any imagined line between diegetic and non-diegetic music.

Monty Python strongly implies that Prince Herbert's propensity toward expressing himself through song is indicative of his sexuality. Though not tolerated by the king, Herbert appears to be living in a musical. As such, the sequence relies on associations between musical theater and gay culture in order for the comedy to work.[74] The link becomes explicit when Lancelot arrives to save Herbert, and the young prince is delighted and ready to run away with the dashing knight. Lancelot articulates his displeasure, stating that he thought Herbert was a woman from his note. Michael Palin brings this point home in the film's commentary when he exclaims, "oh dear, the knight's greatest fear—someone who sings and is gay."[75]

At the end of the sequence, a song finally does emerge in the form of a choral introduction. A low bassoon melody enters, and the chorus begins a repetitive, staccato tune, singing "he's going to tell." Although the texture of the song thickens, including more sustained singing, a drum and additional woodwinds, Lancelot and his squire's dialogue takes precedence in the soundtrack. Since Lancelot makes good his "dramatic" escape (swinging haphazardly over the wedding guests), the scene ends before Herbert gets his chance to actually sing. For the audience, the promise of Herbert's song is never fulfilled before the camera cuts away from the castle. Throughout the over thirteen-minute sequence, the tropes and associations of musical theater loom large while only teasing a big musical number from the apparent musical's star—Herbert.

While the "Camelot Song" and the scenes involving Prince Herbert specifically allude to the musical as genre, other instances of song increase the satirical nature of *Holy Grail*. The first incidence of singing in the film highlights the religious satire and reoccurs throughout the film. In various scenes, the text "Pie Jesu Domine, Dona eis requiem" emulates a plainchant style. The lyrics themselves stem from the end of the "Dies Irae" sequence from the Roman Catholic Requiem Mass. Separating these final lines in this way is a decidedly modern move; select examples of later, more elaborate musical settings of the Requiem include a distinct "Pie Jesu" movement rather than simply concluding the "Dies Irae" with these lines.[76] This brief text translates to "merciful (or pious) Lord Jesus, Give them rest." Given the circumstances of each utterance of the chant, the sentiment conveys another layer of the satire.

Of all of the musical styles represented in *Holy Grail*, this chant contains the most stylistic consistency with documented music from the medieval era. As discussed earlier, the Pythons set their retelling of King Arthur in 932 A.D., adding to the constant anachronistic humor by outlining a highly specific year. Since plainchant signifies the known sacred musical practices of this time period, its use in the film becomes one of the few examples with any sense of musical authenticity. Indeed, John Haines observes that the "Dies Irae" is the Latin liturgical chant that is most frequently heard in medieval film."[77] Of course, Neil Innes, sometime Python collaborator, used an original but simplistic approximation of a chant tune (Example 5.3). While the text parodies the use of "Dies Irae" in film, the music itself only alludes to the style without actually using the melody from the original sequence (Example 5.4). The mixture of a narrow plainchant style range and plodding rhythm (ripe for the self-flagellation displayed in its first appearance) offers an amusing musical take on chant.

The first episode to feature the "Pie Jesu" chant transpires before the actual Grail quest begins. The scene opens on a group of seven monks trudging through a village while chanting. They sing the chant in octaves, marking the end of each phrase by hitting their heads with a board. The angle alternates between an overhead shot of the hooded monks circling the village square and close-ups of Neil Innes as the lead monk's face (Figure 5.4). This chant scene sets up a somewhat ominous atmosphere in its depiction of medieval religiosity. The type of self-harm depicted, however, softens the blow. The scene then becomes an amusing take on the disturbing practice shown.

Both visually and musically, this scene closely parodies the flagellation scene from Ingmar Bergman's *The Seventh Seal* (1957). Ellen Bishop observes that the Monty Python version is "most likely a direct comment on the literally rendered grotesque passage of the flagellants" in Bergman's

Example 5.3 *Holy Grail* Chant. Transcribed from Terry Gilliam and Terry Jones, dirs. *Monty Python and the Holy Grail*. Culver City, CA: Sony Pictures, 1974. DVD.

Example 5.4 Modern Transcription of Original "Pie Jesu" Chant Fragment.

Figure 5.4 Monty Python Monks. Terry Gilliam and Terry Jones, dirs. *Monty Python and the Holy Grail*. Culver City, CA: Sony Pictures, 1974. DVD.

film.[78] *The Seventh Seal*'s scene features a procession of hooded monks with penitents whipping themselves while all sing a version of the actual medieval "Dies Irae" chant (Figure 5.5). Bergman's film draws heavily on the "Dies Irae" throughout its score, but the quasi-diegetic use in this scene is the most remarkable and disturbing. The chanting is interspersed with wailing penitents, and the representation of religious fervor in the wake of the plague is unsettling. This procession is full of visual and aural drama, which disrupts the town (and even a performance by traveling actors).

Figure 5.5 *The Seventh Seal* Flagellants' Scene. Ingmar Bergman, dir. *The Seventh Seal*. New York: The Criterion Collection, 1957. DVD.

The chant itself bursts onto the soundtrack with both men and women's voices, which are punctuated by a drumbeat. Monty Python's version strongly suggests the troubling nature of the scene but as mentioned, softens it with the humorous head banging of the chanting monks. The self-flagellation and rhythmic punctuation of Bergman morph into a visual and aural gag. Additionally, these monks simply make a circuit through a town square and lack both the passion and impact of Bergman's religious fanatics. The monks themselves do not display any of the impassioned vocal style or dramatic physicality that so marks the procession in *The Seventh Seal*. Instead, they sing their chant in a relatively monotonous vocal style. Importantly, the surrounding villagers ignore the chanting monks. They do not inspire either awe or disgust, as in Bergman, but indifference. The entire proceeding comes off as perfunctory. Shouting supplants the chant as the scene transitions to the villagers calling for a woman to be burned at the stake as a witch. Given the translation of the Latin text of the preceding chant, the shift becomes especially jarring. The loud mob clearly wants no peaceful rest for their victim.

After its first appearance, the "Pie Jesu" chant appears twice more during the course of the film. The second iteration is during the animation sequence that precedes "The Tale of Sir Galahad." The chanting remains the same, appearing to be the same track as its first use. The visuals now show Terry Gilliam's animated monks jumping off a cliff one by one. The lemming monks dive into water while uttering gleeful exclamations. One monk misses the mark and lands in an illumination, mooning a delighted woman. The final chant accompanies the presentation of the "Holy Hand Grenade of Antioch," which the knights hope to use against the killer bunny. This nondiegetic presentation of the "Pie Jesu" text is responsorial. A tenor leader calls "Pie Jesu domine," while a male chorus answers "dona eis requiem" in a lower range. The phrases repeat four times. Although still repetitive, the call-and-response coupled with a more disjunct melodic character both act to vary this final iteration of the chant. The variation makes sense as it adds reverence to the presentation of the relic, making the religious veneration of a hand grenade overly serious (and therefore, much funnier). This imitation of chant works to parody religion, especially in its medieval incarnation. Using music to further embed the Python's religious spoof is appropriate given that the nature of the quest itself is highly religious.

"The Tale of Sir Robin" introduces the final song in *Monty Python and the Holy Grail*. The sequence, beginning at thirty-two minutes and forty-five seconds, shows Sir Robin traveling in search of the Grail, escorted by his "favorite minstrels." Unlike Lancelot, Galahad, or Arthur himself, Sir Robin is not a character out of traditional Arthurian legend but a Python creation. Eric Idle wrote the character and his related sketches, and in true Monty Python fashion, the creator realizes the character onscreen. As such, Idle plays the cowardly Sir Robin who prefers to quest with a constant musical accompaniment. The minstrels, led by Neil Innes, follow Robin around, chronicling his experiences as they dance through the forest. Innes sings "The Ballad of Sir Robin" while the additional musicians play a simple accompaniment, doubling the melody at points.

Although Innes attempts a sort of authenticity in the instruments, little documentation and no notation from the appropriate period exist to give an accurate representation of instrumental accompaniment before 1000 C.E. On the other hand, the written monophonic repertoire as well as descriptions of the troubadours and trouvères does survive. This lack of documentation coupled with the discrepancy between stated and actual setting of the film makes the ensemble feel more Renaissance in its make-up and style. Recorders, tabor, and a bagpipe dominate the instrumentation aurally and visually. Despite the lack of instrumental performance practice, Haines notes that the presence of minstrels in film became quickly cliché, stating, "the singing minstrel has become iconic in modern times: the signal stereotype of a musical Middle Ages."[79] It is this stereotype at which the sketches involving Sir Robin and his minstrels poke fun.

Despite the allusion to the singing minstrel trope, it is unsurprising that Innes's music is modern in its compositional style. Similar to the overall aesthetic of the film, Innes provides enough musical tropes of the medieval in order to draw the audience in, and yet ultimately, the musical style is common practice. The lilting $\frac{6}{8}$ meter matches the image of Robin "riding" through the forest, and Innes employs a standard AA'B form. Unlike music from the ostensible time period in which *Holy Grail* is set, "Brave Sir Robin" is firmly tonal, using a minor key. The B section humorously enhances the gruesome lyrics by listing all of the myriad ways that Robin could die in a serious of running eighth notes. The appealing tune and lively rhythmic approach as juxtaposed with the minor mode reinforce the song's joke.

While Innes wrote the music, Idle penned the lyrics to the song. Idle stresses his contribution in his commentary, stating Innes is singing "*my* lyrics."[80] Idle's claim of ownership over the song is important given his creation of a musical based on the film thirty years later. Idle clearly felt a connection to the songs in addition to seeing the potential to expand *Holy Grail* into a full-blown musical. Idle's lyrics humorously chronicle the travels of brave Sir Robin and the increasingly graphic description of ways he might die in the quest. While the opening scene refers to Sir Robin as brave, he quickly puts a stop to the minstrel's horrifying description and soon reveals himself as rather cowardly.

Due to their tendency to dwell on Sir Robin's cowardice, the knight becomes weary of his minstrel companions, and eventually, they must die. After Sir Robin and the minstrels' encounter with the three-headed knight, the traveling minstrel tune begins again. The brief reprise (less than twenty seconds) employs the same music but changes the words to illustrate Sir Robin's retreat from the murderous knight(s). The lead minstrel now sings how Robin "bravely ran away" while Sir Robin himself interjects his objections. In the next animation, which occurs one minute after "The Tale of Sir Robin" has concluded, the minstrels die during the long months of the quest. In their commentary, Cleese, Idle, and Palin frequently refer to the function of the animations as a way to move the plot along or transition from the self-contained adventures of the knights. This final animation fulfills this function while removing extraneous characters. The animation includes a brief instrumental version of the minstrels' music as they travel the land with King Arthur and the Knights of the Round Table. However, the narrator notes that during the harsh winter, "they were forced to eat Robin's minstrels, and there was much rejoicing."[81] Not only does this serve to remove the superfluous characters for the final sequence of the film but acknowledges them as annoying.

While Idle never sings as Sir Robin, song defines the character. Although Eric Idle later famously sings "Always Look on the Bright Side of Life" in the film *The Life of Brian* (1979), his character in *Holy Grail* simply engages with musicians. Throughout *Holy Grail*, the Pythons rely on the stronger voice of Neil Innes as the primary singer. In "The Tale of Sir Robin" sequence, this device allows the minstrels to reveal Robin's cowardice—an aspect of his personality that he actively denies when the minstrels refer to it. The musicians and their song reveal separate facets of Robin's character in such a way that subverts expectations. Sir Robin views the Grail quest as a pleasure trip and displays an affinity towards artistic appreciation. The lyrics of the minstrels' song, ostensibly meant to flatter the knight, in reality reveal Sir Robin's perceived character flaw in a not-so-subtle manner. Taken together, the presence of song and the musicians themselves are integral to Sir Robin's characterization.

Like the earlier literary adaptation by T. H. White, Eric Idle's newly created knight alludes to the myth of Robin Hood rather than Arthurian legend. The connection to White's "Robin Wood" in *The Sword in the Stone* displays a similar loose interpretation of Arthuriana to expand toward a broad depiction of the medieval. The inclusion of Sir Robin and attendant association with Robin Hood offer another opportunity to spoof the swashbuckling Hollywood adventure film genre. While Sir Lancelot's wanton violence engages in one form of parody, Robin's inclination to travel with a gaggle of musicians represents another. Both historically and in cinematic representations, the legend of Robin Hood has been told through the ballad/minstrel tradition.

Despite the fact that the songs are not only few but also short, Monty Python recognizes their importance through sing-along versions of the "Pie Jesu" chant, the "Camelot Song," and "The Tale of Brave Sir Robin" included on the Blu-Ray and DVD special releases. Of course, the insertion of sing-alongs with "bouncy-ball" style lyrics is part of the absurdism of Monty Python's humor. While the "Camelot Song" may lend itself to a funny sing-along, the incongruous, yet even funnier in execution, "Pie Jesu" is nothing more than silly. Additionally, the ability to read the lyrics for Sir Robin's ballad merely enhances the gruesome hilarity of the ways Robin might die in his quest. While *Holy Grail* is not a musical per se, the engagement with the genre is clear and fully enhanced by the emphasis on the songs in the Special Features section of the home release. Given this, it comes as no surprise that Eric Idle would return to one of the troupe's most popular properties and turn it into a musical. With a base of three songs plus Prince Herbert's implied musical numbers, the decision feels natural in a way that many film-to-stage adaptations do not.

6

Notions of Place, Legend, and Broadway
in *Monty Python's Spamalot*

Thirty years after Graham Chapman's Arthur gravely declined to go to
Camelot, Eric Idle created a new version of the character who resolves to put
on a Broadway musical. Although *Monty Python and the Holy Grail* engages
with the musical as a genre throughout its complex of allusions, Idle adapts
the film into a full-blown early twenty-first-century "meta-musical." As the
tagline states, the new musical is "lovingly ripped off from the motion picture."[1] It, of course, uses the original loose plot of *Holy Grail*. At the same
time, *Spamalot* becomes its own unique creative work. Although never
subtle, the intertextual references within *Spamalot* make it a worthy piece
of musical Arthuriana. The fact that the musical can be enjoyed as a comedy
without audiences necessarily considering it in light of the larger Arthurian
legend does not lessen its contribution to that pantheon. The levels of adaptation and remarkably dense intertextuality of this musical comedy make it a
fitting end to this study.

Monty Python's Spamalot premiered on March 17, 2005, in the Shubert
Theatre, eventually running for 1,575 performances. Eric Idle wrote the book
and lyrics, and John Du Prez wrote the music for new songs. The original
cast featured not only Hank Azaria in his Broadway debut but also the inef-
fable Tim Curry as King Arthur, David Hyde Pierce as Sir Robin and other
characters, Christian Borle in roles such as the Historian and Sir Herbert,
and Sara Ramirez as the Lady of the Lake. The show constituted a tremendous commercial success for the creators, which extended to its tour and a
Las Vegas run. Idle would later remark that the show was "the first time in my
life I experienced big money."[2] *Spamalot* garnered thirteen Tony nominations
and won three. After losing the majority of the nominated awards, Idle recalls
director Mike Nichols making his way down to his seat during the ceremony
and saying, "They're going to stiff us . . . You have to think of something to
say."[3] The remembered assumption, however, proved premature once Sara

From Camelot *to* Spamalot. Megan Woller, Oxford University Press (2021). © Oxford University Press.
DOI: 10.1093/oso/9780197511022.003.0007

Ramirez won for Best Featured Actress, Nichols himself took home Best Director, and *Spamalot* won Best Musical of the year.

Growing Popularity and Adaptation of *Holy Grail*

In the decades since the original release of *Monty Python and the Holy Grail*, the British comedy troupe continued to gain a following in the United States. The Pythons' next film, *The Life of Brian* (1979), did incredibly well despite controversy, domestically and in the United States—in fact, the film became the highest grossing British film in the States that year.[4] In 1980, Monty Python performed at the Hollywood Bowl to an audience of thousands. Footage from the live performance was interspersed with additional sketches and received limited theatrical release in 1982 as *Monty Python Live at the Hollywood Bowl*. Even after the troupe went their separate ways into various solo careers in addition to dealing with the death of Graham Chapman, Monty Python's status has continued to rise. Re-releases and live reunions fuel their enduring popularity in the United States and the United Kingdom.[5] Not only are the sketches, songs, and films highly influential but interest in the former members and troupe history also remains strong. Popular nonfiction literature still abounds with the 2018 release of Eric Idle's *Always Look on the Bright Side of Life: A Sortabiography* and the 2019 revised edition of David Morgan's *Monty Python Speaks!: The Complete Oral History*.[6] In the years since the troupe's ultimate split, Monty Python has become a cultural institution.

Unsurprisingly, the film *Monty Python and the Holy Grail* has piggybacked on the lasting success of Monty Python. Indeed, the film has become the best-known and most beloved property of Monty Python's tenure as a comedy troupe. On the one hand, *The Life of Brian* had more box office success and positive critical response as well as being generally considered a better film by many of the Pythons themselves.[7] Yet it is *Holy Grail* that has captured American popular imaginations over time. Eric Idle observes, "in the States, I found that Monty Python was really popular. Everyone knew *The Holy Grail*. It seemed to be a college rite of passage."[8] The film has received multiple home releases, including Special Editions complete with full-length film commentary by the four remaining Pythons and other features.[9] In the mid-1990s, the video game development company 7th Level created a CD-ROM adventure game based on the film called *Monty Python & the Quest for the Holy Grail*. Similarly, a licensed video *Holy Grail*-themed slot machine exists. Given this evidence of cultural consciousness, it follows that Idle would choose to musicalize this particular film.

In adapting *Monty Python and the Holy Grail*, Eric Idle uses the basic premise of the film as the foundation for the stage musical. The loose plot structure of *Holy Grail* provided Idle and collaborators with a good deal of creative freedom for *Spamalot*. In discussing his adaptation of the film, Idle asserts that he always thought *Holy Grail* was perfect for a musical, in part since it offered a "mock-heroic pastiche of Wagnerian grandeur."[10] Due to the sketch-based nature of the narrative, *Spamalot* could follow the original outline and even import specific scenes practically verbatim while making significant changes. In order to tighten the narrative structure, several stand-alone characters from the film become conflated with Arthur's Knights. For example, both the man attempting to dispose of the "not dead yet" plague victim and the dead body collector become Sir Lancelot and Sir Robin, respectively. In the same way, the film's Marxist Dennis turns to Arthur's cause with the help of the Lady of the Lake to become Sir Galahad in *Spamalot*.

Similarly, episodes that functioned as detached sketches now act as the impetuses for significant characters to join King Arthur as Knights of the Round Table. The adventures have more of a through-line (though often nonsensical), and Arthur not only finds the Grail via audience participation but decides to put on a Broadway show. While the self-referential aspect of *Spamalot* differs from the film, it also feels very much in the spirit of Monty Python. As explored in the previous chapter, the troupe embedded *Holy Grail* with dozens of cinematic references. Although the change of medium affects the final product significantly, the drive remains the same.

In its adaptation of the original Monty Python film, *Spamalot* intersects with the Arthurian legend itself in continued, complicated ways. As explored in the previous chapter, *Holy Grail* unequivocally contributes to the modern pantheon of Arthuriana. The combination of Graham Chapman's staid performance as King Arthur coupled with the bleak atmosphere effectively contrasts with anachronisms and sheer silliness. Despite the cinematic intertextuality and careful visuals created by the Pythons, the facts of budget differences impact each of these productions. At the end of the day, *Holy Grail* had meager financial backing, drawn from a number of relatively small investments. *Spamalot*, on the other hand, is a slick Broadway production. Given these considerations, no one can make the claim of "authenticity" often attributed to the original film. *Spamalot* makes no pretense toward medievalism, instead reveling unabashedly in its modern aesthetic and high production values.

Spamalot's Double Audience-Base and Americanization

Spamalot caters to two specific audience sets: Broadway lovers and Monty Python fans. Although a somewhat facile observation given both the adaptation of *Holy Grail* and the self-referential quality of the show, it represents an important aspect of the show's success. In discussing the phenomenon, Hank Azaria (who played Sir Lancelot among other roles in the original Broadway cast) observes, "there's some overlap there but not a ton. And you could sort of tell by the first five minutes in [from] how the audience was responding whether they were a musical crowd or they were a Python crowd."[11] With re-enacted scenes from the film interspersed with "meta" musical jokes, there is plenty for each audience segment to enjoy—a factor which likely expanded the overall audience. Azaria goes on to claim, "on the best nights it kind of would ignite and both factions would get delighted and hit a frenzy. We had a lot of nights like that, it was really gratifying."[12] The Broadway production made around $20 million in advance ticket sales, and the show remained a hot ticket throughout its four-year run.[13]

While popular reception for the show was an unmitigated success, critical reception might be viewed as positive but not exactly glowing. Theater critics emphasize the cast and direction, noting that the show itself is fun if uninspiring. After watching a Chicago preview, Michael Phillips asserts that *Spamalot* consists of "an engaging blend of the extraordinarily faithful and the we'll-try-anything," and goes on to state, "the film had a priceless take-it-or-leave-it quality. The musical's more determined to get you to take it and like it, for better or worse. But that's how most musicals are."[14] Having seen a preview version, Phillips calls the cut song "Burn Her!" the show's lowest point. Inevitably, comparisons to *Holy Grail* abound with cast and lifted scenes often appearing at a disadvantage to those familiar with the original. Ben Brantley ultimately concludes

> Do these disparate elements hang together in any truly compelling way? Not really. That "Spamalot" is the best new musical to open on Broadway this season is inarguable, but that's not saying much. The show is amusing,

agreeable, forgettable—a better-than-usual embodiment of the musical for theatergoers who just want to be reminded now and then of a few of their favorite things.[15]

Others, such as David Rooney, seem to be suffering fatigue from the self-referential trend in 2000s musicals.[16] At the same time, all admit to experiencing enjoyment while watching the show. The familiarity bred from its source of adaptation and the meta-nature work together to ensure that the show is a pleasurable experience for many viewers.

While *Monty Python and the Holy Grail* can be read as influential in an American context, *Spamalot* undergoes a process of Americanization not present in the original film. Although the creators Eric Idle and John Du Prez are British, they insert a decidedly US flavor into the original production, primarily through the heavy reliance on Broadway tropes. Of course, the United States and the United Kingdom have always had a great deal of cultural interchange—a fact to which the proliferation of Arthurian legend attests—and that is most certainly true for musical theater. Since the popularity and influence of British operetta a la Gilbert and Sullivan, there has been much back and forth between the American musical and British counterparts. To be sure, the American composers of Tin Pan Alley, such as Irving Berlin, Cole Porter, and Richard Rodgers, once dominated the genre. In the twenty-first century, however, one cannot deny the importance of British composers, such as Andrew Lloyd Webber, in the history of Broadway. As such, Idle and Du Prez easily draw on multiple musical styles from both sides of the ocean, though with a decided emphasis on the American. The decision to incorporate Broadway's musical history into *Spamalot* thus Americanizes the musical retelling of Arthur in a fashion comparable to, though more delightedly outlandish than, Disney's take on *The Sword in the Stone*.

Similar to the earlier Disney film, *Spamalot* draws on American forms of entertainment but more importantly, American values. In an insightful article exploring the Americanization of both Arthurian legend and Monty Python in *Spamalot*, Laurie A. Finke and Susan Aronstein illustrate how Eric Idle and John Du Prez utilize the conventions of the Broadway musical in order to underpin their show with typical American principles. The diversity of the United States, patriotic feelings, and heteronormative emphasis on marriage and family have become core themes throughout the history of American musical theater. As Raymond Knapp has deftly shown, the American musical has been a prime site for mythologizing America. Knapp notes that "the idealistic tone of nationalism has proven irresistible to Americans, who tend to see nationalism as a kind of super-charged patriotism, and who have, accordingly, enthusiastically produced and embraced their own mythologies."[17] While numerous musicals in the early part of the twentieth century did this cultural work, Knapp identifies post-WWII ideology as fueling this trend. Among the most high-profile examples of these types of American nationalistic musicals are the shows of celebrated collaborators Rodgers and Hammerstein. The duo's focus on community, heteronormative romance, and the nuclear family provide a model for this type of myth making.

Despite being ostensibly set in England and written by British creators, *Spamalot* celebrates the promise of America as a land of opportunity with democratic ideals through its use of American musical conventions. As Finke and Aronstein assert,

> *Spamalot* stages the rejection of the aristocratic ideology that interpellates subjects as chivalric knights and its replacement with an American ideology of democratic possibility and self-actualization that depends upon subjects who misrecognize themselves as individuals free to become whatever they desire, free to "find their grails."[18]

The authors go on to observe that, unlike in *Holy Grail*, Arthur's knights come from the peasantry. In a move that consolidates the dozens of characters present in the film, *Spamalot* turns Dennis into Galahad and two of the peasants in the "Not Dead" plague sketch into Lancelot and Robin. These changes not only give the plot additional continuity but add a "rags-to-riches" element not present in the original film. As such, *Spamalot* conforms more to an American ideology, which is reminiscent of Arthur's humble beginnings and Cinderella-type childhood in Disney's *The Sword in the Stone*. As explored in the opening chapters, the insertion of an actual American everyman, or Yankee, into King Arthur's court presents an explicitly American perspective into the legend. The impulse then to impart this particular aspect of American mythology into Arthurian legend is not only common but also particularly suited to the genre of the musical.

In addition to the democratic ideology, *Spamalot* turns toward the idea of "finding the Grail" as the pursuit of happiness. Unlike in *Monty Python and the Holy Grail*, Arthur and the knights plainly acknowledge what the "Grail" actually is: the cup used at the Last Supper. After Sir Robin expresses skepticism at God's ability to lose a cup, Arthur claims that the Grail is more of a metaphor. Finke and Aronstein assert that unlike the original film, in which the Grail remains unattainable, "Spamalot . . . is full of grails, and all of them are real."[19] At the end of the show, Lancelot and Herbert's grail proves to be each other ("find your male"), while Robin has discovered that musical theater is his grail. Upon receiving the quest instructions from God, Arthur states, "we must all look within us. That is where we'll find the grail." In the song which follows, the Lady of the Lake urges Arthur and the other knights to "find your grail." In their analysis of the song "Find Your Grail," Finke and Aronstein observe the simplicity of both the music and lyrics, dovetailing with the piano-vocal score's identification of the song as an inspirational pop ballad. They emphasize that the song "parodies the earnest sentimentality of the genre (think of "We Are the World") . . . Unlike most of the other songs in Spamalot, this one is delivered earnestly, without comic embellishment."[20]

This assessment, however, fails to take Sara Ramirez's vocal performance into account. As the original Broadway cast recording reveals, Ramirez does a credible diva parody throughout the song. Not only does she include a number of more generalized vocal diva clichés, which include low growls and glottal attack embellishments, she specifically spoofs a number of well-known pop divas. The recording performance includes a healthy dose of Whitney Houston, along with stylistic elements common to Celine Dion, Mariah Carey, Cher, Christina Aguilera, and Barbra Streisand. Ramirez's vocal performance is extremely comedic, using expert vocal manipulation in order to accomplish the parody successfully. In fact, it would be a mistake to sing this song straight; Ramirez's powerhouse, comedic vocal performance paves the way for the Lady of the Lake's Act II number, "Diva's Lament." In true Spamalot fashion, "Find Your Grail" proves the Lady's diva-hood in the most overt and humorous way possible, setting her up to lay claim to the title later in the show.

Additionally, the various instrumental and visual clichés used throughout the song enhance its comic nature. After Ramirez finishes the first half of the song, a dramatic guitar solo enters with soft, choral "ahs" in the background. This bridge offers a spot-on—and amusing—parody of the type of power ballad Finke and Aronstein identify as the target genre being lampooned. Soon after, Tim Curry begins talk-singing, dramatically accompanied by trumpet flourishes at points. With his entrance, the texture starts to thicken, building to the full orchestral complement in the last minute of the song. By the end of the song, the choreography has included moves such as the arm roll a la The Temptations, step-clap, and waving torches in the air as if they were lighters. In this way, the song taps into a number of "inspirational song" clichés. While the "Find Your Grail" message may be earnest, the performance is anything but. Like every song in the musical, this song is a pastiche. Harnessed for comedic purposes, pastiche as part of a self-referential humor fits into two popular trends to which *Spamalot* conforms: satire and stage adaptations of films.

An Early Twenty-First-Century Musical Comedy

Satirical musicals, such as *Urinetown* (2001) and *Avenue Q* (2003), trade on the type of mocking parody and in-jokes upon which *Spamalot* thrives. In particular, *Urinetown* includes a similar type of self-referential style and open acknowledgment that "this is a musical" within the context of the show. Like *Spamalot*, Anne Beggs asserts that *Urinetown* "pays homage to its commodity predecessors on Broadway; the entire process is then turned into marketable postmodernism."[21] Both shows engage in musical pastiche and mock musical theater conventions while simultaneously utilizing them. *Urinetown*, however, offers pointed social and political commentary. Beggs discusses the show's indebtedness to Brechtian ideals.[22] It is here where *Spamalot* differs as its purposeful, emphasized theatricality does not have didactic goals.

Unlike *Urinetown* or even the highly irreverent *Avenue Q*, *Spamalot* uses the "meta" method without engaging in socially relevant content. In fact, the self-referential tactic seems to have felt rather old hat to some reviewers as it invites comparison with the earlier successful and more subversive examples of the trend. As mentioned earlier, David Rooney expresses his fatigue with the meta-musical by this point with so many "imitators" coming on the heels of *The Producers*.[23] In the extremely limited scholarly attention given toward *Spamalot*, it is most often listed as one of "a slew of self-referential postmodern musicals . . . [which] look back on their own legacy with affection and witty insight."[24] In doing so, however, Bud Coleman discerns that these shows "can appear too much of an insider phenomenon . . . suggesting that audiences must know a great deal about musicals in order to get all of the allusions and jokes."[25] Thus, *Spamalot*'s numerous references to the musical as genre throughout both the score and book place the show within a contemporary trend.

The musical pastiche, which occurs throughout the show, takes on some of the most beloved shows and styles of the Broadway stage and indeed, beyond.

Jessica Sternfeld asserts, "there are also no new musicals that do not, at least in some ways, reflect the influence of the 1980s megamusical."[26] *Spamalot* does so in multiple ways, one of which is directly mocking the megamusical. As one of the most prominent musical theater composers, both in the United Kingdom and the United States, Andrew Lloyd Webber is the butt of several musical jokes throughout the show. In style and visual gags (complete with an ostentatious chandelier onstage), "The Song That Goes Like This" represents one of these jokes. The musical does contain several different song types, as I will explore later in this chapter; at the same time, no number really strays from the pastiche style of the show. Although *Spamalot* pokes fun at Lloyd Webber's musical style throughout the show, the reliance on pastiche is quite reminiscent of that very composer.

Indeed, the heavy-handed musical allusions share similarities with Lloyd Webber and Tim Rice's early collaboration *Joseph and the Amazing Technicolor Dreamcoat* (1968). The gentle cowboy song style of *Spamalot*'s "All for One" even reminds one of "One More Angel in Heaven" from *Joseph*. Numerous, easily discernible references to other musical styles, and even specific shows, also occur throughout *Spamalot*. Musical theater aficionados will recognize moments out of the "Dance at the Gym" from *West Side Story* and the klezmer-esque wedding sequence from *Fiddler on the Roof*, among the myriad allusions. Lounge singing, cheerleading, and Vegas shows also add to the musical intertextual density present in *Spamalot*. In short, Idle and Du Prez simply drew on styles and specific shows that they found funny in the context of their show.

Due to the self-referential nature of the musical as well as the title, which hearkens not only to Monty Python's history but Lerner and Loewe's musical version of Arthurian legend, musical reference to *Camelot* seems a natural choice for *Spamalot*'s pastiche approach. Although the most obvious option, Idle and Du Prez include little in the way of direct allusion to that Arthurian musical. The song "Come with Me" bears a striking resemblance in its title to "Follow Me" from *Camelot*. Additionally, each of the songs is sung by the character based on the same legendary figure (more or less): the Lady of the Lake, sometimes called Nimue. However, the Nimue of *Camelot* is Merlin's paramour singing a siren song to lure the wizard, whereas *Spamalot*'s Lady of the Lake urges (Dennis) Galahad to join Arthur's entourage and ultimately turns out to be Guinevere, Arthur's future queen. The title and character performing the song strongly suggests an allusion, but the similarities nearly end there.

"Come with Me" sounds markedly different from "Follow Me," and any musical and lyrical similarities are superficial at best. Frankly, "Come with Me" lacks the harmonic, melodic, and lyric complexity of Lerner and Loewe's song. The focus on repeating the titular phrase represents a simplistic correlation, but "Come with Me" has much shorter lyrics than "Follow Me," making the repetition almost obsessive. "Follow Me" is in a longer form, spinning out the melody more than the briefer "Come with Me" does. The main motives of each certainly have some shared aspects: rising, largely stepwise melodic figures and simple, rhythmic patterns in $\frac{4}{4}$. However, the fact that each contains a three-note motive based on a syllabic presentation of the title hardly constitutes imitation. Both songs feature an emphasis on shimmering strings, but long-standing musical tropes for the representation of the magical account for some resemblance in orchestration. In the original Broadway cast recording, Sara Ramirez does some of her most "old-fashioned musical" singing. She relies on her head voice more than elsewhere throughout the show, utilizing a softer, breathier timbre. The original Broadway cast recording of *Camelot*, however, again reveals key differences in style and performance. Mary Sue Berry sings in a higher range, demonstrating a stronger soprano and clearer timbre than Ramirez does. Based on the highly "meta" nature of *Spamalot*, parody seems likely. At the same time, the superficiality of the likeness makes coincidence just as possible.

Regardless, *Spamalot* certainly packs in the musical references. At the same time, it goes further than simple allusion. Ultimately, we learn that Arthur's entire journey has been a Broadway show *the whole time*. Of course, this "reveal" has been teased throughout the entire show. The opening highlights the fact that we, as an audience, are watching a play. The Historian character, imported from the film but given more prominence, comes on stage in order to set the place and time of the show. While the scene offers more background on Arthur as legendary figure than the film does, it also sets up the running "hey, this is theater" gag. After the Historian gives the setting as England, a song about Finland begins. The "mix-up" both offers an additional Monty Python reference for fans (discussed further later in this chapter) and allows for a "meta"-moment when the Historian yells "I said ENGLAND" from offstage once the song has ended. As Coleman observes, *Spamalot* offers an example of a show which "asks the audience to believe that the production of the musical which they are watching is happening in real time in front of them."[27] The "meta" pleasure takes a step beyond the merely self-referential by breaking the fourth wall in order to forcibly remind the audience that we are watching a play.

This reminder acts as a gag which runs throughout the show in various guises. The most famous, oft-cited example is "The Song That Goes Like This." With an opening lyric that states, "once in every show, there comes a song like this," it certainly earns its self-referential place. As mentioned before, the song explicitly parodies the romantic duets of Andrew Lloyd Webber, taking a pointed stab at *The Phantom of the Opera* in particular. Throughout the song, the lyrics dictate the clichéd musical and staging cues which the song makes fun of: changing keys, singing in each other's faces, and overacting represent just a few examples. Like all of the musical theater parodies in *Spamalot*, the song is funny because it is so on the nose and invites the audience to acknowledge their position as musical theater fans. Arthur's announcement of the Intermission at the end of the first act further emphasizes this. He sings, "have a drink and a pee, we'll be back for Act 3!"; Patsy inserts ". . . two, sir," and Arthur responds with "Two!" Arthur's prompt about Intermission hints at a participatory element, which will come to fruition by the end of the show when "the Grail" can be found at an audience member's seat. As Robin announces, the Grail was cleverly hidden "through the fourth wall" all along. Arthur even invites the audience member onstage, and the cast works their name into a brief song praising them as the "Best Peasant in New York." All in all, the audience is not simply asked to believe they are watching a show unfold but revel in that very fact.

In addition to the satirical, self-referential musical trend, *Spamalot* aligns with the film-to-stage adaptations that gained popularity in the twenty-first century. Although select films were adapted into stage musicals before the year 2000, the turn of the century saw this practice expand greatly. With successes such as *The Producers* (2001) and *Hairspray* (2002), film quickly became a major source for musical adaptations. Indeed, the past twenty years have seen dozens of examples with no sign of stopping before the COVID-19 pandemic shuttered Broadway in March of 2020. As *Spamalot* illustrates, the film-to-stage adaptations often draw an existing fan base. Elizabeth Wollman affirms this popularity, stating, "these musicals appeal to global audiences due to their familiar titles, characters, plots, and, usually, songs from film soundtracks."[28] As Larry Stempel states, a major goal of this trend is to "keep the synergy between the two in the public eye."[29]

Furthermore, this relationship between Broadway musicals and Hollywood products make the musicals' branding a much easier enterprise.

As Jessica Sternfeld has shown, Cameron MacIntosh developed recognizable brands for shows like *Cats*, *The Phantom of the Opera*, and *Les Misérables* in order to enhance the marketing campaigns.[30] With issues such as rising expense, Steven Adler asserts that increased levels of "marketing savvy" are needed for the success of Broadway shows.[31] Employing already recognizable products, film-to-stage adaptations have a head start in this department. In an increasingly difficult financial climate for Broadway shows, the ability to have a broad appeal (especially among tourists) has become an important consideration.[32]

As a musical that fits into these two prevailing trends on Broadway in the early twenty-first century, *Spamalot* invites comparison with the show many consider the primary representative of each: Mel Brooks's *The Producers* (2001). Based on the 1967 film starring Zero Mostel and Gene Wilder, the stage musical opened on April 19, 2001, and starred Nathan Lane and Matthew Broderick as the titular characters. Both the film and the stage version are explicitly about Broadway, sending up conventions and the sometimes indefinable thing that creates a hit show. Alex Symonds claims that Brooks "capitalised on the 'cult' popularity of his 1968 [*sic*] film, by remediating it as the Broadway musical *The Producers*. Aside from the introduction of some highly conventional musical numbers, this show essentially replicated his film on stage."[33] While the 1967 film features the outrageous made-up musical *Springtime for Hitler*, the later show becomes more of a backstage musical. Given the subject matter, *The Producers* is ripe for humorous self-referential songs, which include "Opening Night," "I Wanna Be a Producer," and "Keep It Gay."

All of the elements which make the "meta-musical" and film-to-stage adaptation popular are there, and the show was a massive hit. As of this writing, *The Producers* maintains the record for most Tony Award wins with twelve. The original production was still running when *Spamalot* premiered and continued to run through 2007 for an eventual 2,502 performances. Additionally, the property made it back to the cinema with a 2005 film adaptation of the stage musical. Symonds identifies *The Producers* as part of the "rising trend of pre-sold, over-familiar material, designed for theatre's new 'mass audience,' [which] has been perceived by some scholars to have transformed Broadway theatre into a highly predictable and unchallenging entertainment."[34] Scott Miller states that *The Producers* "allows mainstream audiences to feel edgy and adventurous without having to engage any edgy or adventurous work. *Monty Python's Spamalot* would do the same a few years later and with equally uninspiring results, despite another excellent cast."[35] *Spamalot*, of course, is not trying to be particularly edgy or engage in social commentary. Eric Idle wanted the musical to be fun and funny, and in that goal, it succeeds marvelously.

Beyond critical comparison, *The Producers* and *Spamalot* have been linked by the Pythons themselves. In fact, Eric Idle claims to have approached Mel Brooks in the late 1980s with the idea to turn his film *The Producers* into a musical. Though Brooks declined at the time, Idle asserts, "I was very glad he'd waited, as he single-handedly revived musical comedy and I knew that night I would now be able to find people willing to put on *Spamalot*."[36] Clearly, the creator had a similar musical comedy style in mind as that of *The Producers*. As Idle and Du Prez were writing, Idle sent songs to the other Pythons, which they all seemed to like quite a bit. Terry Gilliam declares, "they were wonderful songs, right up to Mel Brooks's level of songwriting."[37] Indeed, both shows share a self-referential, highly over-the-top humor which audiences ate up.

Love them or hate them, *The Producers* and *Spamalot* are representative of a particular escapist form of American musical theater, which found a stable place on the Broadway stage at the turn of the century. Of course, Broadway has never been short of escapism in its various forms, and scholars often separate the "more serious" efforts from the pure entertainment. John Bush Jones observes that American musical theater has always had what he calls "diversionary" musicals. He states, "even shows that contain little content of social relevance—those I call 'diversionary musicals,' which have always comprised the majority of all professionally produced theatre in the United States—these too are important, if only to raise the question of why certain decades delivered more 'mindless fluff' than others."[38] For *Spamalot*, the post-9/11 context offers one possible explanation. Yet placing too much emphasis on a need for escapist theatrical entertainment in New York City in the years immediately following the September 11 attacks is too simplistic. *The Producers* had already been running on Broadway for nearly five months and was the hottest ticket in town.[39] Indeed, the early 2000s were in the midst of what John Kenrick identifies as a "resurgence of musical comedy."[40] At the same time, both Kenrick and Elizabeth Wollman observe the perceived need for comedy and lighter musical fare in the months after the tragedy, as evidenced by the reactions toward *Mamma Mia!* as the first musical to open after 9/11.[41] Certainly, the trends that *Spamalot* follow are designed to bring in audiences, especially tourists.

This film-to-stage "meta-musical," represents a particular type of "diversionary" musical in Jones's terms. However, Anne McCleer argues, "all films, whatever their historical setting, always speak to the moment of their production in some way" in her discussion of *Mary Poppins* and *The Sound of Music*.[42] Although a different type of diversion than *The Sound of Music*, *Spamalot* offers light entertainment, which might similarly be described as escapist. Regardless of whether a show explicitly addresses social concerns, as McLeer suggests, it is always a product of its time. Adaptations, in particular, reveal much in regard to changing audience tastes and their particular historical moment. As the other case studies in this book illustrate, the changes, additions, deletions, and other such effects of the process of adaptation tell us much. The process of Americanization that *Spamalot* undergoes is indicative of a particular time and place. While the Americanization of Arthurian legend had been an artistic impulse for over one hundred years, the particular ways in which *Spamalot* does so dovetails with the cultural milieu of the early 2000s in its use of nostalgia.

On both the self-referential and adaptation level, *Spamalot* engages in nostalgia in a powerful way. Undeniably, nostalgia has been a potent tool in musical theater. As Jones discusses, the apathy and violence in the political and social realm of the late twentieth century led to a nostalgic trend, and shows such as *Spamalot* might be seen as continuing in that vein.[43] In the early 2000s, the postmodern stylistic lens, which *Spamalot* and similar musicals employ, breathed new life into the nostalgic approach for audiences. In the meta-musical, audiences are invited to laugh at the megamusical, for example, but the implied familiarity allows for at least a modicum of affection. The sheer silliness, camp, and as Eric Idle would put it, almost vaudevillian mode of the sketch-based musical hearkens to an older style of musical comedy. In this way, *Spamalot* reflects Idle's own nostalgia for musical comedy as a genre. The audience is invited to remember and hope for a return to "classic musical comedy"—whatever that means in the eyes of the creators.

At the same time, the near exact lifts from *Holy Grail* offer a different nostalgic experience for Python fans. The French taunters, Knights of Ni, the Black Knight, and Tim the Enchanter represent a few of the well-known scenes included in *Spamalot*. In many cases, these scenes feature dialogue taken almost verbatim from the original film. Additionally, several members of the original cast closely aligned their performances of certain characters with the film's portrayals. Hank Azaria in his minor roles of a French taunter, Knight of Ni, and Tim the Enchanter clearly draws from the film's scenes.

In a later interview, Azaria states, "I probably treated the material with too much reverence . . . The one regret I have, I'm a mimic and I worship John Cleese and all those guys, and so I was trying so much to literally re-create [their performances]."[44] While Azaria may wish he had made the roles more his own, the recreation resonated with audiences through a nostalgic lens. In any case, *Spamalot* presents that appealing blend of familiarity and novelty which adaptations in particular strive for and thrive in when achieved. And the show does so in the way so reminiscent of other meta-musicals from around the same time period.

Nevertheless, scholars tend to dismiss the show for many of the reasons it gained its popularity. For example, Larry Stempel casts *Spamalot* as one of many so-called movicals, which focus on "reproducing their sources as closely as possible on stage."[45] While elements of this statement ring true, the show also certainly makes substantial changes. John Kenrick laments these changes as "dumbing down an already silly spoof of the Arthurian legend."[46] In scholarship, *Spamalot* tends to garner slight mentions such as these, whereas understandably *The Producers* has received more attention. Certainly, *Spamalot* fits neatly into popular trends of the time, and it does not have the serious-minded approach to Arthurian adaptation with which Lerner and Loewe treated *Camelot*. Idle and Du Prez's work, however, deserves a closer look as a piece of musical Arthuriana.

Spamalot and Arthurian Tradition

While the cheeky, barely plotted *Holy Grail* has a complex relationship with the history of Arthurian legend, the unapologetically twenty-first-century *Spamalot* further muddies the Arthurian waters. In keeping with the original film, *Spamalot* maintains the focus on several mainstays of King Arthur's myth. In fact, Arthur himself takes on a bigger role than in *Holy Grail* due to the inclusion of more songs. Arthur sings in eleven of the twenty-one numbers (including reprises) as a featured singer or a member of a larger ensemble. In short, he receives a good deal of stage time. Considering the show's basis consists of a series of vignettes, the increased presence in the stage adaptation matters. Arthur's quest for companionship (and, of course, the Grail) acts as a centerpiece that brings the show together. At the same time, the Python gags are now accompanied by overt Broadway references (not to mention the newly added quest to put on a Broadway musical), which do not bring the show narratively closer to the literary Arthurian tradition.

On the other hand, an Arthurian tale does not have to follow earlier stories in order to adhere to the larger tradition. In point of fact, the longevity of Arthuriana, featuring waves of popularity throughout its history, relies on the inherent flexibility of the myth, which allows for new voices and interpretations. Each of the musical versions considered in this study brings a fresh spin to the legend, often adding new elements and contemporary twists. Like Mark Twain and, of course, the original Monty Python film, *Spamalot* assumes a basic cultural knowledge of King Arthur, the Knights of the Round Table, and the quest for the Holy Grail. Yet *Spamalot* gives more specific information regarding the legendary king than *Holy Grail* does. Both iterations of the story include "the Historian," a character designed to lend credence to the retelling. In *Monty Python and the Holy Grail*, however, the Historian's authority is brutally undermined when an anonymous knight casually cuts him down. This action further allows for the anachronistic inclusion of the police, which ultimately ends the film.

In *Spamalot*, the Historian never suffers such an indignity. Instead, he opens each act by setting up Arthur's England, the importance of the king, and his quest. The Historian is a framing device. In the way of other such narrators (*Candide* comes to mind), the Historian imparts additional information and serves as a way to remind the audience that this is theater. As such, *Spamalot* offers more background to the audience, presupposing less familiarity with the legend and earlier retellings than *Holy Grail*. Under the surface-level silliness, much of the comedic brilliance of *Holy Grail* depends on Arthurian and broader medieval traditions, especially in their cinematic forms. While *Spamalot* does similar comedic work with musical theater, the "Arthurian" humor mostly piggybacks on knowledge of *Monty Python and the Holy Grail* rather than on the literary traditions and films that the original source lampoons. Therefore, the inclusion of supplementary background on Arthur and the aspects of the legend used in *Spamalot* caters to an audience once removed from the original film's intended audience. For musical theater fans, rather than Python fans, this additional framing is potentially required.

The adventures of the knights depend on tropes of chivalry and heroism in order to complete the absurd take on the legend. Laurie A. Finke and Susan Aronstein observe that "*Spamalot* follows the structure of all Grail romances: the appearance of the Grail repudiates the secular ideology of Camelot being celebrated and calls the knights to a more difficult path."[47]

The entire point of the Grail quest is to give purpose and (religious) meaning to the mission of the Knights of the Round Table. In T. H. White's retelling, Arthur himself worries about the increasing violence and restlessness of the knights and implements the quest in order to infuse the notion of Might for Right with a higher purpose. Only the untainted Sir Galahad proves worthy and ascends into Heaven upon finding the Grail, leaving the ideals of the Round Table to ultimately dissolve once Arthur's final attempt to bring about lasting change ends. In a "bit" taken from *Holy Grail*, God himself directly passes the quest onto *Spamalot*'s Arthur and his gathered knights. While the film's Arthur declines to go to Camelot, the Arthur of *Spamalot* revels in the Vegas-themed silliness of the castle. As such, the vulgarities of Vegas represent the "secular ideology" Finke and Aronstein identify, whereas the idea of Broadway will come to represent the sacred quest. In this way, *Spamalot* marries Arthurian legend with a highly American form of self-referential musical theater.

The character which might be viewed as an added Arthurian element—in addition to being a clear concession to Broadway conventions—is the Lady of the Lake. Of course, King Arthur mentions this mystical figure in *Holy Grail*. When the belligerent peasant Dennis questions his authority, Arthur draws on divine right and the presentation of Excalibur as presented by the Lady of the Lake. Naturally, Dennis takes issue, ultimately denouncing Arthur's right with the statement that supreme political power cannot be claimed "just 'cause some watery tart threw a sword at you."[48] Dismissed by an anachronistically communist peasant, the Lady of the Lake is merely an absent character in the film. True to form, *Holy Grail* contains few female characters at all, and those who do appear tend to be either sex objects or played by the Pythons in drag. Idle expands the Lady of the Lake into an actual female lead, albeit one who self-referentially laments her diminished role in the second act.

Sometimes nameless, sometimes referred to as Nimue or Vivianne, the Lady of the Lake has appeared as a staple in Arthurian legend for hundreds of years. Although she is a nebulous and variable character throughout the whole of Arthuriana, she makes several notable appearances in the literary and musical works explored throughout this book. Among other roles, T. H. White includes the Lady of the Lake in the capacity mentioned by Monty Python; she bestows Excalibur upon the young King Arthur. Lerner and Loewe's *Camelot* includes the character in another function. The Lady is explicitly named as Nimue, and her song, "Follow Me," removes Merlin from adult Arthur's court by luring him away to her cave. Thus, expanding the character taps into Arthuriana broadly as well as into earlier musical treatments.

Furthermore, *Spamalot* conflates the Lady of the Lake with another prominent woman from the tradition. The end of the show reveals her name as Guinevere. In this way, she shifts from Arthur's benefactress and a mystical figure to his love interest. As such, the reveal is a gesture to popular understanding of Arthuriana, particularly as espoused by Lerner and Loewe. Additionally, the Knights of the Round Table react with aversion at the disclosure. They obliquely acknowledge the part Guinevere plays in the downfall of Arthur's reign and Camelot as ideal. Interestingly, however, the figure that completes the love triangle has been taken out of the equation. As I will discuss later in this chapter, *Spamalot* outs Lancelot as gay. Therefore, the famed love triangle no longer exists. This allusion goes beyond Monty Python since *Holy Grail* never so much as mentions a possible queen but certainly does fall into the realm of a Broadway "in-crowd" and self-referential pleasure in the reference to *Camelot*.

Like most of the characters in *Spamalot*, the Lady of the Lake's musical characterization includes resoundingly non-Arthurian reference points. As discussed earlier, "Come with Me" has the strongest potential connection to a more traditional musical depiction of the Lady of the Lake. Most of the time, however, the character resolutely develops as a musical theater/pop diva. As both "The Song That Goes Like This" and "Find Your Grail" indicate, the Lady of the Lake's songs draw on tropes of megamusical romanticism and pop power ballads. Her second act song, "Whatever Happened to My Part?" solidifies this characterization in a self-referential song that openly acknowledges that this is a musical. Marked in the piano-vocal score as "Power Ballad (Mid-1970's Streisand)," the intent is clear. The song is rife with dramatic, clichéd key changes, including a funny example on the lyrics "I'm constantly replaced by Britney Spears. Britney Spears!" On the emphatic repetition of Spears's name, Du Prez moves from a B♭ in the melody underpinned by the V of V in the previous key to the new key of E major—complete with the minor second move to a B♮ in the melody on the word "Spears," now acting as the fifth scale degree. This type of clichéd key change directly parodies the power ballad. Of course, Ramirez uses her now familiar vocal manipulation in order to hammer the point home. This type of modern characterization for familiar Arthurian characters is not unique to *Spamalot*, but the overtly referential aspect adds to the show's particular appeal.

Pre-Existing Songs and Musical Arthuriana

Thus far, I have considered the purely referential numbers in *Spamalot*, and while nearly every song contains a "meta" or pastiche aspect, this is not the only song type in the show. In fact, *Spamalot* features two other basic song types: pre-existing numbers (either from *Holy Grail* or other Python material) and "Arthurian" or plot songs. All of the songs discussed up to this point were newly composed by John Du Prez. Although *Spamalot* was Du Prez's first Broadway musical, the composer was a natural choice given his working relationship with Eric Idle and several other Python members. Notably, Du Prez wrote the music for *Monty Python's The Meaning of Life* (1983) in addition to solo projects by various members, including *A Fish Called Wanda* (1988) written by John Cleese and also featuring Michael Palin. Although Innes had written the songs for *Holy Grail*, Du Prez's familiarity with the troupe's comedic style, especially as related to music, supplements the original songs. Du Prez's referential songs combine with pre-existing songs to create the composite score. Though Du Prez's music does not have the familiarity of the original songs, his musical style in *Spamalot* complements the show's goofy, over-the-top aesthetic. Du Prez illustrates none of the simplicity or sustained use of medieval musical stereotypes used by Neil Innes in the original film; however, *Spamalot*'s goal differs from *Holy Grail*, and as such, Du Prez's obvious, yet ingrained, use of Broadway musical styles provides the perfect type of silly, "meta" entertainment for musical theater buffs.

As part of its nostalgic work, *Spamalot* includes two songs drawn from Monty Python excerpts unrelated to *Holy Grail*. These non-*Grail* interpolations offer Python-specific fan service as well as generally funny moments. The first of these numbers is "Finland/The Fisch-Schlapping Dance," performed at the opening of the show. As discussed earlier, this moment begins the running gag which highlights the fact that we are watching a show: the actors "misunderstand" the Historian's opening description that the play is set in England and begin to sing about Finland. The subsequent number combines the song "Finland," written by Michael Palin for the 1980 album *Monty Python's Contractual Obligation Album*, with newly composed material by Du Prez. Palin's melody bookends the "Fisch-Schlapping Dance." Du Prez, however, rearranges the original tune to be in keeping with the pseudo-traditional dance. The pre-existing "Finland" tune now appears in a quicker tempo, sung by the chorus and various small solos, and features an oom-pah style accompaniment in $\frac{4}{4}$. In combination with the use of Palin's song, the middle dance section references the "Fish Slapping Dance" skit from *Flying Circus*. The short sketch features Michael Palin and John Cleese. In a less-than-thirty-seconds dance, Palin prances back and forth with fish in order to slap Cleese in the face. When it seems to be Cleese's turn, he pulls out a large trout and knocks Palin into the water. The dance, which accompanies the "Fisch-Schlapping," in *Spamalot* mimics the television sketch. Musically, Du Prez shifts from the common time of Palin's "Finland" to a lilting $\frac{12}{8}$. The tune follows a long-short rhythmic pattern (quarter to eighth note) and employs a stepwise, arched phrasing in the melody. The "Fisch Schlapping Dance" provides a logical, dance B section to Palin's "Finland." Most importantly, *Spamalot* manages to include two Python references beyond the adaptation of *Holy Grail* in the first few minutes of the musical.

Furthermore, the second act includes the most recognizable Python tune, "Always Look on the Bright Side of Life." Written and performed by Eric Idle for *The Life of Brian* (1979), the catchy song has become iconic. In its original format, the song is irreverent, a bit shocking, and absolutely hilarious. As sung by Idle to the character Brian while being crucified, the song ends the film in a truly Python fashion. Idle came up with the ending, saying it needs to be "A song. Sung from the crosses. A ridiculously cheery song about looking on the bright side. Like a Disney song. Maybe even with a little whistle."[49] Idle then describes how he wrote the tune quickly with lessons learned from a Mickey Baker guitar course and remembered conversations with George Harrison.[50] Although initially recorded with a straight vocal, the final performance features a broad cockney accent based on Idle's Mr. Cheeky character from the film. A light jazzy accompaniment, featuring piano and soft percussion as well as the aforementioned whistling, highlights the inappropriate positioning of the song as Idle and other condemned men sing about the "bright side" of life and death.

"Always Look on the Bright Side of Life" has gained a life outside its original context, especially as performed by Idle in live shows and as sing-alongs in various contexts. And it is in this guise that the song makes its appearance in *Spamalot*. "Bright Side" loses its comedic punch outside of *Life of Brian*. Yet as a funny and highly recognizable song, it does its work in *Spamalot*. Idle credits director Mike Nichols for the inclusion of "Bright Side" in the musical, stating that he had "seen how the audience responded to the song, joining in and singing along happily. He wanted *Spamalot* to end that way too."[51] Indeed, the musical does end that way with "Bright Side" acting as the curtain call number, and audiences singing along. However, Idle and Du

Prez also inserted the song early in Act II. As a whole, the number is longer and showier with a larger orchestral arrangement than the original. The song begins with Arthur's squire and "steed" Patsy singing to cheer up the discouraged king. Since the character is self-proclaimed working-class, the broad accent set up in Idle's original performance fits. However, the vocal quality changes and the accents smooth out once Arthur and the other knights join in. As such, some of the lines, which a broad cockney accent render even funnier (e.g., "life's a piece of shit when you look at it"), must stand alone.

Unable to resist incorporating an additional musical allusion, *Spamalot's* version of "Bright Side" includes a dance break. Arthur and the Knights of the Round Table begin tapping, and when a storm passes through, they use umbrellas in the dance. The result is a group tap number that references Gene Kelly's famous "Singin' in the Rain" dance. And the end of the song resorts to clichéd musical and dance tropes, including Arthur and Patsy forming a kickline duo. Already sewn into the plot via Arthur's malaise, the song further becomes the device in which he finds the shrubbery demanded by the Knights of Ni. Therefore, "Bright Side" becomes one of the few songs in the show that explicitly advances the plot. At the same time, it appeals to both Python and musical fans simultaneously. Of course, the most obvious songs to appeal to existing Python fans are the three pre-existing songs taken directly from *Holy Grail*.

The first song from the original film to make an appearance is the Monks Chant. As discussed in the previous chapter, the "Pie Jesu" chant acts both as a parody of the medieval church as well as a cinematic reference to Bergman. Appearing three times in the film, the Monks Chant represents a musical thread for the satire. As used in *Spamalot*, the chant loses its comedic intelligence and meaning. Instead, it simply becomes one of many allusions throughout the show. The musical reference, however, is not exact. Both the melody and lyrics have been changed from *Holy Grail's* versions. Du Prez's melody has a similar plainchant style to Innes's with a small range and repetition (Example 6.1). The functional nature of each chant likely makes the change unrecognizable to most audiences. Idle also

Example 6.1. Recording Transcription of Monk Chant in *Spamalot*. Eric Idle and John Du Prez. *Monty Python's Spamalot*. New York: Theatrical Rights Worldwide, 2005.

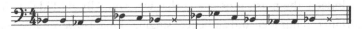

wrote new fake Latin lyrics for the Monks Chant. Rather than using the end of the "Dies Irae," this chant begins with the nonsense Latin "sacrosanctus domine" (head smack). Again, general audiences may not notice the change, but it illustrates a shift in approach. The use of the "Dies Irae" in *Holy Grail* acts as a medieval/Bergman parody while Idle and Du Prez are merely interested in mimicking a famous scene from the film. Interestingly, *Spamalot*'s version incorporates the medieval musical trope of the church bell, which *Holy Grail* lacked. Not bound by the restrictions of the film's locations or religious depiction, the bell signifies stereotypical ideas of the medieval church.[52]

During the show, the monks represent the beginning of the storyline with an obvious yet musically superficial reference to the film. The hooded, head-banging monks simply walk across the stage directly after the "Fisch-Schlapping Dance," thus signifying that we are indeed in *Holy Grail* adaptation territory now. Immediately following the brief song, which lasts for the amount of time it takes for the monks to walk across the stage, Arthur and Patsy appear onstage for the first time. After the coconut and swallows scene, the Monks Chant returns. This brief reprise becomes a short introduction to the song "He Is Not Dead Yet" and is interrupted by the call of "bring out your dead." In fact, this second context is the one used by the original Broadway cast recording. The chant lasts about twenty-five seconds before the dialogue leading "He Is Not Dead Yet" begins. The original "Pie Jesu" lyrics, with their connection to the Requiem Mass, would have certainly offered an amusing juxtaposition to the bright musical comedy number it precedes. The nonsense Latin, however, does not offer any such commentary. As employed in *Spamalot*, the Monks Chant loses its satirical depth.

"The Knights of the Round Table" also changes context and sound in order to fit the musical's own goals. Du Prez and Idle take a roughly one-minute song from *Holy Grail* and spin it into a multi-sectioned production number, which shuffles through a number of musical styles. As it appears in *Holy Grail*, the song occurs in a cutaway that convinces the audience of Arthur's declaration that Camelot is a silly place and therefore, to be avoided. *Spamalot*'s Arthur shows no such qualms. He recognizes and revels in the silliness as represented by the Vegas-like Camelot. The song begins with a flashy introduction that features Vegas showgirls. After a fairly straightforward statement of the song as it appears in the film (with different orchestration), the first expansion occurs in the form of a tap interlude. The vocal statement of the song does include an embedded quotation of the "Toreador" song from *Carmen* when the knights sing about how much they love opera. The knights, all participating in the big number, then sing the song with expanded lyrics.

From this point forward, the musical theater references come fast and thick; *West Side Story* and Kander and Ebb are included in the parody before it once again transitions to a new section and style. Introduced in the way of a lounge act headliner, the Lady of the Lake reprises "Song That Goes Like This." Ramirez performs her best clichéd lounge singer, which features a heavy dose of a Barbra Streisand–like vocal style. Moving into scat, Arthur joins her for a rat pack–esque duet of "Knights of the Round Table." With literal casino sound effects interspersed, the number finally draws to a close with the big chorus finish.

In this way, "Knights of the Round Table" becomes not only a major production number but also an important Arthurian moment in the show in that the expanded, flashy number sets up the need for the Grail quest. As mentioned earlier in this chapter, Finke and Aronstein draw parallels between *Spamalot* and the typical Arthurian romance. It is this scene where the parallel becomes clear. Arthur and the Knights of the Round Table have completely embraced the secular pleasures of Camelot. *Spamalot* represents this path as vice via Las Vegas rather than the wanton violence of earlier versions, yet the same sort of indolence is implied. Although Arthur or a virtuous knight usually suggests the quest as a means of saving Camelot and the knights' goals, God himself interrupts in *Spamalot*. Voiced by John Cleese in the Broadway production, God chides Arthur for playing around in Camelot and sends him and his knights on the quest. The purpose and performance of "Knights of the Round Table" is both thoroughly modern and thoroughly Arthurian.

The final song lifted directly from *Holy Grail* is "The Ballad of Brave Sir Robin." The presentation and sound of the brief number is easily the most faithful to the source film. Once again, Sir Robin "rides" through England questing, accompanied by his own personal minstrels. The song itself last only about one minute with very few alterations to the original version, representing the only song that does not undergo significant change or expansion in the musical. However, instrumentation and vocal style do change in the stage musical. For example, the film version includes bagpipes, while the Original Broadway Cast soundtrack omits that instrument in favor of a high-pitched recorder for a more strident sound. The vocal performance, as sung by Christian Borle, also conforms more closely to Broadway singing styles. Borle sings the tune without significant vocal manipulation but with more vibrato than Innes uses in the film. Still, the overall effect is that "Brave Sir Robin" provides a straightforward reference to the film.

Given Robin's characterization in *Spamalot*, however, the song can be understood a bit differently. From the outset, Robin admits his dislike of fighting as well as his belief that knights mostly dance (an absolutely true notion in the world of *Spamalot*). During "He Is Not Dead Yet," Robin introduces himself and declares his intent to enlist in Arthur's "army." Robin proclaims, "I want to be a knight, but I don't like to fight. I'm rather scared I may simply run away." Although warmongering Lancelot promises to take Robin under his knightly wing, this scene prepares the audience for Robin's eventual displays of cowardice. Since the audience is forewarned so clearly, "The Ballad of Brave Sir Robin" surprises less than it does in the film. Given Robin's stated propensity toward song and dance, it also makes sense that he would travel with minstrels (the usual complement of pipe, lute, and tabor). The minstrels also aid Sir Robin in his subsequent number, "You Won't Succeed on Broadway," and similar to the film, have an even briefer reprise of "Brave Sir Robin." All in all, Robin and his minstrels support the knight's eventual discovery that his personal "grail" is musical theater. His proclivities and accompanying musicians have prepared the way for this ultimate character reveal.

In doing so, *Spamalot* normalizes and explains Robin's perceived cowardice. Susan Aronstein observes that in the context of *Holy Grail*, "Robin's association with music immediately identifies him with the singing and dancing knights left behind in Camelot" and that his encounter with the Three-Headed Knight "confines unseemly behavior safely within the stereotype of the effeminate male."[53] In *Spamalot*, Robin openly acknowledges and ultimately fully embraces this identity. Additionally, the singing and dancing that Robin adores so much is not rejected in the musical. Arthur never turns his back on Camelot, and the king sings and dances frequently. In fact, putting on a Broadway musical (that turns out is already happening) becomes the entire goal for Arthur and his knights. Indeed, Robin's primary musical number, "You Won't Succeed on Broadway," acts as advice for the king's quest to put on a show. Since the condition for succeeding on Broadway includes the involvement of Jews, Idle draws on the Monty Pythonesque trope of simultaneously acknowledging, exploiting, and making fun of stereotypes. The song is openly and purposefully problematic as part of its humor. Du

Prez's musical style, of course, draws directly on Jewish musical styles as used in Broadway shows, becoming increasingly stereotyped throughout the song. The melodic chromaticism, the most obvious markers of klezmer music (such as rhythmically free winds and oompah bass), and a direct quotation from "Hava Nigila" all add to the song's parody. "You Won't Succeed on Broadway" both acts as a self-referential Broadway satire and demonstrates that Robin and his type of masculinity fit right in with this king and his court. As Finke and Aronstein recognize, the musical's version of Arthur and his ideals do not depend on violence in the same way as the film's depiction.

Another knight who embodies this altered representation of knightly masculinity is Sir Lancelot. In fact, Robin and Lancelot are introduced in the same number. In the scene featuring "He Is Not Dead Yet," a sequence lifted from *Holy Grail* changes to bring together the men who will join King Arthur's band of knights. In the song's bridge, Lancelot introduces himself with a simple melody that exudes a heavy emphasis on the downbeat. The section represents a marked change from the overall polka feel of the song, and Lancelot's plodding introduction establishes his simple physicality. Significantly, the insecure Robin mimics Lancelot's music but with more conjunct melodic motion. The men then pick up the original tune and, joined by a chorus, sing and dance their way to Camelot.

In *Holy Grail*, Lancelot simply dismisses the effeminate Prince Herbert and claims a misunderstanding upon finding that he responded to a trapped prince's note (after slaughtering the wedding party). This gender confusion presents an "occasion for a comic hilarity that attempts to shut down" the possibility of gay male sexuality.[54] Eschewing the casual dismissal of homosexuality, *Spamalot* outs Lancelot as gay. In their analysis, Finke and Aronstein lament how Lancelot's gay identity ultimately serves as a

> mere gesture that is quickly placed in the service of the musical's larger conservatism. Not only does his transformation from macho knight to "butterfly" contain homosexuality within a stereotype of effeminacy but also, as it does so, it silences the film's critique of martial violence, arguing that Lancelot's "idiom" stems not from his chivalric identity but from a confused misrecognition of his own sexuality.[55]

Furthermore, Lancelot's homosexuality, and eventual marriage to Herbert, removes him as an obstacle to Arthur and Guinevere's successful marriage.

As Finke and Aronstein aptly point out, Lancelot's sexual identity actually reinforces the heteronormative status quo. Although the knights visibly react to the Lady of the Lake's revelation of her name, her lover of the legend is no longer a concern.

At the same time, the musical does give voice to Lancelot's romantic partner, Herbert. While *Holy Grail*'s version of Herbert never sings once, *Spamalot*'s iteration of the character sings several times. Although his father continues to dislike the impulse and interrupts his songs, Herbert is never completely silenced. Herbert's "song that never was" becomes fully realized and possible in a traditional musical—and more than that, a musical which positively revels in being a musical. The Herbert/Lancelot interaction becomes a song complex in *Spamalot*. Herbert first sings a short ballad fragment "Where Are You?" before his father cuts it off. The tune is directly based on the earlier "Come with Me," sung by the Lady of the Lake to Dennis/Sir Galahad. The familiar tune, which seduced Sir Galahad in Act I, lures Lancelot now. The relationship is clear; Lancelot has found his own love, replacing Guinevere with Prince Herbert. Throughout the show, Christian Borle displays a great deal of vocal manipulation, and he uses this mastery in "Where Are You?" to great effect. He sings the opening verse in a thin tenor similar to Terry Jones's speaking voice in *Holy Grail*. When moving into a more full-throated style, his father strenuously interjects.

Significantly, Herbert sings in other instances as well. Although he does not get to sing about his near-death experience after a brief "He's Going to Tell," Herbert does lead the song "His Name Is Lancelot." He sings the opening verse with its focus on a higher range in a typical Broadway singing style (gone are the overtly thin and "effeminate" singing or over-the-top operatic attempts), then proceeds to lead the chorus. "His Name Is Lancelot" mirrors songs or genres stereotypically associated with gay men, namely the "Copacabana" and disco. Throughout the song, Herbert uses a celebration of stereotyped gay masculinity to further attract Lancelot and lure him away from his violent tendencies. After announcing their impending marriage, Herbert—not Lancelot—sings the reprise of "Find Your Grail" during the finale medley. He intones that one need only "find your male." Despite the justice of Finke and Aronstein's criticisms cited earlier, *Spamalot* does not silence *Holy Grail*'s most gender-bending character. Herbert finds not only his male but also his voice.

182 MONTY PYTHON AS ADAPTERS

Spamalot's King Arthur

One of the most significant changes made from the original film involves the alteration to the character of King Arthur. In *Holy Grail*, Arthur is the only character who might be considered a lead. As mentioned in the previous chapter, Graham Chapman's Arthur is the "straight man" of the film. Everyone and everything around Arthur is patently absurd, but he portrays the legendary king with a gravity which grounds the film. In no way, shape, or form can *Spamalot*'s version of Arthur be considered a serious medieval king. This change in characterization occurs primarily through song and performance. Eleven of the twenty-one songs, including the finale medley, feature Arthur in some way. Unusually for the male lead in a show, Arthur never sings a complete solo number. While he dominates the show and featured soloists, King Arthur always sings either a duet or solo within a larger ensemble. Given the homosocial nature of *Holy Grail* and its musical adaptation, the songs highlight Arthur's constant, nearly exclusively male, companionship. Additionally, his participation in the musical numbers alters the audience's perception of the king.

Although several actors have played Arthur in *Spamalot*, Tim Curry's performance of the king represents a major, and significant, departure from Chapman's performance in the film. As discussed earlier in this chapter, other members of the cast closely aligned aspects of their performance with the original Pythons' portrayals in *Holy Grail*. Curry, on the other hand, brings his highly idiosyncratic style of camp to his depiction of King Arthur. In his autobiography, Idle states, "I had always wanted Tim Curry for King Arthur, and when Mike [Nichols] heard him read the part at my house, so did he."[56] Curry initially rose to prominence as Dr. Frank-N-Furter in the 1975 cult film *The Rocky Horror Picture Show*. In a tour-de-force of camp performance, Tim Curry displays his capacity for archness, vocal manipulation, and over-the-top yet committed acting. All of these characteristics would become trademarks of many of his roles and serve him well in his turn as King Arthur.

Throughout his decades-long career, Tim Curry has released albums, had a number of stage and film roles, and gained experience in voice acting. By the time *Spamalot* premiered, Curry had dozens of theater and film credits to his name. In roles ranging from Rooster Hannigan in the 1982 film adaptation of *Annie* to Wadsworth in the 1985 comedy *Clue* and Long John Silver in *Muppet Treasure Island* (1996), Curry developed as a character actor with well-honed comedic abilities. Using his vocal training and musical experience, Curry released a number of albums in the 1970s and early '80s. In the 1990s, the actor began to do more voice work for television and film, including voicing Nigel Thornberry in the Nickelodeon show *The Wild Thornberrys* (1998–2004). As such, Curry's vast experience and particularly his reputation for camp come into play in his performance as Arthur. Given the idiosyncratic stamp that Curry puts on his performance of Arthur, his version of the character as preserved on the original Broadway cast recording will be explored in the following analysis. Certainly, others have played Arthur in their own ways, and I do not propose to take Tim Curry's interpretation as definitive.[57] At the same time, Idle's insistence that he always had the actor in mind for the part as well as Curry's stark departure from Graham Chapman's rendition make Tim Curry's portrayal of Arthur worth considering.

Unsurprisingly, Arthur introduces himself through song. "King Arthur's Song" is an extremely short verse that introduces Arthur as ruler of England and Scotland (and even "tiny little bits of Gaul") and becomes his theme. The first time this tune appears is during the Historian's description of the legendary king. The orchestra plays the sixteen-bar melody that will later be heard as "Arthur's Song." While the Historian establishes the setting, the accompanying music repeats this melody three times with varied orchestrations. The sixteen bars appear twice in the first Arthurian scene of the show.[58] "Arthur's Song" has the same sense of what the Python's call mock-heroic style as the De Wolfe pieces used in *Holy Grail*, though established in a different way than Arthur's theme in the film. Rather than the brass-heavy, big orchestral theme, "Arthur's Song" instead contains similarities to anthems. The tune is simple to sing and set to a brisk march-like tempo in common time. Although "Arthur's Song" does not feature the large, Romantic orchestral sound of "Homeward Bound," trumpet flourishes do enhance the mock-heroic nature of the song. "Arthur's Song" appears sung or in the underscoring at several points throughout the show in order to characterize Arthur as king.

One of the most significant uses of "Arthur's Song" occurs in the "Laker Girls Cheer," where the short song is embedded into the slightly larger number. On the recording, the track opens with an athletic whistle and snare drums. When Arthur sings his theme, the horns double the melody in order to enrich the sound. Tim Curry's vocal style when he sings this melody is incredibly resonant, displaying Arthur's confidence in his role as king. When the song transitions to the cheer, Arthur interjects with "who's the king" in a booming, almost smug voice. Both Curry and Chapman exude self-assurance in their kingliness. Whereas Chapman simply rides through England and possesses poise, Curry infuses the character with brash con- viction. As an introductory song, *Spamalot*'s "Arthur's Song" invites com- parison with *Camelot*'s "I Wonder What the King Is Doing Tonight." While Arthur is unmarried in both versions, *Spamalot*'s initial presentation of the king is straightforward and "kingly." In contrast, *Camelot*'s song reveals a man unsure of his future as represented by his upcoming arranged marriage. The Arthur of *Spamalot* displays no such insecurities, and from the outset, emphasizes desire for the homosocial comradery embodied by the Knights of the Round Table.

Throughout the entire first act, Arthur participates in several longer songs as part of the ensemble. He has featured solos in several of the larger num- bers, indicating his status. As such, *Spamalot* emphasizes Arthur's position as head of the Knights of the Round Table. After recruiting Galahad, Arthur and the knights stick together for the remainder of the first half. The knights sing the Musketeer-inspired "All for One" in a vaguely cowboy chorus style. In its lyrics and musical allusion to westerns, the song solidifies the homoso- cial milieu of the Knights of the Round of Table. While Bedevere, Galahad, Lancelot, and Robin pass the melody to one another in the second A section, most of the song employs unison singing. In a gentle $\frac{12}{8}$, the melody is simple and easy to sing; stepwise motion or rising thirds predominate with a synthe- sized countermelody enhancing the cowboy allusion.

While "All for One" emphasizes male comradery, "Run Away" depicts their shared cowardice. The song accompanies the French taunter sketch from *Holy Grail*, pitting the cowardly British knights against the French. Arthur and his knights frantically sing "run away" in a quick "Can-Can tempo." The descending stepwise melody with its short-short-long rhythmic pattern followed by quarter note triplets enhance their panic, es- pecially as contrasted by the Frenchmen's staid descending triads on steady quarter notes. Although they will separate after the Intermission, the ho- mosocial milieu is preserved in this number. Of course, *Holy Grail* (like all Monty Python's works) is almost aggressively homosocial—to the point where scholars have criticized the troupe for its misogynistic and homo- phobic tendencies.[59] The few women in the original film are dangerous sexpots (in the Zoot sketch), witches, or Pythons in drag. *Spamalot* cuts several of the minor female characters (the witch and an accompanying song were cut during previews) while adding the Lady of the Lake and various chorus girls. Like its source material, *Spamalot* focuses on the male relationships and interactions. The songs, and Arthur's place in them, enhance this focus. More than that, Arthur embraces the theatrical masculinity of "The Knights of the Round Table" rather than rejecting it as in *Holy Grail*.

Significantly, Arthur rarely sings completely on his own and never partakes in any romance—in song or otherwise—throughout the entire first act. He interacts with the Lady of the Lake, who has a superficial romantic number with Galahad in the form of "The Song That Goes Like This." As the lyrics suggest, the song plays on musical tropes rather than functioning as an actual romantic duet, and any relationship between the Lady and Galahad is never mentioned again. Even within the first act, the rest of the Lady's musical appearances are as singing companion to Arthur. However, they do not display any romantic interest in one another. Instead, the two play off each other for comedic or parodic effect. As mentioned in the earlier discussion of the "Knights of the Round Table," Arthur joins the Lady of the Lake in her lounge act. When the king joins in, the tempo has picked up and the two indulge in a brief scat duel. This highly stylized scatting leads directly into the return of the "Knights of the Round Table" song. Although the Lady has reprised "Song that Goes Like This," Arthur does not yet join her in singing it. They instead return to the homosocial song praising the knights. Both engage in highly over-the-top vocal styles in this section in order to produce a cutely funny riff on the rat pack.

When Arthur sings his verse of "Find Your Grail," he does not engage in the stylistic vocal pastiche used by Sarah Ramirez. Nonetheless, Tim Curry's performance employs its own type of vocal manipulation. He begins using a highly affected talk-singing, which brings this moment in line with Lerner and Loewe's talk-singing Arthur as played by both Richard Burton and Richard Harris. Curry, however, shifts into full-voiced singing—some of his biggest and most dramatic vocalization in the whole show. As his singing escalates, Curry uses a lot of vibrato as well as a growling vocal attack. The style feels appropriate to both the inspirational ballad parody and Arthur's character development. Arthur moves from feeling adrift to having an optimistic confidence as he rejoices in the ability to choose your own path (it is, after all, the American dream). The Lady of the Lake encourages this emotion. While Ramirez may outshine Curry vocally, the Lady of the Lake supports rather than eclipses the king.

The song make-up as it pertains to Arthur looks different in the second act from how it looks in the first. Arthur's entire goal in the first act consists of building a community of knights. He succeeds, and they sing and dance together until sent on their quest by God. Since the knights have dispersed after the incident with the French taunters before Intermission, the second act features episodes following Arthur and his knights as they go their separate ways in order to search for the Grail (and later the means to put on a Broadway show). As such, Arthur becomes less of a featured soloist in ensemble numbers. Neither does he, however, ever sing a true solo song. Although the male-centric community Arthur has built has scattered for the time being, the king is always accompanied by his squire/steed Patsy. Due to this fact, the two inevitably join each other's presumably solo numbers to become duets by the end. "Always Look on the Bright Side of Life" and "I'm All Alone" both illustrate this circumstance. Discussed earlier in this chapter as a pre-existing Python tune, "Bright Side" is repurposed in *Spamalot* in order to cheer up the discouraged king. Curry's performance in this song highlights his particular brand of camp. With his cheeky over-the-top acting and singing, Tim Curry is commanding with a resonant vocal quality but never serious like Chapman.

After the three separate scenes featuring Sir Robin (which does include Arthur), the Lady of the Lake, and Sir Lancelot with Prince Herbert, Arthur sings, "I'm All Alone." Humorously, Arthur does not perform this song alone. "I'm All Alone" begins as a straightforward ballad of loneliness with simple keyboard accompaniment and underlying strings. Tim Curry uses his least affected vocal style of the entire show. His voice is pleasant, simple, and melodic and gives the king a plaintive quality. Of course, Arthur has not been alone throughout the entire show. At the very least, Patsy is literally always with him. As Patsy joins Arthur's ballad, he acknowledges the irony present in the king's complaints and blames class distinctions. Musically, Patsy often directly mirrors Arthur's melody or briefly sings in harmony with him before singing his own eight-measure phrase. The song continues to build on the absurdity of the notion of Arthur's loneliness when the knights join in the chorus for the last third of the song. Once again, Arthur is presented as part of a community of men, albeit a community from which he briefly feels distanced. The perceived disconnect makes way for *Spamalot* to shoehorn in a heterosexual marriage.

As the show itself acknowledges, a conventional Broadway musical comedy "needs" a happy ending (the Grail must be found) and a wedding.

Apparently, the nuptials between Sir Lancelot and Prince Herbert do not fully fit the requirement. *Spamalot* does not settle for anything other than a heteronormative marriage involving the leading male in order to fit the convention. After Arthur's disingenuous reflection on being alone, the Lady of the Lake sweeps in to put herself forward as Arthur's bride. Arthur readily agrees, and the two sing a unison reprise of "The Song That Goes Like This," now called "Twice in Every Show." Having established a flimsy romance between Arthur and the Lady, the community comes back together for the finale in which everyone has found their metaphorical grail; in addition, of course, to the actual cup being found. The happy ending presented in *Spamalot* differs from both Arthurian legend and *Holy Grail*. The latter, of course, has no real resolution at all as the film abruptly ends when modern British police put a stop to the proceedings, and the Grail is never found. In Arthurian legend, Sir Galahad finds the Grail but ascends with it into heaven, and we know where Arthur and Guinevere's marriage leads. Idle and Du Prez knowingly force their ending on the show for their meta-comedic purposes.

Conclusion

Beyond the successful Broadway run, *Spamalot* has had a number of additional productions since it premiered. The West End production opened in 2006, and again featured Tim Curry in the role of Arthur. The first US tour also began in 2006 and continued through 2009. The show also had a short-lived run in Las Vegas.[60] These productions illustrate not only the popularity but also the fundamental variability of *Spamalot* as a musical comedy. Throughout all these productions, changes were made to the show based on location and needs. For example, "You Won't Succeed on Broadway" became "You Won't Succeed in Showbiz" for the West End version of the show. Similarly, Idle peppered small topical references throughout the dialogue and lyrics. These can and were easily changed as the news and location of tours changed.[61] As typical for Vegas shows, Idle slimmed *Spamalot* down to a ninety-minute run with no Intermission, and "All for One" and much of "Run Away!" did not make the cut. Like the musical comedies of the 1920s and 1930s, the topicality, coupled with the idea that *Spamalot* is not a fixed product, is an important aspect of the show.

While not as straightforward as *Camelot*, *Monty Python's Spamalot* extends the Arthurian tradition in musical theater. For hundreds of years, authors, artists, playwrights, and composers have returned to the legend in its various forms. Television series, such as the BBC's *Merlin* (2008–2012), and more recent films, such as Guy Ritchie's *King Arthur: Legend of the Sword* (2017) and *The Kid Who Would Be King* (2019), prove the continued fascination of Arthur and his milieu in popular culture. While some of these works attempt to remain faithful to the best-known of the Arthurian stories, others represent a re-envisioning of Arthuriana; and it is this very malleability that makes the legend so appealing. The myth of King Arthur and his Knights of the Round Table has always been a source of creativity with people changing or adding to the tale according to different preferences and goals. Given this reality, *Spamalot* is absolutely in the spirit of Arthurian legend. Eric Idle and John Du Prez—by way of Monty Python—offer a twenty-first-century retelling, as much a part of its time as a contribution to the pantheon of Arthurian legend.

Conclusion

Although widespread interest in the legend of King Arthur naturally waxes and wanes throughout the years, it never disappears. Between new properties that re-envision and adaptations of classic stories, Arthurian legend continues to grow and change—showing no sign of stopping. Furthermore, the tradition has always been interdisciplinary. Despite the origins in and sheer breadth of Arthurian literature, the artistic realms of visual art, theater, and music have further contributed to the larger pantheon for centuries. It makes perfect sense for musical theater to take up the tale, providing its distinctive spin and approach. With such a massive history, the variability of Arthurian legend represents an important aspect to any adaptations that choose it as subject matter. The purpose and uses of the legend have changed.

In the stage musicals and films discussed in this book, particular trends emerge. While Lerner and Loewe treat Camelot and its inhabitants with romanticism and a feeling of reverence for the idealism of King Arthur, other adapters approach the legend with humor. Traditional adaptations continue—tales of heroes, magic, and forbidden love. On the other hand, some twentieth- and twenty-first-century incarnations ignore or upend the tragedy in favor of a lighthearted or comedic approach. Whether playing with the possibilities of socio-political commentary in the ways that Mark Twain and the original Monty Python troupe prefer or employing musical comedy tropes like Fields, Rodgers, and Hart and Idle and Du Prez, modern treatments often shy away from the high-mindedness of many traditional stories. Indeed, the very longevity of the tale offers seemingly infinite possibilities for finding fodder for satire or just plain parody. Importantly, drama, tragedy, and comedy now co-exist in musical Arthuriana.

While the 1975 film *Monty Python and the Holy Grail* demonstrates a group of British comedians making fun of their own heritage, the other properties represent an American view. Even the American context for *Holy Grail* and eventual transformation into *Spamalot* illustrates a US-based engagement with the British legend. Of course, Arthurian tradition has stories and cycles in many countries as written in many languages, and therefore, the American versions are part of the larger whole. As explored in this book's case studies, the US-based engagement with the legend of King Arthur also epitomizes the history of cultural exchange between the United Kingdom and the United States.

In the musical versions of Mark Twain's *A Connecticut Yankee in King Arthur's Court*, juxtaposition between not only old and new but also British and American form the basis of the humor. Martin/Hank symbolizes modern American ingenuity as well as a fascination with Britishness. At the same time, the Yankee directly influences his surroundings and certainly sees himself as superior. The people of Camelot do not live in an idealistic utopia in the Twain retellings. Mark Twain, followed by Monty Python, pierces the fantasy. Lerner and Loewe's adaptation of T. H. White, on the other hand, does emphasize the idealism while making clear that it is doomed. *Camelot* is easily the most traditional retelling considered in this book, illustrating a type of veneration for Camelot not present in the other musicals. Close on its heels is Disney's *The Sword in the Stone*—at the same time, the American animation company uses the legend for its own purposes. Finally, Monty Python spoofs the notions of chivalry, the medieval, and the idealism of King Arthur. For American audiences, the shifts between satire, captivation, longing for the past, and absurdity reflect various ideas regarding the history of colonialism, politics, and cultural exchange between the two countries. Regardless of the approach, Arthurian legend remains familiar ground, and these musicals play a part in that continued presence.

Through song, the selected case studies tell their own versions of Arthuriana with their specific characterizations of the familiar characters. The very fact that each of these stage musicals and films attracted some of the most significant songwriters and entertainers in American popular culture attests to the centrality of Arthuriana. Each of the goals and styles represented throughout the book are indicative of the time of creation and production. They are artifacts that show us how Arthurian legend continues to evolve in the United States. At the same time, some of these works still resonate with audiences—certainly *Holy Grail* has taken on cult classic status. *Camelot* and *Spamalot* both enjoy a presence in community theater productions, and Disney+ allows new generations of children fuller access to *The Sword in the Stone* than was previously possible. While the Twain musical adaptations may be the most niche properties, they are nonetheless influential, and, certainly, the novel itself remains a popular adaptation property. As a whole, Arthurian musical retellings contribute to the continuation of the legend in their original incarnations as well as via new productions or lasting influence on new works. From *Camelot* to *Spamalot*, Arthurian musicals offer both beauty and silliness, and they are here to stay.

Notes

Introduction: Arthur Adapted

1. Megan Woller, "The Lusty Court of *Camelot* (1967): Exploring Sexuality in the Hollywood Adaptation," *Music and the Moving Image* 8, no. 1 (Spring 2015): 3–18 and Megan Woller, " 'Happ'ly-Ever-Aftering': Changing Social and Industry Conventions in Hollywood Musical Adaptations, 1960–75," PhD diss., University of Illinois Urbana-Champaign, 2014.
2. Linda Hutcheon, *A Theory of Adaptation* (New York: Routledge, 2006), 16.
3. Hutcheon, 21.
4. For representative examples from within this discourse, see Dudley Andrew, "Adaptation," in *Concepts in Film Theory* (New York: Oxford University Press, 1984), 96–106; Thomas Leitch, *Adaptation and Its Discontents: From* Gone with the Wind *to* Passion of the Christ (Baltimore: Johns Hopkins University Press, 2007), 93–126; and David T. Johnson, "Adaptation and Fidelity," in *The Oxford Handbook of Adaptation Studies*, ed. Thomas Leitch (New York: Oxford University Press, 2017), 87–100.
5. David L. Kranz, "Trying Harder: Probability, Objectivity, and Rationality in Adaptation Studies," in *The Literature/Film Reader: Issues in Adaptation*, ed. James M. Welsh and Peter Lev (Lanham: Scarecrow, 2007), 77–102.
6. Bradley Stephens, "Great Voices Speak Alike: Orson Welles's Radio Adaptation of Victor Hugo's *Les Misérables*," in *The Routledge Companion to Adaptation*, ed. Dennis Cutchins, Katja Krebs, and Eckart Voigts (New York: Routledge, 2018), 256.
7. Lisette Lopez Szwydky, "Adaptations, Culture-Texts and the Literary Canon: On the Making of Nineteenth-century Classics," in *The Routledge Companion to Adaptation*, ed. Dennis Cutchins, Katja Krebs, and Eckart Voigts (New York: Routledge, 2018), 130.
8. Szwydky, 131.
9. Woller, "Happ'ly Ever Aftering."
10. Geoffrey Block, *Enchanted Evenings: The Broadway Musical from* Showboat *to* Sondheim and Lloyd Webber, 2nd ed. (New York: Oxford University Press, 2009), 153–92 and 300–332.
11. Block, 153–54.
12. Danielle Birkett and Dominic McHugh, eds., *Adapting the Wizard of Oz: Musical Versions from Baum to MGM and Beyond* (New York: Oxford University Press, 2019); Kathryn M. Grossman and Bradley Stephens, eds., *Les Misérables and Its Afterlives: Between Page, Stage, and Screen* (New York: Routledge, 2015); Dominic McHugh, ed., *The Oxford Handbook of Musical Theatre Screen Adaptations* (New York: Oxford University Press, 2019).

13. Block, *Enchanted Evenings*; Raymond Knapp, *The American Musical and the Performance of Personal Identity* (Princeton: Princeton University Press, 2006); Dominic McHugh, *Alan Jay Lerner: A Lyricist's Letters* (New York: Oxford University Press, 2014); Dominic McHugh and Amy Asch, eds., *The Complete Lyrics of Alan Jay Lerner* (New York: Oxford University Press, 2018); Dominic Symonds, *We'll Have Manhattan: The Early Works of Rodgers and Hart* (New York: Oxford University Press, 2015).

14. James Bohn, *Music in Disney's Animated Features: Snow White and the Seven Dwarfs to The Jungle Book* (Jackson: University Press of Mississippi, 2017).

15. For a key example, see Kevin J. Harty, ed., *Cinema Arthuriana: Twenty Essays*, rev. ed. (Jefferson, NC: MacFarland, 2002).

16. Andrew Lynch, "Imperial Arthur: Home and Away," in *The Cambridge Companion to Arthurian Legend*, ed. Elizabeth Archibald and Ad Putter (New York: Cambridge University Press, 2009), 181.

Prelude: Twain as Adapter

1. Gary P. Henrickson, "Mark Twain, Criticism, and the Limits of Creativity," *Creativity Research Journal* 15, no. 2 (2003): 258–59.

2. Lydia R. Cooper, "Human Voices: Language and Conscience in Twain's *A Connecticut Yankee in King Arthur's Court*," *Canadian Review of American Studies* 39, no. 1 (2009): 65–84 and Lee Clark Mitchell, "Lines, Circles, Time Loops, and Mark Twain's *A Connecticut Yankee in King Arthur's Court*," *Nineteenth-Century Literature* 54, no. 2 (September 1999): 230–48.

3. Cooper, 69.

4. Everett Carter, "The Meaning of *A Connecticut Yankee*," *American Literature* 50, no. 3 (November 1978): 427.

5. See Stephen Knight's chapter on Mark Twain and Arthurian legend for a detailed discussion of how the novel includes pointed contemporary commentary. Stephen Knight, "'A New Deal': Mark Twain's *A Connecticut Yankee at King Arthur's Court* and the Modern Arthurian Legend," in *Arthurian Literature and Society* (London: Palgrave MacMillan, 1983), 187–202.

6. Mark Twain, *A Connecticut Yankee in King Arthur's Court* (New York: Nelson Doubleday, 1889), 202.

7. See Twain for full episode.

8. Carter, 423.

9. Carter, 422.

10. Cooper, 73.

11. Twain, 72.

12. Rebecca A. Umland and Samuel J. Umland, *The Use of Arthurian Legend in Hollywood Film: From Connecticut Yankees to Fisher Kings* (Westport, CT: Greenwood Press, 1996), 10.

13. For example, see Twain, 110–11 for a story of knight errantry taken from Malory's account.

14. Alan Lupack and Barbara Tepa Lupack, *King Arthur in America* (New York: D.S. Brewer, 1999), 93.

Chapter 1

1. In many ways, my work on this show is indebted to the previous scholarship that has considered the work of Rodgers and Hart. Geoffrey Block's foundational research on Richard Rodgers provides an important starting point. As Block notes, Rodgers and Hart have been more widely recognized for their songs than entire shows (with exceptions such as *Pal Joey*). Block's research considers the process of developing and revising a show, looking at deleted songs and key differences between the 1927 Broadway production and 1943 revival. In his monograph, Dominic Symonds usefully and insightfully explores the early partnership of Rodgers and Hart. As their biggest commercial success of the decade, the 1927 production of *A Connecticut Yankee* garners an entire chapter. Symonds discusses the major known aspects of the musical, and I refer readers to his work for an essential consideration of this show. See Geoffrey Block, *The Richard Rodgers Reader* (New York: Oxford University Press, 2002); Geoffrey Block, *Richard Rodgers* (New Haven, CT: Yale University Press, 2003); and Dominic Symonds, *We'll Have Manhattan: The Early Work of Rodgers and Hart* (New York: Oxford University Press, 2015).

2. Bruce Kirle, *Unfinished Show Business: Broadway Musicals as Works-in-Process* (Carbondale: Southern Illinois University Press, 2005), 2.

3. See Symonds, chapter 7. In particular, I point interested readers to the listing of musical numbers reconstructed from four different productions on p. 203.

4. Stephen Knight, "'A New Deal': Mark Twain's *A Connecticut Yankee at King Arthur's Court* and the Modern Arthurian Legend," in *Arthurian Literature and Society* (London: Palgrave MacMillan, 1983), 197.

5. Richard Rodgers discusses their initial interest in gaining the rights to the story after seeing the 1921 silent film. See Richard Rodgers, *Musical Stages: An Autobiography* (New York: Da Capo Press, 1995), 106–7.

6. Symonds, 189.

7. See Knight, "'A New Deal,'" 187–202.

8. T. H. White did not publish his first Arthurian work, *The Sword in the Stone*, until 1938. While the first three books may have been familiar to some by the 1943 revival, White's finished novel, *The Once and Future King*, was published in 1958.

9. See Symonds, 81–82 for full discussion.

10. Herbert Fields, Lorenz Hart, and Richard Rodgers, *A Connecticut Yankee* (New York: R&H Theatricals, 1977), Act I, Scene 2, p. 30.

11. William A. Everett, "King Arthur in Popular Musical Theatre and Musical Film," in *King Arthur in Music*, ed. Richard Barber (Rochester, NY: D.S. Brewer, 2002), 147.

12. See Ethan Mordden, *Make Believe: The Broadway Musical of the 1920s* (New York: Oxford University Press, 1997), 199 and Block, *Rodgers*, 54 for contemporary reactions.

13. Symonds, 13.

14. Mordden, 114.

15. Larry Stempel, *Showtime: A History of the Broadway Musical Theater* (New York: W. W. Norton, 2010), 244–45.

16. Symonds, 205.

17. Interestingly, the exception to this is Neil Innes's approach to the songs in *Monty Python and the Holy Grail* as discussed in Chapter 5.

18. See Symonds, 192–97.

19. Stempel, 247.

20. Rodgers, 107.

21. Allen Forte, "My Heart Stood Still," in *The Richard Rodgers Reader*, 26–29.

22. For an extended analysis of "Thou Swell," see Allen Forte, *The American Popular Ballad of the Golden Era, 1924–1950* (Princeton: Princeton University Press, 1995), 179–83.

23. Block, *Reader*, 20–30.

24. Quoted in Block, *Reader*, 38.

25. Lorenz Hart and Richard Rodgers, "Knight's Opening," *A Connecticut Yankee*, Piano-Conductor Score (New York: R&H Theatricals, 1977), 79. See John Haines, *Music in Films on the Middle Ages: Authenticity vs. Fantasy* (New York: Routledge, 2014) for a full discussion of medieval musical tropes in film.

26. Symonds, 197.

27. Symonds, 201.

28. The 1955 televised production cut Galahad, Evelyn, and their songs in order to reduce running time.

29. Symonds, 197.

30. Jeffrey Magee, "From Flatbush to *Fun Home*: The Broadway Musical's Cozy Cottage Trope," in *Rethinking American Music*, ed. Tara Browner and Thomas L. Riis (Urbana: University of Illinois Press, 2019), 34–49.

31. Mark Twain, *A Connecticut Yankee in King Arthur's Court* (New York: Nelson Doubleday, 1889), 89.

32. Symonds, 207.

33. Symonds, 190.

34. See Symonds, 205–6 for a discussion of "Evelyn, What Do You Say?" and the possible connection to Busby Berkeley's romance with actress Evelyn Ruh.

35. "To Keep My Love Alive," Holograph piano-vocal score in pencil, Box 4, Folder 17, Richard Rodgers Collection, Music Division, Library of Congress, Washington, DC.

36. Everett, 149.

37. See Block, *Rodgers*, 68–70 on how this song presages Rodgers and Hammerstein in style.

38. Block, 71–74.

39. Rental materials available from the Rodgers and Hammerstein organization.

40. See Chapter 6 for Idle's comments.

Chapter 2

1. "Top Grossers of 1949," *Variety*, January 4, 1949, 59.

2. *Variety* staff, "A Connecticut Yankee in King Arthur's Court," *Variety*, December 31, 1948 and Edwin Schallert, "Bing Crosby Jousts with Olden Knights," *Los Angeles Times*, April 29, 1949, A6.

3. *Variety* staff, "A Connecticut Yankee in King Arthur's Court."

4. Bosley Crowther, "The Same Old Crosby Playing 'Connecticut Yankee' for King Arthur, at Music Hall City Across the River," *New York Times*, April 8, 1949.

5. Robert Bookbinder, *The Films of Bing Crosby* (Secaucus, NJ: The Citadel Press, 1977), 47.

6. Gary Giddens, *Swinging on a Star: The War Years, 1940–1946* (New York: Little, Brown and Company, 2018), 89.

7. Gary Giddens, "Introduction: Bing Crosby—Nothing Is What It Seems," in *Going My Way: Bing Crosby and American Culture*, ed. Ruth Prigozy and Walter Raubicheck (Rochester, NY: University Rochester Press, 2007), 5.

8. Bernard F. Dick, "Crosby at Paramount: From Crooner to Actor," in *Going My Way: Bing Crosby and American Culture*, ed. Ruth Prigozy and Walter Raubicheck (Rochester, NY: University Rochester Press, 2007), 87.

9. Dick, 90.

10. See Giddens, *Swinging on a Star* for description and Gary Crosby and Ross Firestone, *Going My Own Way* (New York: Doubleday, 1983).

11. Gary Giddens, *A Pocketful of Dreams: The Early Years 1903–1940* (New York: Little, Brown and Company, 2001) and Giddens, *Swinging on a Star*.

12. Will Friedwald, "Conclusion: Bing Crosby—Architect of Twentieth-Century Style," in *Going My Way: Bing Crosby and American Culture*, ed. Ruth Prigozy and Walter Raubicheck (Rochester, NY: University Rochester Press, 2007), 164.

13. "Sir Cedric Hardwicke Is Dead; Actor on Stage and in Films, 71; Created Roles in Shaw Plays and Excelled in Character Parts for Many Years," *New York Times,* August 7, 1964.

14. J. Roger Oserholm, *Bing Crosby: A Bio-Bibliography* (Westport, CT: Greenwood Press, 1994), 267.

15. Crowther, "The Same Old Crosby."

16. David Carson Berry, "The Popular Songwriter as Composer: Mannerisms and design in the Music of Jimmy Van Heusen," *Indiana Theory Review* 21(Spring/Fall 2000): 48. Although he does not analyze the song in his essay, Berry includes "Once and For Always" in his broad survey of Van Heusen's stylistic trends.

17. Quoted in Osterholm, 267.

18. Rebecca A. Umland and Samuel J. Umland, *The Use of Arthurian Legend in Hollywood Film: From Connecticut Yankees to Fisher Kings* (Westport, CT: Greenwood Press, 1996), 47.

19. Elizabeth Archibald and Ad Putter, *The Cambridge Companion to Arthurian Legend* (New York: Cambridge University Press, 2009) and Alan Lupack, *The Oxford Guide to Arthurian Literature and Legend* (New York: Oxford University Press, 2007).

20. Susan Aronstein, *Hollywood Knights: Arthurian Cinema and the Politics of Nostalgia* (New York: Palgrave Macmillan, 2005), 175.

21. Stephen C. Shafer, "From Crooner to American Icon: Caricatures of Bing Crosby in American Cartoons from the 1930s to the 1950s," in *Going My Way: Bing Crosby and American Culture*, ed. Ruth Prigozy and Walter Raubicheck (Rochester, NY: University Rochester Press, 2007), 130.

22. Berry, 18–20.

23. Cue Sheets: *A Connecticut Yankee*, Jimmy Van Heusen Papers (Collection PASC 127-M). UCLA Library Special Collections, Charles E. Young Research Library, UCLA.

24. Symonds, 208.

25. Aronstein, 8.

Chapter 3

1. Irene Morra, "Constructing Camelot: Britain and the New World Musical," *Contemporary Theatre Review* 19, no. 1 (2009): 23.

2. Paul H. Santa Cruz, *Making JFK Matter: Popular Memory and the Thirty-Fifth President* (Denton: University of North Texas Press, 2015), 191.

3. Both *Brigadoon* (1947) and *My Fair Lady* (1956) by Lerner and Loewe have British settings and/or origins.

4. Ad Putter and Elizabeth Archibald, "Introduction," in *The Cambridge Companion to Arthurian Legend*, ed. Elizabeth Archibald and Ad Putter (New York: Cambridge University Press, 2009), 2.

5. T. H. White, *The Once and Future King* (New York: G.P. Putnam's Sons, 1958).

6. Norris J. Lacy, "The Arthur of the Twentieth and Twenty-First Centuries," in *The Cambridge Companion to Arthurian Legend*, ed. Elizabeth Archibald and Ad Putter (New York: Cambridge University Press, 2009), 123.

7. Alice Grellner, "Two Films That Sparkle: *The Sword in the Stone* and *Camelot*," in *Cinema Arthuriana: Twenty Essays*, rev. ed., ed. Kevin J. Harty (Jefferson, NC: McFarland & Co., 2002), 118.

8. Elisabeth Brewer, *T. H. White's* The Once and Future King, *Arthurian Studies* 30 (Woodbridge: D.S. Brewer, 1993), 93.

9. White, 497.

10. See John K. Crane, *T. H. White* (New York: Twayne Publishers, Inc., 1974), 105 and Brewer, 87–90.

11. Brewer, 90.

12. White, 353 and 376.

13. See Crane for discussion of Lancelot's love for Arthur and the role of God and Guenever in this tangle, 101–4.

14. Reference quoted in Brewer, 82.

15. Quoted in Brewer, 99.

16. Brewer, 100.

17. Brewer, 95–98.

18. Crane, 113–14.

19. Julie Andrews, et al., "My Favorite Things: Julie Andrews Remembers," *The Sound of Music*, directed by Robert Wise (Beverly Hills, CA: Twentieth Century Fox Home Entertainment, 1965), DVD.

20. Quoted in Edward Jablonski, *Alan Jay Lerner: A Biography* (New York: Henry and Holt Co., 1996), 173.

21. Dominic McHugh, *Alan Jay Lerner: A Lyricist's Letters* (New York: Oxford University Press, 2014), 109.

22. Joseph Swain, *The Broadway Musical: A Critical and Musical Survey* (Lanham, MD: The Scarecrow Press, 2002), 215.

23. Quoted in McHugh, 234.

24. Miles Kreuger, telephone conversation with author, June 12, 2018.

25. Miles Kreuger, telephone conversation with author, June 12, 2018.

26. Ethan Mordden, *Open a New Window: The Broadway Musical in the 1960s* (New York: Palgrave Macmillan, 2001), 27.

27. See Mordden, 28 for more on this anecdote.

28. For further discussion of the development and production of *Camelot*, see both Mordden, 23–33, and Scott Miller, *Deconstructing Harold Hill: An Insider's Guide to Musical Theatre* (Portsmouth, NH: Heinemann, 2000), 1–23.

29. Harold Taubman, "'Camelot' Partly Enchanted: Lerner-Loewe Musical Opens at Majestic," *New York Times*, December 5, 1950.

30. Swain, 216.

31. Gene Lees, *The Musical Worlds of Lerner and Loewe* (Lincoln: University of Nebraska, 1990), 171.

32. Geoffrey Block gives an excellent overview of integration in his essay "Integration," in *The Oxford Handbook of the American Musical*, ed. Knapp et al. (New York: Oxford University Press, 2011), 97–110.

33. Elizabeth Wollman, *A Critical Companion to the American Stage Musical* (New York: Bloomsbury, 2017), 112.

34. Raymond Knapp, *The American Musical and the Performance of Personal Identity* (Princeton: Princeton University Press, 2006), 171.

35. As early as Parthy in *Show Boat*, villains or unlikeable characters in musicals do not sing at all as music represents empathy and likeability in the genre.

36. See Knapp, 170–80 for full musical analysis.

37. Knapp, 174.

38. Dominic McHugh and Amy Asch, eds., *The Complete Lyrics of Alan Jay Lerner* (New York: Oxford University Press, 2018), 290.

39. Box 2, Folder 9, Frederick Loewe Collection, Music Division, Library of Congress.

40. See Knapp, 174–75 for a discussion for how the opening songs of the main characters build on one another, reinforcing their connection.

41. William A. Everett, "King Arthur in Popular Musical Theatre and Musical Film," in *King Arthur in Music*, ed. Richard Barber (New York: D.S. Brewer, 2002), 153.

42. Knapp, 171.

43. Mordden, 27.

44. Everett, 154.

45. McHugh and Asch include lyrics for the cut song, "The Quests," which would have been a set piece depicting the questing of Lancelot and other knights. The song, though adding to the already lengthy musical, would have provided another key connection to White's novel. For full lyrics, see McHugh and Asch, 318–21.

46. McHugh and Asch, 305.

47. Box 2, Folder 8, Frederick Loewe Collection, Music Division, Library of Congress. Also, quoted in McHugh and Asch, 314.

48. Knapp, 176.

49. Knapp, 176.

50. Knapp, 176.

51. Megan Woller, "The Lusty Court of *Camelot* (1967): Exploring Sexuality in the Hollywood Adaptation," *Music and the Moving Image* 8, no. 1 (Spring 2015): 13–14.

52. Richard Harris, et al., "*Camelot* World Premiere," special features, *Camelot*, directed by Joshua Logan (Burbank, CA: Warner Home Video, 1998), DVD.

53. Box 99, Folder 19, Joshua Logan Papers, Manuscript Division, Library of Congress, Washington, DC.

54. Box 99, Folder 10, Joshua Logan Papers, Manuscript Division, Library of Congress, Washington, DC.

55. Box 99, Folder 12, Joshua Logan Papers, Manuscript Division, Library of Congress, Washington, DC.

56. Box 99, Folder 11, Joshua Logan Papers, Manuscript Division, Library of Congress, Washington, DC.

57. Matthew Kennedy, *Roadshow!: The Fall of Film Musicals in the 1960s* (Oxford University Press, 2014), 89.

58. Bosley Crowther, "Screen: *Camelot* Arrives at Warner: Film Hasn't Overcome Stage Plays Defects," *New York Times*, October 26, 1967.

59. Charlie Champlin, "*Camelot* Opens at Cinerama Dome," *Los Angeles Times*, November 3, 1967.

60. Richard L. Coe, "*Camelot* Tommyrot," *The Washington Post*, November 9, 1967.

61. Marjorie Adams, "*Camelot* Vanessa's Vehicle to the Stars," *The Boston Globe*, November 2, 1967; Roger Ebert, "Camelot," *Chicago Sun Times,* October 30, 1967; "Camelot Review," *Variety*, October 25, 1967.

62. The 1961 film adaptation of *West Side Story* makes a similar shift by switching the song order positions of "Cool" and "Officer Krupke" in order to highlight the tragedy.

63. Raymond Knapp, "Getting Real: Stage Musical versus Filmic Realism in Film Adaptations from *Camelot* to *Cabaret*," in *The Oxford Handbook of Musical Theatre Screen Adaptations*, ed. Dominic McHugh (New York: Oxford University Press, 2019), 55–84.

64. Knapp, "Getting Real," 62.

65. Sheldon Hall and Steve Neale, *Epics, Spectacles, and Blockbusters: A Hollywood History* (Detroit: Wayne State University Press, 2010), 5.

66. Interview from 12 minutes into the documentary. Joshua Logan, et al., *The Story of Camelot* from *Camelot*, directed by Joshua Logan (Burbank, CA: Warner Bros., 1998), Special Edition DVD.

67. Box 99, Folder 15, Joshua Logan Papers, Manuscript Division, Library of Congress, Washington, DC.

68. Knapp, *Personal Identity*, 172.

69. Miller, 5.

70. Box 1, Folder 8, Alan Jay Lerner Papers, Music Division, Library of Congress.

71. Box 1, Folder 8, Alan Jay Lerner Papers, Music Division, Library of Congress.

72. Box 1, Folder 8 and Box 2, Folder 1, Alan Jay Lerner Papers, Music Division, Library of Congress.

73. Box 99, Folder 21, Joshua Logan Papers, Manuscript Division, Library of Congress, Washington, DC.

74. Box 99, Folder 19, Joshua Logan Papers, Manuscript Division, Library of Congress, Washington, DC.

75. Knapp, "Getting Real," 55–84.

76. Knapp, "Getting Real," 64.

77. Richard Harris, et al., "*Camelot* World Premiere," special features.

78. Miller, 10–11.

79. Alan Jay Lerner and Frederick Loewe, *Camelot: A New Musical* (New York: Random House, 1961), 87.

80. Woller, 14–15.

81. Box 2, Folder 1, Alan Jay Lerner Papers, Music Division, Library of Congress.

82. Alan Jay Lerner, Final Screenplay, 89. Box 2, Folder 1, Alan Jay Lerner Papers, Music Division, Library of Congress.

83. Woller, 12–15.

84. Woller, 3–18.

85. Brewer, 78.

86. Woller, 9–14.

87. Elizabeth Archibald, "Malory's Lancelot and Guenevere," in *A Companion to Arthurian Literature*, ed. Helen Fulton (Malden, MA, Wiley-Blackwell, 2009), 312.

88. See Brewer's analysis for an encapsulation of this reading.

89. Thomas L. Riis and Ann Sears, "The Successors of Rodgers and Hammerstein from the 1940s to the 1960s," in *The Cambridge Companion to the Musical*, ed. William A. Everett and Paul R. Laird (New York: Cambridge University Press, 2008), 183–84; David Walsh and Len Platt, *Musical Theater and American Culture* (Westport, CT: Greenwood, 2003), 116; Jones, 169–70; Knapp, 170–1; Stacy Wolf, *A Problem Like Maria: Gender and Sexuality in the American Musical* (Ann Arbor: University of Michigan Press, 2002), 161.

90. Lerner and Loewe, 15.

91. Quoted in Mark Steyn, *Broadway Babies Say Goodnight: Musicals Then and Now* (New York: Routledge, 1999), 151.

92. Knapp, 170–9 and John Bush Jones, *Our Musicals, Ourselves: A Social History of the American Musical Theatre* (Lebanon, NH: Brandeis University Press, 2003), 169.

93. Jones, 169.

94. Kennedy, 91.

95. This song was cut as part of the extensive revision process which occurred during the first few months of the Broadway run.

96. Walsh and Platt also look at the connections between Kennedy's administration and subsequent assassination with *Camelot*. See Walsh and Platt, 116.

97. Box 15, Folder 22, Alan Jay Lerner Papers, Music Division, Library of Congress.

Chapter 4

1. See Elisabeth Brewer, *T. H. White's* The Once and Future King (Cambridge: D. S. Brewer, 1993).

2. Brewer, 32.

3. Kurth Sprague, *T.H. White's Troubled Heart: Women in* The Once and Future King (Rochester: Boydell & Brewer, 2007), 90.

4. C. M. Adderley, "The Best Thing for Being Sad: Education and Educators in T. H. White's *The Once and Future King*," *Quondam et Futurus: A Journal of Arthurian Interpretations* 2, no. 1 (Spring 1992): 60.

5. Adderley, 63.

6. T. H. White, *The Once and Future King* (New York: G.P. Putnam's Sons, 1958), 120–9.

7. White, 172.

8. White, 196.

9. White, 197.

10. Douglas Brode, *Multiculturalism and the Mouse: Race and Sex in Disney Entertainment* (Austin: University of Texas Press, 2005); Eleanor Byrne and Martin McQuillan, *Deconstructing Disney* (Sterling, VA: Pluto Press, 1999); Henry A. Giroux and Grace Pollock, *The Mouse That Roared: Disney and the End of Innocence* (New York: Rowman and Littlefield, 2010); Elizabeth Bell, Lynda Haas, and Laura Sells, eds., *From Mouse to Mermaid: The Politics of Film, Gender, and Culture* (Bloomington: Indiana University Press, 1995); Annalee R. Ward, *Mouse Morality: The Rhetoric of Disney Animated Film* (Austin: University of Texas Press, 2002); Janet Wasko, *Understanding Disney: The Manufacture of Fantasy* (Malden, MA: Blackwell, 2001).

11. Ward's *Mouse Morality* as well as Giroux and Pollock's *Mouse That Roared*, in particular, make this argument.

12. Ward, 2.

13. Jack Zipes, "Breaking the Disney Spell," in *From Mouse to Mermaid: The Politics of Film, Gender, and Culture*, ed. Elizabeth Bell, et al. (Bloomington: Indiana University Press, 1995), 33.

14. Wasko, 113.

15. For more information, see Janet Wasko, *Understanding Disney*.

16. For further discussion, see Chris Pallant, *Demystifying Disney: A History of Disney Feature Animation* (New York: Continuum, 2011), 3–13.

17. Pallant, 11.
18. Michael J. Barrier, *Hollywood Cartoons: American Animation in Its Golden Age* (New York: Oxford University Press, 1999), 567.
19. Barrier, 567–68.
20. Bosley Crowther, "Eight New Movies Arrive for the Holidays," *New York Times*, December 26, 1963.
21. Crowther, "Eight New Movies."
22. *Variety* staff, "The Sword in the Stone," *Variety*, December 31, 1962.
23. James Bohn, *Music in Disney's Animated Features: Snow White and the Seven Dwarfs to The Jungle Book* (Jackson: University Press of Mississippi, 2017), 190.
24. Bohn, 188.
25. Brode, 218.
26. White spells the wizard's name as Merlyn; Disney uses the spelling Merlin.
27. Bohn, 180.
28. Quoted in Robert B. Sherman and Richard M. Sherman, *Walt's Time: From Before to Beyond* (Santa Clarita: Camphor Tree, 1998), 141.
29. Quoted in David Tietyen, *The Musical World of Walt Disney* (Milwaukee, WI: Hal Leonard, 1990), 128.
30. Sherman and Sherman, 28.
31. Sherman and Sherman, 28.
32. Brode, 219.
33. Wasko, 113.
34. Bohn, 190.
35. Wolfgang Reitherman, "Never Before Seen Alternate Opening: Where Wart Meets Merlin," special feature, *The Sword in the Stone*, 50th Anniversary Edition (Burbank, CA: Disney, 2013).
36. Raymond H. Thomson, "The Ironic Tradition in Four Arthurian Films," in *Cinema Arthuriana: Twenty Essays*, rev. ed. (Jefferson, NC: MacFarland, 2002), 112.
37. Giroux and Pollock, 92.
38. George Rodosthenous, "Introduction," in *The Disney Musical on Stage and Screen: Critical Approaches from 'Snow White' to 'Frozen'*, ed. George Rodosthenous (New York: Bloomsbury, 2017), 5.
39. Brode, 221.
40. Richard M. Sherman and Robert B. Sherman, "Music Magic: The Sherman Brothers," special feature, *The Sword in the Stone*, 50th Anniversary Edition (Burbank, CA: Disney, 2013).
41. Sherman and Sherman, *Walt's Time*, 29.
42. Wasko, 117–19.
43. Wasko, 119.
44. Grellner, 119 and Thomson, 111.
45. Grellner, 118.
46. Elisabeth Brewer, *T. H. White's* The Once and Future King, *Arthurian Studies* 30 (Woodbridge: D.S. Brewer, 1993), 214.

47. Ross Care, "Makes Walt's Music: Music for Disney Animation, 1928–1967," in *The Cartoon Music Book*, ed. Daniel Goldmark and Yuval Taylor (Chicago: A Cappella Books, 2002), 34.

48. Sherman and Sherman, "Music Magic."

49. Bohn, 236–37.

50. Leonard Maltin, *The Disney Films*, 4th ed. (New York: Disney Editions, 2000), 216–18.

51. Bohn, 187.

52. William Everett, "King Arthur in Popular Musical Theatre and Musical Film," in *Arthurian Studies: King Arthur in Music*, ed. Richard Barber (New York: D.S. Brewer, 2002), 157.

53. Sherman and Sherman, "Music Magic."

54. Sherman and Sherman, "Music Magic."

55. Bohn, 188.

56. Brewer, 33.

57. Reference from opening sequence: Uther's death ushers in a dark age. Wolfgang Riethermann, *The Sword in the Stone* (Burbank, CA: Disney, 1963).

Chapter 5

1. Raymond H. Thomson, "The Ironic Tradition in Four Arthurian Films," in *Cinema Arthuriana: Twenty Essays*, ed. Kevin J. Harty (Jefferson, NC: McFarland, 2002), 114.

2. Susan Aronstein, *Hollywood Knights: Arthurian Cinema and the Politics of Nostalgia* (New York: Palgrave Macmillan, 2005), 112.

3. Rebecca A. Umland and Samuel J. Umland, *The Use of Arthurian Legend in Hollywood Film: From Connecticut Yankees to Fisher Kings* (Westport, CT: Greenwood Press, 1996), 67.

4. Umland and Umland, 63.

5. Elizabeth Murrell, "History Revenged: Monty Python Translates Chrétien De Troyes's Perceval, or the Story of the Grail (Again)," *Journal of Film and Video* 50, no. 1 (1998): 50.

6. Daniel L. Hoffman, "Not Dead Yet: Monty Python and the Holy Grail in the Twenty-First Century," in *Cinema Arthuriana: Twenty Essays*, ed. Kevin J. Harty (Jefferson, NC: McFarland, 2002), 137.

7. Andrew Lynch, "Imperial Arthur: Home and Away," in *The Cambridge Companion to Arthurian Legend*, ed. Elizabeth Archibald and Ad Putter (New York: Cambridge University Press, 2009), 181.

8. Kevin J. Harty, "An Overview," in *Cinema Arthuriana: Twenty Essays*, ed. Kevin J. Harty (Jefferson, NC: McFarland, 2002), 19.

9. Darl Larsen, *A Book about the Film Monty Python and the Holy Grail: All the References from African Swallows to Zoot* (New York: Rowman and Littlefield, 2015).

10. Hoffman, 138.

11. Vincent Canby, "*Monty Python and the Holy Grail,*" *The New York Times*, April 28, 1975.

12. "Commentary with John Cleese, Eric Idle and Michael Palin," special features, *Monty Python and the Holy Grail*, 40th Anniversary Blu-Ray Edition, directed by Terry Gilliam and Terry Jones (Culver City, CA: Sony Pictures, 2015) and "Commentary with Terry Gilliam and Terry Jones," special features, *Monty Python and the Holy Grail*, 40th Anniversary Blu-Ray Edition, directed by Terry Gilliam and Terry Jones (Culver City, CA: Sony Pictures, 2015).

13. Gilliam and Jones, "Commentary," 01:30–01:52.

14. Larsen, xx.

15. See Jeffrey Miller, *Something Completely Different: British Television and American Culture* (Minneapolis: University of Minnesota Press, 2000) and Ellen Bishop, "Bakhtin, Carnival and Comedy: The New Grotesque in *Monty Python and the Holy Grail,*" *Film Criticism* 15, no. 1 (Fall 1990): 49–64.

16. Umland and Umland, 64.

17. Hoffman, 137.

18. Jones, "Commentary," 10:45.

19. Hendrik Hertzberg, "Naughty Bits," *The New Yorker*, March 29, 1976.

20. Larsen, 68.

21. Jones, "Commentary," 10:10–10:50.

22. Jones, "Commentary," 10:25–10:50.

23. Martha W. Driver, "What's Accuracy Got to Do With It?: Historicity and Authenticity in Medieval Film," in *The Medieval Hero Onscreen: Representations from Beowulf to Buffy*, ed. Martha W. Driver and Sid Ray (Jefferson, NC: MacFarland, 2004), 21.

24. William F. Woods, "Authenticating Realism in Medieval Film," in *The Medieval Hero Onscreen: Representations from Beowulf to Buffy*, ed. Martha W. Driver and Sid Ray (Jefferson, NC: MacFarland, 2004), 48.

25. Woods, 39.

26. Woods, 43.

27. Martha W. Driver and Sid Ray, eds., *The Medieval Hero Onscreen: Representations from Beowulf to Buffy* (Jefferson, NC: MacFarland, 2004).

28. David Day, "*Monty Python and the Holy Grail:* Madness with a Definite Method," in *Cinema Arthuriana: Twenty Essays*, ed. Kevin J. Harty (Jefferson, NC: McFarland, 2002), 131.

29. Day, 131.

30. Palin, "Commentary," 27:18–27:22.

31. Terry Jones, ed., *Monty Python and the Holy Grail (Book)* (London: Eyre Methuen, 1977).

32. Several stories referenced in the following paragraphs appear in a number of books, television interviews, and film features. For major examples, see John Cleese, Terry Gilliam, et al., *The Pythons: Autobiography by the Pythons* (New York: Thomas Dunne, 2003) and David Morgan, *Monty Python Speaks!: The Complete Oral History*, rev. ed. (New York: Harper Collins, 2019).

33. See Morgan, 151–52.

34. Morgan, 156.

35. Morgan, 148–88.

36. For more on this style, see Cleese, Gilliam, et al.

37. See Cleese, "Commentary" for some particular stories.

38. See Morgan, 167 and Gilliam and Jones, "Commentary," 7:18–7:40.

39. Quoted in Morgan, 192.

40. Quoted in Morgan, 192.

41. Miller, 111.

42. See Morgan for ABC show and subsequent lawsuit, 209–19.

43. Quoted in Morgan, 201.

44. Cleese, Gilliam, et al., 269.

45. Internet Movie Database, "*Monty Python and the Holy Grail*," accessed February 24, 2020, https://www.imdb.com/title/tt0071853/.

46. Vincent Canby, "*Monty Python and the Holy Grail*," *The New York Times*, April 28, 1975.

47. Gene Siskel, "Now Comes King Arthur to Cut 'em off at the Pass," *Chicago Tribune*, June 9, 1975.

48. Miller, 113.

49. Miller, 131.

50. Gary Hardcastle and George Reich, "'What's All This Then?': The Introduction," in *Monty Python and Philosophy: Nudge Nudge, Think Think!*, ed. Gary L. Hardcastle and George L. Reisch (Peru, IN: Open Court, 2006), 2.

51. Giorgio Biancorosso, *Situated Listening: The Sound of Absorption in Classical Cinema* (New York: Oxford University Press, 2016), 3.

52. De Wolfe Music, "Nitrate // Bitrate: 100 Years of De Wolfe Music," accessed February 24, 2020, https://www.dewolfemusic.com/page/nitrate_to_bitrate.

53. Idle, "Commentary," 12:09–12:25.

54. Idle, "Commentary," 12:30.

55. Jones, "Commentary," 02:30–02:35.

56. Jones, "Commentary," 02:30–02:35.

57. Idle, *Pythons*, 264.

58. Haines writes a chapter detailing the sound and examples of each of these types. John Haines, *Music in Films on the Middle Ages: Authenticity vs. Fantasy* (New York: Routledge, 2014).

59. Haines, 19.

60. Haines, 134.

61. Gilliam, "Commentary," 02:15.

62. Haines, 46–47.

63. Haines, 71.

64. Palin, "Commentary," 55:39 and Idle, "Commentary," 55:55.

65. Palin, "Commentary," 51:08

66. Gilliam, "Commentary," 22:55.

67. Aronstein, 112.

68. Larsen, 247.

69. Larsen, 251.
70. Palin, "Commentary," 23:00.
71. Larsen, 244; Jones, ed., "Camelot, It Is a Silly Place," scene 10.
72. Larsen, 244.
73. Cleese, "Commentary," 22:32.
74. John M. Clum argues that beyond the stereotype, musical theater does indeed play a role in gay culture. See John M. Clum, *Something for the Boys: Musical Theater and Gay Culture* (New York: St. Martin's Press, 1999).
75. Palin, "Commentary," 56:15.
76. Gabriel Fauré's "Pie Jesu" movement may be the most well known.
77. Haines, 128.
78. Bishop, 60.
79. Haines, 88.
80. Idle, "Commentary," 33:19.
81. Graham Chapman, et al., *Monty Python and the Holy Grail*, directed by Terry Gilliam and Terry Jones (Culver City, CA: Sony Pictures, 1974), Blu-Ray, 1:04:55–1:05:00.

Chapter 6

1. Eric Idle and John Du Prez, *Monty Python's Spamalot* (New York: Theatrical Rights Worldwide, 2005).
2. Eric Idle, *Always Look on the Bright Side of Life: A Sortabiography* (New York: Crown Archetype, 2018), 220.
3. Idle, 217.
4. "*Life of Brian*: Facts and Figures," *Telegraph*, October 11, 2011, accessed March 2, 2020, https://www.telegraph.co.uk/culture/8818328/Life-of-Brian-facts-and-figures.html.
5. See David Morgan, *Monty Python Speaks!: The Complete Oral History*, rev. ed., *Revised and Updated Edition* (New York: Harper Collins, 2019), 319–30 for pre-*Spamalot* reunion in Aspen.
6. Both of these popular works were released during the research of this book.
7. See Morgan, 317–18 for Palin and Cleese's statement about *The Life of Brian* as the best Python film.
8. Idle, 190.
9. At the time of this writing, the most recent release was the 40th Anniversary Blu-Ray, and Netflix has the film available. Additional releases include a 2001 Special Edition DVD and a 35th Anniversary Blu-Ray.
10. Idle, 205.
11. Quoted in Morgan, 342.
12. Quoted in Morgan, 342.
13. *Spamalot* also made $1.6 million the day after it opened, a little over half of *The Producers* record but more than respectable. Jesse McKinley, "Arts, Briefly; 'Spamalot'

Gives Broadway a Boost," *New York Times*, March 19, 2005. For complete statistics, see https://www.ibdb.com/broadway-production/spamalot-384262#Statistics, accessed July 8, 2019.

14. Michael Phillips, "Is Spamalot Digestible?," *Chicago Tribune*, January 10, 2005.
15. Ben Brantley, "A Quest Beyond the Grail," *New York Times*, March 18, 2005.
16. David Rooney, "*Monty Python's Spamalot*," *Variety*, March 17, 2005.
17. Raymond Knapp, *The American Musical and the Formation of National Identity* (Princeton: Princeton University Press, 2005), 122.
18. Laurie A. Finke and Susan Aronstein, "Got Grail? Monty Python and the Broadway Stage," *Theatre Survey* 48, no. 2 (November 2007): 295.
19. Finke and Aronstein, 302.
20. Finke and Aronstein, 303.
21. Anne Beggs, "'For Urinetown Is Your Town . . .': The Fringes of Broadway," *Theatre Journal* 62, no. 1 (2010): 51.
22. Beggs, 42–43.
23. Rooney, "*Monty Python's Spamalot*."
24. Jessica Sternfeld and Elizabeth A. Wollman, "After the Golden Age," in *The Oxford Handbook of the American Musical*, ed. Raymond Knapp, Mitchell Morris, and Stacy Wolf (New York: Oxford University Press, 2011), 123.
25. Bud Coleman, "New Horizons: The Musical at the Dawn of the Twenty-First Century," in *The Cambridge Companion to the Musical*, ed. William A. Everett and Paul R. Laird, 2nd ed. (New York: Cambridge University Press, 2008), 292.
26. Jessica Sternfeld, *The Megamusical* (Bloomington: Indiana University Press, 2006), 334.
27. Coleman, 291.
28. Elizabeth L. Wollman, *A Critical Companion to the American Stage Musical* (New York: Bloomsbury Methuen Drama, 2017), 181.
29. Larry Stempel, *Showtime: A History of the Broadway Musical Theater* (New York: W. W. Norton, 2010), 635.
30. Sternfeld, 77–79.
31. Steven Adler, *On Broadway: Art and Commerce on the Great White Way* (Carbondale: Southern Illinois University Press, 2004), 189.
32. See Adler, 189–90.
33. Alex Symonds, *Mel Brooks in the Cultural Industries: Survival and Prolonged Adaptation* (Edinburgh: Edinburgh University Press, 2012), 163.
34. Symonds, 164.
35. Scott Miller, *Strike Up the Band: A New History of the Musical Theatre* (Portsmouth, NH: Heinemann, 2007), 225.
36. Idle, 155.
37. Quoted in Morgan, 335.
38. John Bush Jones, *Our Musicals, Ourselves: A Social History of the American Musical Theatre* (Lebanon, NH: Brandeis University Press, 2003), 2.
39. See Sternfeld, 344–48, for a discussion of the effect of 9/11 on Broadway shows, such as *The Producers*, in the weeks and months after the attacks. *Spamalot* was several

years removed, and Broadway settled back into a routine, but an impact surely remains.

40. John Kenrick, *Musical Theatre: A History* (New York: Continuum, 2008), 371.

41. Kenrick, 372–4 and Wollman, 180.

42. Anne McLeer, "Practical Perfection? The Nanny Negotiates Gender, Class, and Family Contradictions in 1960s Popular Culture," *NWSA Journal* 14, no. 2 (Summer 2002): 81.

43. Jones, 305–30.

44. Quoted in Morgan, 340.

45. Stempel, 636.

46. Kenrick, 375.

47. Finke and Aronstein, 302.

48. Graham Chapman, et al., *Monty Python and the Holy Grail*, directed by Terry Gilliam and Terry Jones (Culver City, CA: Sony Pictures, 1975).

49. Idle, 101.

50. Idle, 101.

51. Idle, 206.

52. John Haines, *Music in Films on the Middle Ages: Authenticity vs. Fantasy* (New York: Routledge, 2014), 26–44.

53. Susan Aronstein, "'In My Own Idiom': Social Critique, Campy Gender, and Queer Performance in *Monty Python and the Holy Grail*," in *Queer Movie Medievalisms*, ed. Kathleen Coyne Kelly and Tison Pugh (Burlington, VT: Ashgate, 2009), 122.

54. Aronstein, "In My Own Idiom," 122.

55. Finke and Aronstein, 306.

56. Idle, 208.

57. In fact, it should be noted that a 2010 UK Cast Album featuring Marcus Brigstocke as King Arthur is readily available via streaming services such as Spotify as well as on CD. This album is based on a short British touring production from 2010.

58. Note that the original Broadway cast recording omits brief reprises of the shortest songs, including "King Arthur's Song." As the sixteen-bar verse lasts about fifteen seconds, it appears only in conjunction with the "Laker Girls' Theme." It is, however, Arthur's theme.

59. See Aronstein, "In My Own Idiom," 115–16 for some general discussion on this issue.

60. The theater at the Wynn hotel had initially housed *Avenue Q*, but the show did not do as well as expected and closed. As such, the theater was renamed the Grail theater and contracted *Spamalot* for an expected decade run. This show similarly did not do as well as expected and closed after one year. See Hilary Baker, "From Broadway to Vegas: The Triumphs and Tribulations of *Avenue Q*," *Studies in Musical Theatre* 5, no. 1 (2011): 71–83 and Idle, *Always Look on the Bright Side*, 220–24.

61. A small example of this is changing any references to New York to the tour stops. When I saw *Spamalot* in 2008 in South Bend, Indiana, the audience member with the Grail seat was the "best peasant in South Bend."

Archival Collections

Alan Jay Lerner Papers, Music Division, Library of Congress, Washington, DC.

Frederick Loewe Collection, Music Division, Library of Congress, Washington, DC.

Jimmy Van Heusen Papers (Collection PASC 127-M). UCLA Library Special Collections, Charles E. Young Research Library, UCLA.

Joshua Logan Papers, Manuscript Division, Library of Congress, Washington, DC.

Richard Rodgers Collection, Music Division, Library of Congress, Washington, DC.

Bibliography

Adderley, C. M. "The Best Thing for Being Sad: Education and Educators in T. H. White's *The Once and Future King.*" *Quondam et Futurus: A Journal of Arthurian Interpretations* 2, no. 1 (Spring 1992): 55–68.

Adler, Steven. *On Broadway: Art and Commerce on the Great White Way.* Carbondale: Southern Illinois University Press, 2004.

Andrew, Dudley. "Adaptation." In *Concepts in Film Theory,* 96–106. New York: Oxford University Press, 1984.

Archibald, Elizabeth, and Ad Putter, eds. *The Cambridge Companion to Arthurian Legend.* New York: Cambridge University Press, 2009.

Archibald, Elizabeth. "Malory's Lancelot and Guenevere." In *A Companion to Arthurian Literature,* edited by Helen Fulton, 312–325. Malden, MA: Wiley-Blackwell, 2009.

Aronstein, Susan. *Hollywood Knights: Arthurian Cinema and the Politics of Nostalgia.* New York: Palgrave Macmillan, 2005.

Aronstein, Susan. "'In My Own Idiom': Social Critique, Campy Gender, and Queer Performance in *Monty Python and the Holy Grail.*" In *Queer Movie Medievalisms,* edited by Kathleen Coyne Kelly and Tison Pugh, 115–128. Burlington, VT: Ashgate, 2009.

Baker, Hilary. "From Broadway to Vegas: The Triumphs and Tribulations of *Avenue Q.*" *Studies in Musical Theatre* 5, no. 1 (2011): 71–83.

Barrier, Michael J. *Hollywood Cartoons: American Animation in Its Golden Age.* New York: Oxford University Press, 1999.

Beggs, Anne. "'For Urinetown Is Your Town . . .': The Fringes of Broadway." *Theatre Journal* 62, no. 1 (2010): 41–56.

Bell, Elizabeth, Lynda Haas, and Laura Sells, eds. *From Mouse to Mermaid: The Politics of Film, Gender, and Culture.* Bloomington: Indiana University Press, 1995.

Beloin, Edmund. *A Connecticut Yankee in King Arthur's Court.* Directed by Tay Garnett. Universal City, CA: Paramount Pictures, 1949. DVD.

Bellamy, Gladys C. *Mark Twain as a Literary Artist.* Norman: University of Oklahoma Press, 2012.

Berry, David C. "The Popular Songwriter as Composer: Mannerisms and Design in the Music of Jimmy Van Heusen." *Indiana Theory Review* 21 (Spring/Fall 2000): 1–51.

Biancorosso, Giorgio. *Situated Listening: The Sound of Absorption in Classical Cinema.* New York: Oxford University Press, 2016.

Birkett, Danielle, and Dominic McHugh, eds. *Adapting the Wizard of Oz: Musical Versions from Baum to MGM and Beyond.* New York: Oxford University Press, 2019.

Bishop, Ellen. "Bakhtin, Carnival and Comedy: The New Grotesque in *Monty Python and the Holy Grail.*" *Film Criticism* 15, no. 1 (Fall 1999): 49–64.

Block, Geoffrey. *Enchanted Evenings: The Broadway Musical from* Showboat *to Sondheim and Lloyd Webber.* 2nd ed. New York: Oxford University Press, 2009.

Block, Geoffrey. "Integration." In *The Oxford Handbook of the American Musical,* edited by Raymond Knapp et al, 97–110. New York: Oxford University Press, 2011.

Block, Geoffrey. *Richard Rodgers.* New Haven, CT: Yale University Press, 2003.

Block, Geoffrey. *The Richard Rodgers Reader*. New York: Oxford University Press, 2002.

Bohn, James. *Music in Disney's Animated Features: Snow White and the Seven Dwarfs to the Jungle Book*. Jackson: University Press of Mississippi, 2017.

Bookbinder, Robert. *The Films of Bing Crosby*. Secaucus, NJ: The Citadel Press, 1977.

Brewer, Elisabeth. *T. H. White's The Once and Future King*. Woodbridge: D.S. Brewer, 1993.

Brode, Douglas. *Multiculturalism and the Mouse: Race and Sex in Disney Entertainment*. Austin: University of Texas Press, 2005.

Budd, Louis J. *Mark Twain: The Contemporary Reviews*. Cambridge: Cambridge University Press, 1999.

Byrne, Eleanor, and Martin McQuillan. *Deconstructing Disney*. Sterling, VA: Pluto Press, 1999.

Carter, Everett. "The Meaning of A Connecticut Yankee." *American Literature* 50, no. 3 (1978): 418–40.

Cleese, John, Terry Gilliam, et al. *The Pythons: Autobiography by the Pythons*. New York: Thomas Dunne, 2003.

Clum, John M. *Something for the Boys: Musical Theater and Gay Culture*. New York: St. Martin's Press, 1999.

Cohan, Steven, and Ina R. Hark. *The Road Movie Book*. London: Psychology Press, 1997.

Coleman, Bud. "New Horizons: The Musical at the Dawn of the Twenty-First Century." In *The Cambridge Companion to the Musical*, edited by William A Everett and Paul R. Laird, 356–80. New York: Cambridge University Press, 2008.

Cooper, Lydia R. "Human Voices: Language and Conscience in Twain's 'A Connecticut Yankee in King Arthur's Court.'" *Canadian Review of American Studies* 23, no. 1 (2009): 65–85.

Covici, Pascal. *Mark Twain's Humor: The Image of a World*. Dallas, TX: Southern Methodist University Press, 1962.

Crane, John K. *T. H. White*. New York: Twayne, 1974.

Crosby, Gary, and Ross Firestone. *Going My Own Way*. New York: Doubleday, 1983.

Cutchins, Dennis, Katja Krebs, and Eckart Voigts, eds. *The Routledge Companion to Adaptation*. New York: Routledge, 2018.

DeWolfe Music. "Nitrate // Bitrate: 100 Years of DeWolfe Music." Accessed February 24, 2020. https://www.dewolfemusic.com/page/nitrate_to_bitrate.

Dobski, Bernard J., and Benjamin A. Kleinerman. "'We Should See Certain Things Ye, Let Us Hope and Believe': Technology, Sex, and Politics in Mark Twain's Connecticut Yankee." *The Review of Politics* 69, no. 4 (Fall 2007): 599–624. https://doi.org/10.1017/S0034670507000976.

Driver, Martha W., and Sid Ray, eds. *The Medieval Hero Onscreen: Representations from Beowulf to Buffy*. Jefferson, NC: MacFarland, 2004.

Dunne, Michael. "Bing Crosby's Cinematic 'Song of the South.'" *Journal of Popular Film & Television* 32, no. 1 (Spring 2004): 31–38.

Everett, William A. "King Arthur in Popular Musical Theatre and Musical Film." In *Arthurian Studies: King Arthur in Music*, edited by Richard Barber, 145–60. New York: D.S. Brewer, 2002.

Fields, Herbert, Lorenz Hart, and Richard Rodgers. *A Connecticut Yankee*. New York: R&H Theatricals, 1977.

Fields, Herbert, Lorenz Hart, and Richard Rodgers. *A Connecticut Yankee*. Directed by Max Liebman. Pleasantville, NY: Video Artists International, 1955. DVD.

Finke, Laurie A., and Susan Aronstein. "Got Grail? Monty Python and the Broadway Stage." *Theatre Survey* 48, no. 2 (Fall 2007): 289–311.

Fulton, Helen. *Companion to Arthurian Literature.* Chichester, UK: Wiley-Blackwell, 2012.

Gehring, Wes D. *Forties Film Funnymen: The Decade's Great Comedians at Work in the Shadow of War.* Jefferson, NC: McFarland, 2014.

Giancarlo, Matthew. "Mark Twain and the Critique of Philology." *ELH* 78, no. 1 (Spring 2011): 213–37. https://www.jstor.org/stable/41236540.

Giddins, Gary. *Bing Crosby: A Pocketful of Dreams: The Early Years 1903-1940.* New York: Little, Brown and Company, 2001.

Giddins, Gary. *Bing Crosby: Swinging on a Star: The War Years 1940-1946.* New York: Little, Brown and Company, 2018.

Gilliam, Terry, and Terry Jones, dirs. *Monty Python and the Holy Grail.* Culver City, CA: Sony Pictures, 1974. DVD.

Giroux, Henry A., and Grace Pollock. *The Mouse That Roared: Disney and the End of Innocence.* New York: Rowman and Littlefield, 2010.

Grant, Barry K. "Introduction: Movies and the 1960s." In *American Cinema of the 1960s: Themes and Variations,* edited by Barry Keith Grant, 1–21. New Brunswick, NJ: Rutgers University Press, 2008.

Grossman, Kathleen M., and Bradley Stephens, eds. *Les Misérables and Its Afterlives: Between Page, Stage, and Screen.* New York: Routledge, 2015.

Grudens, Richard. *Bing Crosby: Crooner of the Century.* New York: Celebrity Profiles, 2003.

Haines, John. *Music in Films on the Middle Ages: Authenticity vs. Fantasy.* New York: Routledge, 2014.

Hall, Sheldon, and Steve Neale. *Epics, Spectacles, and Blockbusters: A Hollywood History.* Detroit, MI: Wayne State University Press, 2010.

Hardcastle, Gary, and George Reich. "'What's All This Then?': The Introduction." *Monty Python and Philosophy: Nudge Nudge, Think Think!,* edited by Gary L. Hardcastle and George L. Reisch, 1–10. Peru, IN: Open Court, 2006.

Harty, Kevin J, ed. *Cinema Arthuriana: Twenty Essays.* Jefferson, NC: McFarland, 2002.

Henrickson, Gary P. "Mark Twain, Criticism, and the Limits of Creativity." *Creativity Research Journal* 15, no. 2 (Summer 2011): 253–60. https://doi.org/10.1080/10400419.2003.9651417.

Hertzberg, Hendrik. "Naughty Bits." *The New Yorker,* March 1976. Accessed February 22, 2020. https://www.newyorker.com/magazine/1976/03/29/naughty-bits

Holden John B. "Mark Twain's A Connecticut Yankee: A Genetic Study." *American Literature* 18, no. 3 (1946): 197–218. https://www.jstor.org/stable/2920832.

Hutcheon, Linda. *A Theory of Adaptation.* New York: Routledge, 2006.

Idle, Eric. *Always Look on the Bright Side of Life: A Sortabiography.* New York: Crown Archetype, 2018.

Idle, Eric, and John Du Prez. *Monty Python's Spamalot.* New York: Theatrical Rights Worldwide, 2005.

Internet Movie Database. "Month Python and the Holy Grail." Accessed February 24, 2020. https://www.imdb.com/title/tt0071853/.

Jablonski, Edward. *Alan Jay Lerner: A Biography.* New York: Henry and Holt, 1996.

Johnson, Joel A. "A Connecticut Yankee in Saddam's Court: Mark Twain on Benevolent Imperialism." *Perspectives on Politics* 5, no. 1 (2007): 49–61. https://www.jstor.org/stable/20446349.

Jones, John B. *Our Musicals, Ourselves: A Social History of the American Musical Theatre*. Lebanon, NH: Brandeis University Press, 2003.

Jones, Terry, ed. *Monty Python and the Holy Grail (Book)*. London: Eyre Methuen, 1977.

Kennedy, Matthew. *Roadshow!: The Fall of Film Musicals in the 1960s*. New York: Oxford University Press, 2014.

Kenrick, John. *Musical Theatre: A History*. New York, NY: Continuum, 2008.

Kirle, Bruce. *Unfinished Show Business: Broadway Musicals as Works-in-Process*. Carbondale: Southern Illinois University Press, 2005.

Knapp, Raymond. "Getting Real: Stage Musical versus Filmic Realism in Film Adaptations from *Camelot* to *Cabaret*." In *The Oxford Handbook of Musical Theatre Screen Adaptations*, edited by Dominic McHugh, 55–84. New York: Oxford University Press, 2019.

Knapp, Raymond. *The American Musical and the Performance of Personal Identity*. Princeton: Princeton University Press, 2006.

Knight, Stephen. "'A New Deal': Mark Twain's *A Connecticut Yankee at King Arthur's Court* and the Modern Arthurian Legend." In *Arthurian Literature and Society*, 187–216. London: Palgrave Macmillan, 1983.

Kruse, Horst H. "Mark Twain's 'A Connecticut Yankee:' Reconsiderations and Revisions." *American Literature* 62, no. 3 (1990): 464–83. https://www.jstor.org/stable/2926742.

Langford, Barry. *Post-Classical Hollywood: Film Industry, Style, and Ideology Since 1945*. Edinburgh: Edinburgh University Press, 2010.

Larsen, Darl. *A Book About the Film Monty Python and the Holy Grail: All the References from African Swallows to Zoot*. New York: Rowman and Littlefield, 2015.

Lees, Gene. *The Musical Worlds of Lerner and Loewe*. Lincoln: University of Nebraska Press, 1990.

Leitch, Thomas. *Adaptation and Its Discontents: From* Gone with the Wind *to* Passion of the Christ. Baltimore: Johns Hopkins University Press, 2007.

Leitch, Thomas, ed. *The Oxford Handbook of Adaptation Studies*. New York: Oxford University Press, 2017.

Lerer, Seth. "Hello, Dude: Philology, Performance, and Technology in Mark Twain's 'Connecticut Yankee.'" *American Literary History* 15, no. 3 (Autumn 2003): 471–503. https://www.jstor.org/stable/3568083.

Lerner, Alan J., and Frederick Loewe. *Camelot: A New Musical*. New York: Random House, 1961.

Lev, Peter, and James M. Welsh. *The Literature/Film Reader: Issues in Adaptation*. Lanham: Scarecrow, 2007.

Lupack, Alan. *The Oxford Guide to Arthurian Literature and Legend*. New York: Oxford University Press, 2007.

Macfarlane, Malcolm. *Bing Crosby: Day to Day*. Metuchen, NJ: Scarecrow Press, 2001.

Magee, Jeffrey. "From Flatbush to Fun Home: The Broadway Musical's Cozy Cottage Trope." In *Rethinking American Music*, edited by Tara Browner and Thomas L. Riis, 34–49. Urbana: University of Illinois Press, 2019.

Maltin, Leonard. *The Disney Films*. New York: Disney Editions, 2000.

McHugh, Dominic. *Alan Jay Lerner: A Lyricist's Letters*. New York: Oxford University Press, 2014.

McHugh, Dominic, ed. *The Oxford Handbook of Musical Theatre Screen Adaptations*. New York: Oxford University Press, 2019.

McHugh, Dominic, and Amy Asch, eds. *The Complete Lyrics of Alan Jay Lerner*. New York: Oxford University Press, 2018.

McLeer, Anne. "Practical Perfection? The Nanny Negotiates Gender, Class, and Family Contradictions in 1960s Popular Culture." *NWSA Journal* 14, no. 2 (Summer 2002): 80–101.

Miller, Jeffrey. *Something Completely Different: British Television and American Culture.* Minneapolis: University of Minnesota Press, 2000.

Miller, Scott. *Deconstructing Harold Hill: An Insider's Guide to Musical Theatre.* Portsmouth, NH: Heinemann, 2000.

Miller, Scott. *Strike Up the Band: A New History of the Musical Theatre.* Portsmouth, NH: Heinemann, 2007.

Mitchell, Lee C. "Lines, Circles, Time Loops, and Mark Twain's 'A Connecticut Yankee in King Arthur's Court.'" *Nineteenth-Century Literature* 54, no. 2 (1999): 230–48. https://www.jstor.org/stable/i345793.

Mordden, Ethan. *Make Believe: The Broadway Musical of the 1920s.* New York: Oxford University Press, 1997.

Mordden, Ethan. *Open a New Window: The Broadway Musical in the 1960s.* New York: Palgrave Macmillan, 2001.

Morgan, David. *Monty Python Speaks!: The Complete Oral History, Revised and Updated Edition.* New York: Harper Collins, 2019.

Morra, Irene. "Constructing Camelot: Britain and the New World Musical." *Contemporary Theatre Review* 19, no. 1 (2009): 22–34.

Morris, Christopher D. "The Deconstruction of the Enlightenment in Mark Twain's 'A Connecticut Yankee in King Arthur's Court.'" *Journal of Narrative Theory* 39, no. 2 (Summer 2009): 159–85. https://www.jstor.org/stable/41427203.

Murrell, Elizabeth. "History Revenged: Monty Python Translates Chrétien De Troyes's Perceval, or the Story of the Grail (Again)." *Journal of Film and Video* 50, no. 1 (1998): 50–62.

O'Keefe, Arthur S. "The Morally Imperative Lie in Twain's 'Connecticut Yankee.'" *Midwest Quarterly* 54, no. 1 (Autumn 2012): 11–22.

Oserholm, J. Roger. *Bing Crosby: A Bio-Bibliography.* Westport, CT: Greenwood Press, 1994.

Pallant, Chris. *Demystifying Disney: A History of Disney Feature Animation.* New York: Continuum, 2011.

Pfitzer, George M. "'Iron Dudes and White Savages in Camelot:' The Influence of Dime-Novel Sensationalism on Twain's 'A Connecticut Yankee in King Arthur's Court.'" *American Literary Realism* 27, no. 1 (Fall 1994): 42–58. https://www.jstor.org/stable/27746595.

Prigozy, Ruth, and Walter Raubicheck. *Going My Way: Bing Crosby and American Culture.* Rochester, NY: University of Rochester Press, 2007.

Quirk, Tom, and Mark Twain. *The Portable Mark Twain.* New York: Penguin Books, 2004.

Reitherman, Wolfgang, dir. *The Sword in the Stone.* Burbank, CA: Disney, 1963. DVD.

Riis, Thomas L., and Ann Sears. "The Successors of Rodgers and Hammerstein from the 1940s to the 1960s." In *The Cambridge Companion to the Musical*, edited by William A. Everett and Paul R. Laird, 203–29. New York: Cambridge University Press, 2008.

Robertson Pamela W., and Arthur Knight. *Soundtrack Available: Essays on Film and Popular Music.* Durham, NC: Duke University Press, 2001.

Rodgers, Richard. *Musical Stages: An Autobiography.* New York: De Capo Press, 1995.

Rodosthenous, George. "Introduction." In *The Disney Musical on Stage and Screen: Critical Approaches from 'Snow White' to 'Frozen'*, edited by George Rodosthenous, 1–14. New York: Bloomsbury, 2017.

Santa Cruz, Paul H. *Making JFK Matter: Popular Memory and the Thirty-Fifth President.* Denton: University of North Texas Press, 2015.

Schofield, Mary A. "Marketing Iron Pigs, Patriotism, and Peace: Bing Crosby and World War II—A Discourse." *The Journal of Popular Culture* 40, no. 5 (2007): 867–81.

Sherman, Richard M., and Robert B. Sherman. "Music Magic: The Sherman Brothers." *The Sword in the Stone.* Burbank, CA: Disney, 2013. DVD.

Sherman, Robert B., and Richard M. Sherman. *Walt's Time: From Before to Beyond.* Santa Clarita, CA: Camphor Tree, 1998.

Sprague, Kurth. *T. H. White's Trouble Heart: Women in* The Once and Future King. Rochester, NY: Boydell & Brewer, 2007.

Stempel, Larry. *Showtime: A History of the Broadway Musical Theater.* New York: W. W. Norton, 2010.

Sternfeld, Jessica, and Elizabeth A. Wollman. "After the Golden Age." In *The Oxford Handbook of the American Musical*, edited by Raymond Knapp, Mitchell Morris, and Stacy Wolf, 111–24. New York: Oxford University Press, 2011.

Sternfeld, Jessica. *The Megamusical.* Bloomington: Indiana University Press, 2006.

Steyn, Mark. *Broadway Babies Say Goodnight: Musicals Then and Now.* New York: Routledge, 1999.

Storey, Mark. "Huck and Hank got to the Circus: Mark Twain Under Barnum's Big Top." *European Journal of American Culture* 29, no. 3 (Spring 2011): 217–28. https://doi.org/10.1386/ejac.29.3.217_1.

Strout, Cushing. "Crisis in Camelot: Mark Twain and the Idea of Progress." *The Sewanee Review* 120, no. 2 (Spring 2012): 336–40. https://www.jstor.org/stable/41495407.

Swain, Joseph. *The Broadway Musical: A Critical and Musical Survey.* Lanham, MD: The Scarecrow Press, 2002.

Symonds, Alex. *Mel Brooks in the Cultural Industries: Survival and Prolonged Adaptation.* Edinburgh: Edinburgh University Press, 2012.

Symonds, Dominic. *We'll Have Manhattan: The Early Work of Rodgers and Hart.* New York: Oxford University Press, 2015.

Tietyen, David. *The Musical World of Walt Disney.* Milwaukee, WI: Hal Leonard, 1990.

Twain, Mark. *A Connecticut Yankee in King Arthur's Court.* New York: Nelson Doubleday, 1889.

Umland, Samuel J., and Rebecca A. Umland. *The Use of Arthurian Legend in Hollywood Film: From Connecticut Yankees to Fisher Kings.* Westport, CT: Greenwood Press, 1996.

Walsh, David, and Len Platt. *Musical Theater and American Culture.* Westport, CT: Greenwood, 2013.

Ward, Annalee R. *Mouse Morality: The Rhetoric of Disney Animated Film.* Austin: University of Texas, 2002.

Wasko, Janet. *Understanding Disney: The Manufacture of Fantasy.* Malden, MA: Blackwell, 2001.

White, T. H. *The Once and Future King.* New York: G.P. Putnam's Sons, 1958.

Wolf, Stacey. *A Problem Like Maria: Gender and Sexuality in the American Musical.* Ann Arbor: University of Michigan Press, 2002.

Woller, Megan. "'Happ'ly-Ever-Aftering': Changing Social and Industry Conventions in Hollywood Musical Adaptations, 1960–75." PhD diss., University of Illinois Urbana-Champaign, 2014.

Woller, Megan. "The Lusty Court of *Camelot* (1967): Exploring Sexuality in the Hollywood Adaptation." *Music and the Moving Image* 8, no. 1 (Spring 2015): 3–18.

Wollman, Elizabeth. *A Critical Companion to the American Stage Musical.* New York: Bloomsbury, 2017.

Zipes, Jack. "Breaking the Disney Spell." In *From Mouse to Mermaid: The Politics of Film, Gender, and Culture*, edited by Elizabeth Bell, et al, 21–42. Bloomington: Indiana University Press, 1995.

Index